A Student Guide to Writing Research Reports, Papers, Theses and Dissertations

This useful guide for students combines all the guidance, advice and key tips needed to write successful research reports, theses or dissertations, exploring, in detail, each of the elements involved in writing an academic paper.

The book will guide you through all the key sections of a report including the introduction, literature review, method, results, discussion and more. Each chapter contains instructions and advice aimed at three different levels of report writing experience – 'The basics' covers the basic purpose and structure of each section as well as the most common mistakes, 'Refinements' helps you to develop your report writing skills beyond the basics, adding polish and depth, and 'Advanced' offers advice and insight into the most complex issues in report writing. In addition to the guidance, there are examples to show you the principles of report writing in action and exercises which allow you to test your understanding as you learn.

An essential reference for any student writing an academic paper, *A Student Guide to Writing Research Reports, Papers, Theses and Dissertations* is the ideal resource to be used as part of your independent study or when working with a supervisor.

Cathal Ó Siochrú is a Senior Lecturer and Researcher in Education Studies at Liverpool Hope University, UK.

A Student Guide to Writing Research Reports, Papers, Theses and Dissertations

Cathal Ó Siochrú

Routledge
Taylor & Francis Group

LONDON AND NEW YORK

Cover image: © Getty Images

First published 2023
by Routledge
4 Park Square, Milton Park, Abingdon, Oxon OX14 4RN

and by Routledge
605 Third Avenue, New York, NY 10158

Routledge is an imprint of the Taylor & Francis Group, an informa business

© 2023 Cathal Ó Siochrú

British Library Cataloguing-in-Publication Data
A catalogue record for this book is available from the British Library

ISBN: 978-0-367-62103-2 (hbk)
ISBN: 978-0-367-62104-9 (pbk)
ISBN: 978-1-003-10796-5 (ebk)

DOI: 10.4324/9781003107965

Typeset in Bembo
by codeMantra

To Jules, without whom none of this would have been possible.

Contents

Foreword

Just another book on how to do research? Well, no: this is the book that we have needed for a long time. The book that guides you to success in the job that is done by practically every student in further and higher education, every researcher, everyone carrying out an investigation: writing that final report. It's the end-product of all your work and it's the way you tell the world about it.

So many of those books on research methods include, if we're lucky, a chapter near the end on writing up research, almost as an after-thought. But writing the report is surely the most important part of your investigation. It's probably the longest piece of writing you'll do, it's complicated and it's a highly specialised form of writing. Getting it wrong is easy and good guidance can be hard to find!

I've taught in higher education for many years and helped students with hundreds of dissertations, special studies and reports; so I should be good at it, but there are always difficult questions. For example, many of my students were writing library studies on early years learning theories and they'd ask, "What do I write in the methods bit? Do I just say I've been reading books and journal articles?" I remember that question most of all because it was a repeated one, and I never felt I really answered it properly.

This book gives explicit guidance in producing the ideal final report for research in all forms and in all subjects. Like all good teachers, Cathal has carefully judged the way ideas and materials are presented and explained to make sense to the reader. Each chapter offers three levels of access: for the undergraduate beginner through to the experienced researcher and tutor, so all can read selectively. He also helps you to check and reflect on what you have learned, so the exercises at the end of each chapter give a thorough testing of your understanding. The structure of the report is explained chapter by chapter on each of its different sections, but I would draw your attention to Chapter 9 on 'Academic Writing'. This is often left unexplained, but is a skill which many students find new and challenging. The chapter will help you explicitly to take up the style and type of writing you need to convince your reader that you are a serious academic. You may also want to check out Chapter 8, which talks about how to write a report on a library study or non-empirical research, offering guidance on many aspects, including that tricky methods section.

Cathal Ó Siochrú uses all his experience as researcher and teacher to spark your enthusiasm for each of the sections of your report and help you become a confident and skilled report writer.

Stephen Ward
Emeritus Profesor of Education
Bath Spa University

Author biography

Cathal Ó Siochrú is a Senior Lecturer and Researcher in the areas of student feedback, learning-related beliefs and assessment methods. He teaches on the topics 'Psychology of Education' and 'Research Methods', developing research methods courses for many universities and supervising countless undergraduate, postgraduate and doctoral theses.

Overview

▶ WHAT IS A REPORT AND WHY DO WE WRITE THEM?

Sir Isaac Newton, famed for his research on gravity, motion and light among other things, is supposed to have written "If I have seen further it is by standing on the shoulders of giants". There is some debate over what he meant by that, but the most common interpretation is that Newton was acknowledging all the previous researchers whose work was the foundation for his discoveries. All new research owes a debt to previous research in this way: benefiting from their discoveries, learning from their mistakes, starting at the point that the previous research left off. However, for this process to work, it is essential to know about the findings of other researchers and it is the writing and publication of research reports which makes all of that possible.

A research report is part history, part recipe and part announcement. It is a history, because it talks about the previous research that inspired the report writer to attempt the current research. It is a recipe, because it contains a step-by-step explanation as to how that current research was carried out. It is an announcement, because it offers a summary of the findings of the current research and an explanation of what those findings mean. In this way, a research report enables other researchers to repeat the current research to see if they get the same findings, vary the design to see if they find something new or tackle a new question that was posed but left unresolved by the findings of the current research. This process, where researchers build on and respond to the research of others, is sometimes referred to as 'academia' or 'academic discourse'. It is a conversation between researchers, with each research report representing a contribution to that conversation, agreeing, disagreeing or adding to the points that others have made.

DOI: 10.4324/9781003107965-1

Because research reports are intended for an audience of other researchers, report writers need to learn to use a specific language and layout in the report. Learning the language of report writing can sometimes mean learning a special terminology, words that have a specific agreed meaning which helps researchers to understand each other. At other times, learning the language of report writing is more about learning a style of writing which is used in reports and other academic written work, again to ensure clear communication. Just as important as learning the language is learning the layout of the report, which involves knowing how a report is structured and the rules regarding which information is provided in each section. As with the rules concerning language, the rules concerning layout are there to guarantee clear communication, ensuring that the report contains all the information the audience will want to know and that each piece of that information is located where the audience expects it to be.

You should always approach the writing of any research report as if you are writing for an audience of other researchers. This is true even if the report is being written as part of a course of study, will never be published and may only ever be read by the person who is marking it. Even if the report is a piece of coursework, the examiner will want you to demonstrate you can master the rules of language and layout used in writing published research reports. For this reason, throughout the book I will always refer to those who are reading your report as your 'audience', making no distinction between an audience of one, as in the case of a piece of coursework, and an audience of countless researchers, as in the case of published research.

While the idea of learning all of these rules about language and layout can feel daunting at first, you should not forget that, like Newton, you will have help. You too can rely on those that came before you to give you a helping hand, sharing their experiences about learning how to write research reports. This book contains the lessons about report writing which were learnt by myself, my students, my colleagues and all of those who advised and inspired us. You are welcome to 'stand on my shoulders', and the shoulders of all those others, to give you a helping hand in your report writing career, hopefully enabling you to see further than you did before.

▶ WHY DOES THIS BOOK FOCUS ON REPORT WRITING?

Speaking in very broad terms you could divide the research process into three stages.

1   Developing the research design.
2   Implementing that design.
3   Writing the research report.

The primary purpose of this book is to provide guidance on the third stage, the writing of the report. Any mention of the development and implementation stages in this book will usually focus on things that should be done during those first two stages in order to help you with the report writing stage.

The main reason that this book focuses almost entirely on the report writing stage is to allow for the time and space needed to properly explore report writing and offer detailed guidance on it. Whenever you are writing something for publication, whether it is a research report or a book about writing reports, you always have a limited amount of space to work with. It would be impossible for me to explore the writing of research reports in the kind of depth and detail that I provide in this book if I was also trying to squeeze in an in-depth discussion of the other two stages as well. The majority of other textbooks which offer guidance on the research process seem to have reached a similar conclusion, with most books choosing to focus on the development and implementation stages, leaving the report writing stage with only a comparatively brief mention. This brief discussion of report writing in the other books, offering only a limited amount of guidance, is unlikely to help a first-time report writer to approach their first report with confidence or to provide a more experienced writer with the advice they need to develop their skills further.

I have always had a problem with this approach, taken by so many textbooks on the research process, where they offer much less guidance on the report writing stage than the other stages. In my experience, both as a teacher of research methods and a researcher myself, I find the report writing stage is critical. All of the researcher's hard work in the other stages can be undone by a poorly written report which presents that research in a bad light. This book is an attempt to address all of that, giving the report writing stage the attention it deserves and offering report writers at all levels of experience the guidance they need to progress.

It is for all these reasons that the bulk of this book focuses on the report writing stage. That being said, it does offer some guidance on the design and implementation stages as well. For example, the guidance in this book on the introduction and literature review sections of the report contain a good deal of useful advice regarding things you should be doing during the design stage. Similarly, guidance in this book on the method and results sections highlights a number of things to watch out for during the implementation stage as well. As such, it is recommended that you consult the basic guidance in those chapters when completing the earlier stages in the research process, so you lay the foundations for a really good report. In this way, this book should be useful to you throughout the research process, while offering the greatest level of detail and guidance in the report writing stage.

If you want more guidance on the development and implementation stages than can be found in this book, the good news is that guidance on those stages is very widely available. As I have said before, most other textbooks on the research process will discuss those stages in detail. Furthermore, guidance on development and implementation of a research design tends to be the bulk of what is taught in most research methods courses. As such, you should see this book as part of a lager toolkit, working alongside other books and research training but offering what they do not: detailed guidance on the report writing stage so that your research is being presented in the best light by a high-quality research report.

▶ HOW TO USE THIS BOOK

Chapter contents

The majority of this book follows the structure of a typical research report. Chapters 2 to 6 cover the five main sections of the report (introduction, literature review, method, results and discussion) with each section discussed in a separate chapter. Chapter 7 discusses three minor sections (abstract, references and appendices) all within a single chapter. It is worth noting that this 'typical' report structure is the one used in empirical research, which is research that involves the collection and analysis of data. Chapters 8 and 9 do not focus on sections from this kind of report. Instead, Chapter 8 discusses writing reports for non-empirical research, also known as 'desk-based research', and Chapter 9 discusses the academic writing style. Below you will find a brief summary of the contents of each chapter.

Chapter 2: The introduction

The introduction is where you explain the setting and purpose behind your research. You discuss the wider context to which your research is related, before focusing in on a specific research area within that context. You then outline the theoretical model that you will use to explore that research area and finish off by stating the questions that your research seeks to answer. By the end of your introduction, your audience should have a clear idea of what your research is about, the research questions that you are trying to answer and why those answers matter.

Chapter 3: The literature review

The literature review is where you review the claims and findings made within those parts of the literature which are closely related to your research. You explain how the claims, findings and unresolved questions in that literature inspired your research. By the end of your literature review, your audience should have a clear idea of the key questions in the literature which remain unresolved and how your research proposes to answer them.

Chapter 4: The method

The method is where you tell your audience how your research was carried out. You explain your research design, who took part, what they did, any equipment used and ethical precautions taken. By the end of the method section, your audience should understand exactly how your research was done.

Chapter 5: The results

The results is where you announce the findings of your research. You discuss the analyses you carried out, identifying the methods of analysis, key findings and the relevance of those findings to the research questions. By the end of the results section, your audience should know what your research has found, how it was found and what the findings have to say about the research questions.

Chapter 6: The discussion

The discussion is where you explore and apply the findings of your research, while also critically evaluating the research itself. You review the answers to your research questions and explore the links between the findings of your research and the findings of the previous research. You also evaluate your research design, consider practical applications for your findings as well as future research ideas. By the end of the discussion section, your audience should be aware of the theoretical and practical implications of your research.

Chapter 7: Abstracts, references and appendices

This chapter covers three sections. The abstract section is where you summarise the entire report in a single paragraph, including the wider context, research area, research questions, methodology, key findings and discussion topics. It provides your audience with an overview of the entire research. The references section is where you provide the information needed to locate every source that is relevant to your research. This enables your audience to evaluate or locate those sources. The appendices section is where you include important information which was not suitable for inclusion in any of the other sections of the report. You create a separate appendix for each type of information you wish to include. The information in each appendix should make an important contribution to the audience's understanding of the report.

Chapter 8: Desk-based research

This chapter explores the specific requirements for writing research reports for two types of non-empirical desk-based research: a systematic literature review and theoretical research. A systematic literature review involves the review of literature in order to determine the impact that the theoretical assumptions and methodology used in that literature had on findings in a given research area. Theoretical research involves the critical evaluation of the fundamental assumptions, definitions and validity of evidence relating to a concept, theory or issue which is widely mentioned by the literature in a given research area. In this chapter, guidance on writing a report for each of these desk-based research methods is combined with elements of the general advice on report writing found in the other chapters of the book.

Please note: If you are writing a report for desk-based research it is recommended that you **read this chapter first**, before reading the rest of the book.

Chapter 9: Academic writing

This chapter discusses the academic writing style used in research reports. Academic writing aims to provide insightful answers by presenting evidence and drawing conclusions from that evidence, all of which is done within a pre-arranged report structure which helps to ensure clarity and consistency. When done correctly, the academic writing style ensures that your report is read and understood by the widest possible audience, and that the points you make are seen as credible and persuasive.

The structure of each chapter

Each chapter begins with an overview of the structure and purpose of the report section under discussion. This is followed by a prep work checklist which identifies the steps in your research that should be completed before trying to write that section. The rest of the chapter is divided into four parts, with the different parts offering guidance at different levels of complexity and challenge, ranging from basic guidance to advanced concepts. A summary of each part and its aims can be found below.

The basics

This is aimed at a first-time report writer. It will cover the basic purpose and structure of that section of the report, before walking you through the steps involved in providing all the essential content that is expected in that section. If you are new to report writing, or out of practice and badly in need of a refresher, this is where you should begin.

Common mistakes

This is also aimed mainly at the first-time report writer, looking at some of the most common mistakes made when tackling that section of the report. It is worth noting that, although the mistakes discussed here are more likely to be made by first-timers, they can be made by any level of report writer if they are not being careful. As such, a review of this part of the chapter is also recommended as a refresher for report writers at intermediate and advanced levels of experience as well.

Refinements

This is aimed at the intermediate level report writer, someone who feels they have a good grasp on the basic elements of report writing for that section and is looking to advance their skills to the next level. Guidance here often involves returning to some of those same elements that are mentioned in 'the basics' and considering what can be done to enhance those elements. This usually means adding additional details or complexity which go above and beyond the bare minimum standards that are expected at the basic level.

Advanced

This is only recommended for the more experienced researcher, offering advice and insight on some of the more complex concepts and issues in report writing.

This can involve introducing an entirely new element into the section or a new way of looking at the section itself. You won't find any simple answers in this part of the chapter, but you will find some new and interesting questions or challenges for you to consider the next time you come to write this section.

The chapters are structured in this way to help avoid information overload, allowing you instead to focus on those elements which are most appropriate to your current level of experience in report writing. That way, you will not need to wade through content you already know, or be asked to master concepts which put you out of your depth. Of course, there is no rule which says you have to stick to just one part of the chapter at a time. A sneak-peek at the advice being given at a more advanced level may help you to prepare for what is to come, or possibly a glance back through the earlier levels may offer a useful refresher on the things you should already know. However you do it, remember to pace yourself. Report writing is a complicated skill and you need to give yourself time to master the various sub-skills involved. Patience and practice are the foundations of good report writing.

Call outs

Throughout this book, you will see call outs in the text. These call outs will appear in brackets and will mention the title and page number of another section of this book. For example, here is a call out to a section in the chapter on the introduction which talks about how to present your research questions in your report (See: Research questions, p. 18). Call outs are used when a topic is only briefly mentioned in one section of the book, but is discussed in more detail in another section. In effect, the call out is letting you know that if you want to learn more about this topic, you can read about it in the section that the call out is highlighting.

Exercises

At the end of each chapter are exercises which can be used to test your learning about the section which was the focus of that chapter. There is a multiple-choice exercise which tests both your knowledge and understanding of a broad range of concepts about that section. There is also a sorting exercise which tests your understanding of the purpose of that section within the report. The answers to these exercises can be found at the end of the chapter. Each answer will include a recommendation to review specific topics within that chapter, either to better understand the answer or to avoid misunderstandings which lead to incorrect answers. It is not necessary for you to have read the entire chapter before attempting the exercises. A reading of the 'basics' and 'common mistakes' parts of the chapter should be enough to enable you to attempt all the questions in both exercises. If the answers recommend reviewing parts of the chapter you have not read yet, you can use these recommendations as signposts for where to go next, when you feel ready for it.

Common questions

What are the differences between reports, research papers, dissertations and theses?

Throughout this book, I refer to the piece being written as a research report. However, when you look at the structure of what I call a research report, you may find you know it by a different name. To some, it would be called a research paper, to others a dissertation or a thesis. The question as to whether these are all simply different labels for the same thing, or labels for different things, is a matter of debate. One perspective is that a research paper and research report are similar things in terms of size and structure, but the label 'paper' is more commonly used in the humanities and 'report' in the sciences. Linked to this view is the idea that research papers focus on theoretical research, whereas research reports focus on empirical research. Yet another way of distinguishing between them is by level of study. Research papers and reports are at the lowest level, typically undergraduate, with dissertations at the next level, such as in final year undergraduate or masters, while a thesis would be at the highest level, namely doctoral or post-doc. All of these pieces have similar structures, although the higher the level of study, the longer and more complex the piece is expected to be.

Presented in this way it can all sound very neat and tidy, with what looks like a clear system of labels. Unfortunately, not everyone follows this system. Sometimes, the exact same piece of academic writing may be referred to as a research report in one place, a dissertation in the second and a research paper in the third. As such, it is often better to ignore the labels and focus on the purpose of what you are writing instead. If what I call a 'research report' has the same overall purpose and much the same structure as what you call a paper, dissertation or a thesis, then this book can still help you to do a better job of writing that paper, dissertation or thesis. In the end, it is the guidance you can find here and not the labels used that will matter. Whether you call it a report, a paper, a dissertation or a thesis, this book will help you to write a better one.

Does it matter if the labels for the sections and sub-sections in my report do not match the ones in the book?

In much the same way that a 'research report' may also be known as a 'thesis' or 'dissertation', the labels used for the sections or sub-sections in that report can vary. For example, what is called the 'discussion' section in this book can sometimes be called the 'conclusions' section instead, with similar alternatives existing for many other section and sub-section labels. Most of the time, this difference in the label for a section or sub-section is just cosmetic, changing the name but not the section itself.

As such, if you are unsure whether to follow the guidance in this book because the label you use for a section is different from the label used in this book, you should check the purpose of that section, which is explained at the start of the chapter. If the section discussed in that chapter has the same purpose, but a different label, as the section you are trying to write, then it is OK to apply the guidance in that chapter to the section you are writing.

If, on the other hand, you cannot find a section with a similar purpose in this book to the section you are trying to write, then it may be a section which is unique to your subject area or type of research. As this book is offering general guidance on report writing, it cannot cover every possible variation in report writing that might occur in all the different subjects that use the research report format. In such cases, you should look for guidance on that section from your supervisor or editor. Alternatively, you could look at similar reports in the same subject area for guidance on how that section is to be written.

What should I do if the book gives different advice to my supervisor/editor?

Before a report can reach the wider audience of researchers for which it is intended, it first needs to be judged to see if the report and research behind it meet the required standards. In the case of a report that will be published, this is known as 'peer review' and the judges are selected researchers. In the case of a report that will be submitted as an assignment on a course, the judges are the examiners. There is usually a person, whose role is to provide the report writer with guidance on how to approach the research and the writing of the report, so as to be successful when the report is judged. For a report to be published, that person is the editor, and for an assignment on a course, that person is the supervisor. For simplicity's sake, I will use the label of 'supervisor' to refer to both. The guidance in this book is intended to work alongside, not replace, the guidance from your supervisor. Your supervisor's guidance will contain rules and expectations about report writing which are the part of the system to which the supervisor belongs. Following those rules is a necessity if you want your report to be successful when it comes time for it to be judged within that system.

What this means is, if the guidance in this book appears to differ from or even contradict the guidance from your supervisor, then it is always your supervisor's guidance you should follow. Or to put it another way, 'supervisor always beats book'. Hopefully these differences will be rare, or may even not happen at all. If they do happen, it is always worth discussing these apparent differences in guidance with your supervisor. This may reveal a misunderstanding of that guidance which, when cleared up, causes the apparent differences in the guidance to disappear. Other times, the differences between the guidance in book and from your supervisor may be on issues which are a matter of choice or are trivial. In these cases, your supervisor may give you the choice to follow whichever guidance you prefer, but it is still your supervisor who is allowing you to make that choice. So, as you can see, in all situations and on all issues, whenever there is a disagreement in guidance between supervisor and book, the basic rule remains that 'supervisor always beats book'.

Are the citations used in the examples fact or fiction?

Throughout the book, alongside the guidance, I have included some written examples of the section under discussion, examples which demonstrate the writing principles being discussed at that time. A word of warning, though: in these examples, I include example citations for 'sources' which supposedly support the points being made in the example. **All of these citations are fictional, all of the 'sources' they refer to have been invented by me.** These fictional citations are included only for appearances sake, to demonstrate what that section of the report would look like. The only point of these examples is to demonstrate the style and structure of the section being discussed, they are not being used to share any real facts or information on the research areas that they appear to be discussing.

As such, these fictional citations and invented sources should never be used to support any points in any real pieces you are writing. Also, none of the claims being made in these examples should be taken as true based only the example. If you want to know the actual research findings in any of the research areas mentioned in an example, you need to conduct your own literature review and read the real sources. The 'facts' on display in these examples are like wax fruit, only there to resemble the real thing, so don't try and swallow them!

Do I have to follow the guidance in this book?

This book contains guidance, not orders, and so it is always your choice as to what extent you choose to follow that guidance. Robotically following the guidance without ever asking why or, even worse, when the guidance seems inappropriate to the report you are writing, is not good practice. This is why the guidance in this book will always combine directions on what you should do with an explanation as to why you should do it that way. Even so, this may still leave you in a situation where you do not fully understand why you are doing something, or where you can think of other ways to do it. Even in those cases, there are still many good reasons to follow the guidance in this book. One such reason is that reports often follow set patterns and rules because it helps to make them predictable, ensuring that everyone can find the information they are looking for where they expect to find it. Ignoring the guidance, and the rules behind that guidance, can end up confusing your audience and undermining the effectiveness of the report. The other issue to keep in mind is that experience requires patience. Often we follow guidance without fully understanding the rules behind that guidance so as to gain the experience which will, eventually, help us to understand why the rules were needed in the first place. As such, when in doubt and while you are still learning, it is advisable to follow the guidance in this book wherever you can.

Eventually, your experience will grow beyond the need for guidance, leaving you with an entirely new relationship with the rules behind that guidance. There is a saying about playing jazz that tells us, "It's not the notes you play, it's the notes you don't play". One interpretation of that saying is that mastery of any skill involves the ability to improvise and reinterpret the rules. This is true for many different skills, including report writing, with experienced researchers reinterpreting the rules regarding report writing and enhancing the effectiveness of their reports as a result. But, before you take this as a licence to ignore the rules and hand in your own entirely original interpretation a research report, you should consider if you have reached that level of mastery. You should also consider whether those who evaluate your report will see you as an expert. After all, ignorance and improvisation can look very similar, and your attempt to re-interpret the rules could be mistaken for not understanding those rules. In most subject areas, mastery in research and report witting is usually demonstrated at doctoral and post-doctoral levels. At that point, you probably won't need this book or its guidance any more. However, until that time, you should aim to do the best job you can within the rules, and the guidance provided in this book will help you do just that.

2 The introduction

The introduction is the section where you explain the purpose behind your research: what you are trying to do and why you are trying to do it. You do this by first talking about the wider context to which your research is related, before focusing in on the research area within that context that your research will explore in greater detail. You will also need to outline the theoretical model you plan to use when conducting that exploration. You finish off by stating the questions that your research seeks to answer as well as what the research aims to achieve. In that way, by the end of your introduction, your audience should have a clear idea of what your research is about, the research questions that you are trying to answer and why those answers matter.

▶ BEFORE YOU BEGIN THIS CHAPTER...

Before you are ready to begin writing your introduction, there are a number of steps in the research process you will need to complete first.

- Identify an issue or topic that interests you.
- Conduct a scoping review of any research which relates to that issue.
- Based on that review, make note of any key findings and potential research areas.
- Locate a suitable supervisor.
- Discuss the key findings and potential research areas with your supervisor.
- Agree on a research area and aims of the research with your supervisor.

Once you have completed all of these steps, you are ready to begin writing this section of the report.

DOI: 10.4324/9781003107965-2

▶ THE BASICS

The basic structure of the introduction comes in five parts. First, you establish the wider research context. Second, you identify the specific research area within that context that your research will focus on. Third, you outline the theoretical model you plan to use to explain this area. Fourth, you identify the research's aims and objectives before finally stating the research questions and hypotheses.

Introduce the research context

Your first job in the introduction is to help your audience to see the wider relevance of your research. In essence, you are explaining why you carried out the research and why the findings will matter. This is why you start off your introduction by talking about the 'real world' issues and situations that your research is connected to, also known as the research 'context'. Your aim when talking about the research context is to convince your audience that there is a problem in need of a solution and/or an issue which needs to be better understood. In other words, you need to make the case that the problem or issue is important enough to justify researching it.

> *Luke is planning to research possible causes of surgical errors. To set up the research context, Luke will talk about the nature and potential seriousness of surgical errors and the range of outcomes that can result from such an error. He will also offer statistics on the number of surgical errors which occur each year and the efforts made to reduce this number. He will finish this section by putting his research forward as important step toward a better understanding of this issue, with the potential for offering a method of reducing the number of errors.*

Exactly how you make the case justifying your research is up to you. Your justifications could be financial, humanistic, moral or logical, anything from improving the bottom line to saving lives. The only reason which is not acceptable is saying you did the research because you 'had to' as a requirement of your course or your career. Even if that was a big part of your motivation for doing the research, you still need to find a research topic that matters to someone other than yourself and you need to explain why it matters at the start of the introduction. However you do it, your hope is that once you have made your case, your audience will agree that this is an issue worth researching.

Identify the research area

Once you have established the research context, you then need to identify the area within that context which will be the focus of your research. It would not be practical for any one piece of research to try to study the entire context. You would get overwhelmed by all the 'surface features', those elements of the context that are already widely known and understood. A study of the surface features may tell you what is happening in a situation, but it is unlikely to offer any insights as to *why* those things are happening. Instead, you should be trying to get past the surface of your research context and find out what is going on underneath. To do that, your research will need to limit its focus to a small section of the context, also known as picking a research 'area'. Like a scientist staring into a microscope, this focus means you only see a very small part of the whole picture, but you see it in the kind of detail needed to learn something new.

Which area you focus on is up to you, with the only requirement being that you should be able to explain to your audience why you have focused on that area. For example, you could cite a few of the other researchers who have also focused on the same research area and found things which show that area is important to the wider context. It also helps if you can identify questions which have been left unresolved by the previous research. Be aware though that the previous research and unresolved questions are things you will talk about in more detail in your literature review (See: Identifying the foundations and unresolved questions, p. 41). As such, all your audience needs here in the introduction is a brief mention of both, just enough to understand your choice of research area.

[In Luke's Research area] *This research will focus on the relationship between the instruments that a surgeon has available to them and the number of surgical errors made. The importance of this relationship has already been demonstrated in other research which found that the quality of the instruments (Frye, 2020) and the surgeon's level of familiarity with them (Orozoco, 1998) both influence the likelihood of surgical errors. However, Bowen (2009) found that, despite having better quality instruments and training, some wealthier hospitals still experience higher levels of surgical error than expected, which suggests there are other factors involved which are not yet fully understood.*

Outline the theoretical model

Having established the context and research area, the next step is to sketch an outline of the theoretical model you will use to explore this area. The 'theoretical model' refers to the collection of theories and concepts you will be using in your research. Outlining your theoretical model means identifying the key theories and concepts that are relevant to your research area, explaining how they relate to each other and showing how they will help to better understand your research area.

[In Luke's Theoretical model] *At the heart of this research are the concepts of working memory and attentional resources. The large variety of instruments available to the surgeons in wealthy hospitals is overloading their working memory which, according to Whitworth (2006) is the part of memory used in everyday decision making. The surgeons are devoting so much of what Kish (2014) calls 'attentional resources' to keeping track of all their instruments while they operate, it is distracting them and this leads to more errors.*

In order to keep your introduction short and focused, and to avoid too much repetition between the introduction and the literature review, you should only give a basic explanation of the concepts and how they relate to the research area. You may want to cite at least one foundational source for each key concept that you mention or claim you make. You won't need to go into much detail about these sources or other related research here in the introduction; you can do all of that in your literature review (See: Identifying the foundations and unresolved questions, p. 41). Think of this part of the introduction like the trailer, and the literature review is the feature film; you want to tell your audience enough to get them interested but not so much that you give away the ending. Judging how much to explain here in the introduction and how much to leave to the literature review is a tricky balancing act, especially for the first-time report writer, but with experience it gets easier.

Aims and objectives

Having discussed what the research is about, at this point in the introduction, you are ready to say what the research hopes to achieve and how it will achieve it. The research aims are statements which summarise what the research hopes to achieve. They do this by explaining how applying concepts from the theoretical model to the situation outlined in the research area will help to tackle issues in the wider context. While there are many ways you can structure a statement of research aims, a common structure would be, "*We aim to research X which will show us Y and that will enable us to do Z.*", where X is a concept you are applying to a situation, Y is what you hope to find and Z is the benefit that will come from that finding. Depending on how many concepts and issues you are juggling, your research may have only one aim or several. To ensure you don't overlook any of your aims, you should use the following questions to identify all the instances of these elements (X, Y and Z) in your research.

1   Can you think of one thing you are trying to understand and the concept are you using to try and better understand it? (X)
2   What do you hope to reveal/demonstrate as a result of that better understanding? (Y)

3   If it is successful, what difference will this part of your research make to the wider context? (Z)

> [In Luke's Aims] *The aim of this research is to explore the role of attentional resources on doctors' use of surgical tools, as a potential cause for surgical errors. Making this connection should help to reduce the rate of surgical errors by helping surgeons to better manage and protect those attentional resources.*

After stating the aims, the next step is to state the research objectives, which are the steps the researcher will need to take to achieve the aims. Most research has what I would call a 'standard design' which means they all have a similar set of objectives, namely, conducting a literature review, designing a methodology, gathering data, analysing it and then writing a report. Since the objectives in a standard design are so commonplace, I would argue that they are not worth stating as objectives and can instead be taken for granted. In this situation, you would not need to state any objectives in your introduction.

Stating objectives is recommended if the research design differs from that standard design in some meaningful way. A common example would be if the research was made up of two or more separate phases of data collection. You should consider your data collection to have more than one phase if you have sets of data that are going to be analysed separately. A separate analysis is typically either a result of having different types of data gathered using different methods or if the results of separate analyses will be used to answer different research questions. Another example of a non-standard design would be if your research included both an empirical phase, which focuses on collecting and analysing data, followed by an applied phase, where the results of the empirical phase are then used to make changes in a real-life situation. For all of these non-standard designs, it is worthwhile stating your objectives when talking about your research in the introduction.

> *Luke's original research plan was to research the relationships between the number of instruments present, a surgeon's level of focus and the number of errors made. Although Luke was measuring a few different things, they were all part of a single analysis used to answer one research question, which meant he had a standard design and so did not need to state his objectives. However, he now plans to add in a second phase of data collection where he shares the results of his analysis with the surgeons and asks them to reflect on their experiences of trying to divide their attention during surgery. This will produce a different type of data, requiring a separate analysis and the results of that analysis will be used to answer a different research question. As such, he will state that his first objective is to measure and analyse the link between attention and errors, while his second objective is to explore the doctors' views on the findings of his first analysis.*

Research questions

Having summarised the purpose and plan for your research in your aims and objectives, you are now ready to pose your research questions. A research question is a question that you are trying to answer by carrying out your research. It should not be confused with a survey or interview question, which are questions that are answered by the participants in your research. Instead, the answer to a research question will come from analysing the data you collect. You can have more than one research question and each research question should be specific, focusing on one or two elements within the research area and clearly identifying something you would like to know about those elements.

> [In Luke's Research questions] *There are three research questions which I hope to answer in this research. First, is there a relationship between the number of instruments present in the operating theatre and the surgeon's level of focus? Second, is there a relationship between a surgeon's level of focus and the number of surgical errors that occur? Third, how do the results of the analysis from the first two questions compare to the surgeons' experience of managing their attention during surgery?*

Each research question should connect to some part of your analysis. As I said before, the answers to the research questions will come from the analysis of the data collected. As we will see in the chapter on the results section, it's the analysis which allows us to get beyond the surface of what is happening and better understand some of the deeper mechanisms which can explain why those things are happening (See: The basics, p. 14). However, the findings of that analysis also need to be linked back to the theoretical model, because it's only with a theoretical model that we can identify which deeper mechanism it is that the findings are revealing. Connecting the findings to the theoretical model also enables us to achieve insight, by which I mean it enables us to make connections between the answer to this one research question and a new way of looking at the whole research area and wider context.

> *If Luke didn't have a theoretical model based on attentional resources, and instead just found statistical evidence of a direct relationship between the number of instruments and number of errors, that result would be hard to interpret. Without a theoretical model, his finding is interesting but not insightful because he wouldn't be able to explain why there is a relationship between number of instruments and number of errors. It's the model that helps him to understand the link between the number of instruments and errors because of the relationship both those things have with attentional resources of the surgeon. In addition, knowing about the role of attention in this relationship provides the insight that the number of instruments may be only one thing that acts as a drain on a surgeon's attentional resources. It suggests that we should look for other things which act as a drain*

on these valuable resources, like noise, smells and other distractions. Finally, it raises the possibility that we should examine the impact of things outside of the surgery which could reduce or increase the levels of attentional resources that the surgeon has to begin with, such as diet, sleep or mood.

That is the difference a research question makes, the difference between an interesting finding, which tells you an isolated fact, and an insightful finding which opens your eyes to new possibilities in the way you think about the wider context. Thus, each research question should act like a bridge, connecting your analysis to your theoretical model, allowing you to use the model to make sense of what the analysis has found (See: Relevance of the findings, p. 97).

Stating your hypotheses (quantitative research only)

Although the research questions are usually the final part of your introduction, sometimes you will go further than simply posing research questions in your introduction; you will also predict the answers that you expect to find. These predictions are known as 'hypotheses'. Each hypothesis will predict the answer to one of your research questions. The intention is that during the analysis of your data, you will test the hypothesis to see if the data supports it or not. Do the results match the prediction? (See: Findings of the analysis, p. 93) Since this kind of test requires some form of statistical analysis, you typically only find hypotheses in research that is gathering quantitative (numerical) data.

The wording of a hypothesis is related to the type of statistical analysis you will be using to test that hypothesis. For example, if your hypotheses contained a prediction about a difference between groups, then you would need to use a statistical test which tests for differences (such as a t-test or ANOVA). In this example, your hypothesis might predict no difference between the groups or that one group will have a higher or lower average score compared to the others. A hypothesis should always refer to specific variables and specific groups so that it is clear which variables or which groups the predictions in that hypothesis relate to.

Vincent is researching how personality variables can influence charitable behaviour. His theoretical model predicts that people are more likely to donate to a charity whose aims match their personal values. Vincent will statistically compare the average donation amount made to the two types of charity (matching and non-matching). His first hypothesis will state...

Hypothesis one is that the average donation amount to a value-matching charity will be significantly higher than the average donation amount to a non-matching charity.

It is a good idea to give each hypothesis a number, referring to them as hypothesis one, hypothesis two and so on. This will help later on when you need to refer to a specific hypothesis since you can use the number of the hypothesis as a quick way to identify which one you are talking about.

▶ COMMON MISTAKES

In the introduction, your research is still in the future

A common mistake when writing the introduction is to write about your research in the past tense. The fact that many sections of the report, such as the results and discussion, refer to the research in the past tense is likely to be one reason the past tense is used in the introduction as well. Also, many first-time report writers tend to put off writing up their report until the research itself is complete, in which case it is understandable that they think of the research in the past tense from the very first line they write. However, in the introduction, when you are referring to your research you should use the future tense, not the past tense. You should write about your research as if it is just about to happen.

The report should be about the research not about the course you are taking

Most research reports written by undergraduate students are completed as part of an assignment for one of their courses. It is likely that the first steps in the research process involved elements of that course: lectures or tutorials on the topic of research, meetings with a supervisor, searching for relevant previous research in the library. A lot of first-time report writers think that they need to mention some of these activities when talking about their research. These descriptions usually take on a shape similar to a reflective diary with mentions of their personal thoughts and opinions on the process, alternative research ideas that were discarded, suggestions from their supervisor, difficulties locating previous research and so on.

However interesting these points might be, most of them are not essential to understanding your research. Most research reports need to fit within a tightly specified word limit and providing too much detail here can leave you without the space you need to include more important information later on. Even if you do not run out of space, too much detail on every twist, turn or minor obstacle you faced could leave your reader bored or impatient for you to get on to the more important topics in your report. As a rule-of-thumb, the only place in your report where you will describe how you actually carried out your research is in the procedure section of the method where you offer an example of how your data collection was carried out (See: Procedure, p. 70). Apart from that, your audience does not need a step-by-step description of how the research was carried out or how you wrote your report.

Any mention of your methodology should be brief

Your introduction is not the place for a detailed explanation of how you are going to carry out your research, also known as your methodology. As such, in the introduction, you should avoid going into detail about who is taking part, what equipment or tests you are planning to use or your data collection methods. This information will be covered in detail in the method section (See: The basics, p. 14).

This does not completely rule out mentioning the methodology in the introduction; it is more about keeping any mention of it very brief, only mentioning what is necessary. For example, you might find it's necessary to mention a few methodological details when talking about your research to help your audience to understand your research questions and hypotheses.

[In Vincent's Research questions] *In this research I will measure people's personal values and then, a week later, arrange for an assistant to approach all the participants with a request to donate to a charity which either matches or doesn't match their values.*

One other reason you might need to discuss your method in your introduction is when some aspect of your methodology is new or important. In this situation, you should mention why this aspect of the methodology was important and worth mentioning.

[In Vincent's Research questions] *I will arrange for a donation opportunity to be offered to each participant which either does or doesn't match their values. This has not been done before in any of the previous research and should allow me to establish if matching values is the cause of the donating behaviour, something other research has speculated about but not been able to prove.*

Your research area should not be too broad

The purpose of picking a research area is to narrow your focus onto a small section of the wider context, so that it is possible to cover that area in one piece of research. A lot of first-time report writers are too ambitious and set out to study research areas that would take dozens of people, working as a team, years to cover properly.

As a rule of thumb, most first-time report writers will need to narrow the focus of their research area several times before it is narrow enough. This means that, whatever your first choice of research area is, your next step is to ask yourself "Are there a few different types of that situation, issue or behaviour?" If there are, then narrow your focus to just one example and then repeat the process again, starting with that one specific type of behaviour or situation and looking for different sub-types, so you can again focus on just one. Keep going until you have narrowed it down to a situation or behaviour which is so specific that it is hard to think of any sub-types. At that point, your research area has a narrow enough focus.

> *Vincent started off with an interest in why people help each other. He considered several types of helpful behaviour, ranging from dramatic rescues to helping the disadvantaged. After deciding to focus on helping the disadvantaged, Vincent considered several sub-types of help you can give (volunteering, donating goods and donating money) and decided to focus on donating money. He plans to use a theoretical model which talks about the impact that your values can have on your behaviour, to focus on the people's values as the explanation for why they do or do not donate.*

Remember that even a suitably narrow research area will still be too complex for you to research all the elements present. This is why you will be using your theoretical model to focus on a few specific elements within the research area. All this means that your research will end up focused on what can feel like a very small set of issues, which some first-time report writers can find a little disappointing. But don't despair, major scientific discoveries can come from very small events, like the flight of a moth or the fall of an apple.

Hypotheses that predict multiple things at the same time

It is important to ensure that each hypothesis predicts only one thing at a time. Predicting only one thing ensures that a hypothesis will either be supported by the evidence or not supported, but never both. If you attempt to predict more than one thing at a time you can end up with a situation where some of those things happen, but others don't. As a result, your hypothesis ends up being partially true. At best, this can be complicated and confusing to explain, or at worst it may be impossible to tell which predictions within the hypothesis were supported and which were not supported. It is for reasons like these that I argue that hypotheses work best when they stick to predicting one thing at a time. If you find that your hypothesis is predicting multiple things in this way, the solution is to separate each of the predictions into a separate hypothesis.

[In Vincent's hypotheses – First Daft]

Hypothesis one is that the average donation amount and levels of volunteering to a value-matching charity will be significantly higher than the average donation amount made and levels of volunteering to a non-matching charity.

[In Vincent's hypotheses – Second Daft]

Hypothesis one is that the average donation amount to value-matching charity will be significantly higher than the average donation amount made to a non-matching charity.

Hypothesis two is that the average level of volunteering to value-matching charity will be significantly higher than the average level of volunteering to a non-matching charity.

▶ REFINEMENTS

Scope the literature first, then pick a research area

Many first-time researchers tend to make life hard for themselves by the way they go about conducting their research. Choosing a research area that is too advanced or that requires a special population are two good examples of this kind of rookie error. But one of the most common mistakes is to decide on a research area first and then go looking for previous research on that area.

Why is this approach a bad idea? The easiest way to explain that is to use a fishing analogy. Imagine for a moment that you were going fishing in a river for the first time. Without asking anyone what kind of fish live in that river, you decide that you are going after one specific type of fish and only that type of fish. What do you think will happen? Chances are that you will end up throwing back all the other types of fish that you catch waiting for this one type that you decided on before you even began. You will almost certainly spend a lot more time fishing and the specific fish you are looking for may never turn up. It might not even live in that river! At the end of the day, you could end up having caught a lot of fish but going home empty-handed (and hungry). Not a smart way to fish and equally not a smart way to go about reviewing literature either.

What I hope is clear from that analogy, is just how risky and potentially inefficient it is to pick your research area before doing an initial review of literature.

Picking your area first means restricting yourself to just the previous research that falls within your chosen area, before you know how much research even exists in that area or if you can find any of it. A tell-tail sign that a report writer may have made this mistake is if their literature review contains a phrase along the lines of "There is not much research in this area". That is rarely true; what more likely is that they could not find much research in that area. As well as potentially struggling to find what you want, just like the fishing analogy, you may end up discarding plenty of previous research which was easy to find and could have been the basis for perfectly good research of your own. The final disadvantage of picking your area first is that the research which relates to that area could take far longer to locate, and that is assuming you ever locate it. Since most research takes place against a deadline, this is time that you cannot afford to waste.

The other limitations you need to keep in mind when choosing your research area are the limits to the journal subscriptions for your library. No matter how big the budget may be for your library, no one can afford to subscribe to all the journals out there. If you chose a research area before checking out your library journal subscriptions, you run the risk that even if you are lucky enough to find articles which are relevant to your chosen research area, they may be published in journals that your library does not subscribe to. It is a common complaint among students that all the interesting or relevant articles they need for their research are the ones they cannot access because the library does not subscribe to them. These students will often blame the library for letting them down by not having the things they need. They are missing the fact that their own decisions, such as picking a research topic before seeing what subscriptions the library has, could be the real root of their problems.

For all these reasons, it is a better plan to do an initial search, also known as a 'scoping review', looking at a wide variety of research before then deciding on your research area based on what you can find. By searching for inspiration among the journals and books that your library subscribes to you, are also making the best use of the resources available. The first step is to come up with a research context you are interested in, but no specific research area or research questions. Once you have picked your context, you read-up on any sources you can find which refer to that context. You are looking for sources that interest you or previous research that gives you an idea for new research. When you find a piece of research or two that inspire you in this way, they become the core of your literature review. It is also at this point that you are ready to write your first draft of your theoretical model as well as the research aims, objectives and questions. This is why I state that a scoping review is one of the things you should do before you attempt to write your first draft of your introduction.

Your research questions will decide your methodology

Although you may not notice it the first few times you come up with research questions, it will eventually dawn on you that the way you phrase your research questions practically decides your methodology. The reason for this is that each type of research question requires a certain kind of methodology to answer it. The most obvious way this connection can be demonstrated is in the link between the phrasing of the research question and the choice between qualitative and quantitative research methods.

On the one hand, if the question asks whether one thing is the cause of another or even if one thing is merely related to another, then a quantitative methodology is best suited to answer that question. This is because establishing causality or a relationship between two or more things is what statistics are intended to do. If you are not entirely sure whether a question is about causality or a relationship of this type, then there are certain signpost words to look out for. Examples include, if your research question asks whether one thing is better or worse than an alternative, what the effect of something is or whether we can consider it effective, or if one thing is associated, linked or related to another. However, it is the combination of these signpost words with key words such as 'if', 'is' or 'whether' which really confirms that a quantitative-type research question is present. This is because these key words mean you are asking 'if' that effect or relationship exists, and it is a quantitative methodology alone which can test for the existence of something, such as an effect or relationship. Answering this type of research question, by analysing that data collected, will either verify or undermine the theoretical model. If the findings of the analysis are consistent with the causality or relationship mentioned in the research question, then that supports the theoretical model which inspired that research question. On the other hand, if the findings of the analysis do not support the causality or relationship, then that undermines the credibility of the theoretical model.

One the other hand, if the question asks why or how something is happening then a qualitative methodology is best suited to answer that question. This is because achieving a better understanding of people's reasons or their experiences is what a qualitative methodology and analysis are designed to do. As with the quantitative-type questions, there are signpost words which indicate that a qualitative-type question is present. They include asking about the reason for something, the meaning of something to someone or the experience/understanding that someone has of something. Again, it is the combination with a key word such as 'why', 'what' or 'how' that confirms it is a qualitative-type question. By using these key words, you show that you are not questioning the existence of the thing being studied; instead you are trying to better understand the nature of that existence, a task for which qualitative methods are ideal. Answering this type of research question, by analysing the data collected, will add to our understanding of the theoretical model that inspired the research question. Depending on what the findings are, they could potentially suggest new additions to the model that can then be verified by later research.

> *Vincent's research question asks if the similarity between the values of the person and the values of the charity affect how much they donate to the charity. The keyword 'if' combined with the signpost 'affect' tells Vincent he will need to use quantitative methods. However, if Vincent were to add a research question to ask what are people's reasons behind their decision to donate or not to donate to a charity, then the keyword 'what' and the signpost 'reason' show that he will need to use qualitative methods to answer that second question.*

You will find this link between research question and methodology goes even deeper than simply deciding the choice between qualitative or quantitative methods. As we saw earlier, a research question about differences between groups would require both the data and the statistical test used to measure group differences. This raises an interesting point of caution when posing your research questions; you need to make sure you either know, or are ready to learn, the methodologies needed to both gather the data and carry out the analysis needed to answer that question. From a pragmatic point of view, it may be in your interest to pick research questions which will require data collection and analysis methods you know well (See: Know your analysis, p. 103). This is definitely worth considering if you are conducting your research as part of a course of study and will be graded on the outcome. You may need to balance the competing motivations to push your limits and demonstrate your ability to learn new things, against playing to your strengths and showing off the polished performance that comes from experience and practice.

Does my research need to be original?

There is a lot of debate as to whether a piece of research that is carried out as part of a course of study needs to be original in terms of the research area, theoretical model and research questions. Assuming you gather your own data and write it up in your own words, is it acceptable to entirely replicate the methods, model and research questions of a previous piece of research? To many academics, the answer to this question depends on your level of study. In many institutions, the official rules state that so-called 'original research' is a requirement in a doctoral thesis (also known as a PhD) but not below that level. As such, if you are carrying out research as part of an undergraduate or master's degree, it would be entirely within the rules in those institutions to simply replicate another piece of research. However, just because you *can* do something doesn't mean you should.

The problem with entirely replicating another piece of research is not about breaking some rule, but about the problems this creates when you come to write up your research. The problem first rears its head when you come to explain the aim of the research in the introduction. You need to explain how your research will help with understanding the research area or resolving an issue in the wider context. However, it will be hard to convince anyone that your research will make a valuable contribution when there is an identical piece of previous research which has already made all the same contributions. You will find this problem crops up again when you come to report your findings in the results and discussion (See: Wider implications, p. 118 and Past research, p. 119). On the one hand, if you find the same results as the previous research, then they beat you to it and steal all the glory. Even your discussion of what results mean will sound like a pale imitation of the discussion in the previous research, which will have said much the same things. On the other hand, if you find a different result to the previous research that's not much better, since it will be hard to explain why your results differ if your design is an exact copy of theirs, with nothing added or changed. It will be hard to shake the impression that it is your research which contains some mistake, and any claims you make that the previous research is the flawed one will sound a little self-serving.

Based on all the reasons offered here, I would argue that there should always be some originality in your research. It is not a problem if you want to confirm the results of a piece of previous research as part of your research, just as long as it is not all you are doing. By adding something new to your methodology or theoretical model, you will be better able to argue that one of the aims of your research is to increase understanding of the research area. It will also allow you to talk about the value that this increased understanding will bring. This helps you when it comes to the results as well. Finding what the previous research found is OK this time because now it is not the only thing you found. Not finding what the previous research found can be better managed too, by using the changes you made to shed light on why you found a different result. Maybe your changes caused the difference in results, which would suggest there is a potentially 'confounding variable', a variable that was unknown to the first piece of research but which can have an impact on the issue both you and they were exploring. As I hope you can see now, the addition of something new returns a sense of purpose to your research.

What you change is up to you, but it is important to note that simply changing something for the sake of being different from the previous research is not guaranteed to produce strong new research. It is better if you have a reason for making that specific change, some basis on which you can argue that making this change will have a meaningful impact on the research area being studied. You can find the basis for that argument in the same source as most (if not all) good research ideas, a literature review of the previous research. In that sense 'original research' does not come from you dreaming up a new research method or theoretical model out of thin air. It comes from a synthesis of previous research, combing research methods or concepts from a variety of research to produce an original combination. Thus, even if originality is not a requirement of the rules wherever you are completing your studies, it's always part of the recipe for good research.

▶ ADVANCED

Should the introduction acknowledge changes to the research plan?

More often than not, the introduction section ends up being written (or re-written) at the same time as the rest of the report, namely after the research has been completed. However, unlike the rest of the report, the introduction seems to be intended to capture your point of view as it was beforehand: a statement of your research plans and intentions. If this is the case, then how should your introduction reflect those parts of the research which did not go as planned?

Almost all research plans change. A researcher who ends up carrying out the same exact research design that they first dreamt up is the exception not the rule. The process of reviewing the literature almost always knocks a few holes in the original research idea by revealing certain research avenues as dead-ends or by introducing new variables and new ideas to the researcher. Furthermore, when the researcher actually comes to collect the data, unexpected difficulties can turn what was planned as the main data collection into an unplanned pilot study, which is then used to iron-out problems with the methodology. This can result in the data collection needing to begin again with new methodologies and even new variables. Even at the relatively late stage of data analysis, unexpected results may require the researcher to re-assess their expectations and find new theoretical models to make sense of their findings. In the military, they say "no plan survives first contact with the enemy", and similarly in academia, few research plans survive the research process unchanged.

One question raised by all this revision is whether you should mention these changes in your introduction. Should you present the final version of your research as if it were all part of the original plan? If you changed your theoretical model or research questions as a result of your literature review, should you mention those changes or simply present the revised model as if it were the one you planned to use all along? How far should you take these revisions? Is it OK to alter your research questions after you complete your analysis so as to better match your findings? If you don't find what you expected, do you quietly drop the previous research that would have supported the findings you did not get from your literature review and replace it with other research that supports what you did find? Some would view this as dishonest; like changing your bet after the race is over. Others fear that 'tidying up' in this way and reporting research without acknowledging dead-ends, mistakes or revisions can present an image of research that is too perfect, giving the impression that 'good' research always works out exactly as planned.

Ultimately, this may end up being a question of practicality rather than honesty. Most research reports need to fit within a tightly specified word limit, and with space at a premium, it can feel like there is no room to discuss the wrong turns and dead-ends. Instead, you can feel limited to discussing the final plan, the one that worked. The one exception seems to be the doctoral thesis where there is both the space to explore some of the messiness of the research process and an expectation to do so. Thus, if you are not writing a doctoral thesis, you can always tell yourself that there is no spare room to talk about wrong turns and changes. While that may be true, efficient report writing is always about making the best use of the space available and that means making space to include the things that are important. If you agree with those who feel it is important to acknowledge the messiness of research, then you can and should make space in your introduction to talk about at least some of those twists and turns your research has taken. Admitting such changes and mistakes should not be seen as diminishing the research in any way. From Pavlov to Pasteur, the history of research is littered with illuminating accidents and fortuitous mistakes.

What is a theoretical model (and why do I need one)?

The purpose of most research is to develop an explanation for why things are the way they are or to better understand how something works. Most of the research that is not developing a new explanation is trying to put an existing explanation to the test, usually by applying it to the real world. We can refer to these explanations as 'theoretical models' or just 'models'.

When we think of the word 'model', the mental image we get are models of planes or ships made from plastic or wood. These physical models are a much smaller and simpler representation of the real thing. They can be built for decorative purposes but they can also have a practical use such as the models of aeroplanes and other vehicles used in wind tunnel tests. A model will almost always be a simplified representation of the real thing, leaving out details that aren't important to the model builder, often focusing on those details that will allow the builder to use the model to explore qualities of the real thing by using the model in its place. If I have a new aeroplane design, I don't need to go as far as building a real aeroplane based on my new design to see if it will fly, I can build a scale model and test that.

Just like those physical models, a theoretical model is a simplified representation of some situation in the real world. The model will pick out certain elements of the situation it is trying to explain and then make predictions about the relationships between those elements as an attempt to explain how that situation works. For example, if I am trying to understand why those students in my class who have part-time jobs are doing poorly on their assessments, I could construct a theoretical model of that situation. In my model, the elements I would include are time spent on a part-time job, time spent on studies and performance in their assessments. The model would predict that as the time spent on a part-time job increases, time spent studying decreases and that has an impact on performance. I can then design my methodology so that I gather data about these three things and use a statistical analysis to test the relationships between them that the model predicts. If the results show that the relationships work the way my model has predicted, then that lends support to my model as a valid explanation for that situation. If enough research finds evidence to support my model, it can become the standard model used to explain the impact of part-time work on a student's studies. On the other hand, if my results do not support the relationships the model predicts, then it is back to the drawing board either to change the model or completely replace it.

When it comes to deciding which elements to include in the model and what relationships to predict between those elements, this is best done based on the previous research. When constructing a model, it works best if the majority of the elements that you plan to include in that model have already been shown to be important in that situation by previous research. It is even possible that some of the relationships between those elements, predicted by my model, have also already been demonstrated in previous research. The new model then takes all these established elements and relationships and adds something new, maybe adding in a new element, a new relationship or combining them all for the first time. In this way, the new model is not making a wild stab in the dark in its predictions. It is taking a small step from what is known out into the unknown. These small steps make it possible for the researcher to make sense of what they find by limiting the number of unknowns. Like a jigsaw with missing pieces, the more pieces you already have, the easier it is to look at the picture as a whole and figure out what appears on the bits that are missing.

▶ CHAPTER 2: EXERCISES

Exercise I: MCT

1) The goal of the introduction is...
   A. to explain the purpose behind your research.
   B. to explore the previous research that has inspired your research.
   C. to explain the methodology you will use in detail.
   D. All of the above.

2) You tell your audience about the research context because it helps them to _____ and the reason it is important for you to do that is because it helps you to _____.
   A. see the wider relevance of your research, justify why the research is necessary.
   B. understand the previous research that has been carried out, establish your theoretical model.
   C. see where you got your ideas from, illustrate the twists and turns that occur in real research.
   D. None of the above.

3) What are the two main benefits that come from your research area having a narrow focus?
   A. Fewer surface elements to distract you. Easier to show the relevance to the research context.
   B. Easier to show the relevance to the research context. Increased chances of finding relevant research.
   C. Easier to cover in one piece of research. Fewer surface elements to distract you.
   D. Increased chances of finding relevant research. Easier to cover in one piece of research.

4) The purpose of a theoretical model is to...
   A. summarise the key concepts and theories that are central to your research.
   B. predict how the various elements of a situation relate to each other.
   C. identify which deeper concept or mechanism that the results of the analysis are revealing.
   D. All of the above.

5) When talking about your research, the _____ tell us what the research is trying to find out, the _____ tell us why the research matters and the _____ tell what the researcher will do to find the answers they are looking for.
   A. aims, objectives, research questions
   B. objectives, aims, research questions

C. research questions, aims, objectives
D. research questions, objectives, aims

6) Where do the answers to the research questions come from?
   A. The participants.
   B. The analysis.
   C. The literature review.
   D. The methodology.

7) If you link a research question to the theoretical model, then the answer to that question is more likely to provide insight, which help you to make connections between....
   A. the concepts looked at in this research and other concepts which might have a similar effect.
   B. the answer to that research question and new perspectives on the wider research context.
   C. your research and potential future research.
   D. All of the above.

8) A hypothesis is used to...
   A. Predict the answer to one of the research questions.
   B. Restate the research question using quantitative/statistical terminology.
   C. Explain the relevance of the research question to the research context.
   D. Link the research question to the findings of the analysis.

9) In my research, my three research questions ask: first, if short one-to-one tuition sessions are more effective than longer group sessions in improving student performance; second, what do students in group sessions understand to be the role of the teacher; third, if there is a relationship between a student's level of confidence and the level of benefit they get from group teaching. The methodologies I will need to answer these questions are _____ for the first question, _____ for the second and _____ for the third.
   A. Quantitative, Quantitative, Qualitative
   B. Qualitative, Qualitative, Quantitative
   C. Qualitative, Quantitative, Qualitative
   D. Quantitative, Qualitative, Quantitative

10) Carrying out original research means ensuring that your research is not just a replication of a piece of previous research. Why is this important?
   A. Carrying out research which copies the methodology and theoretical model of other research is against the rules.
   B. By adding something new you give your research a clearer purpose than it would have if it was only a replication.

C. Your research will be a lot more impressive, and get a higher grade, if you can demonstrate that you came up with every part of it yourself.

D. It's only important for a doctoral thesis, that is the only form of research that has to be original.

Exercise 2: How serious are these mistakes?

A common problem faced by many first-time report writers is judging the relative importance of all the different rules and requirements involved in report writing. How important is it to refer to your research in the future tense? How serious is it to leave out your aims? With this in mind you will find, in alphabetical order, 12 common mistakes made by first-time report writers when writing their introduction. You need to put each of them in one of three categories of importance: serious errors, moderate errors and minor errors.

- Carrying out research which is entirely replicating a piece of previous research.
- Choosing research aims which aspire to achieve nothing more than answering the research questions.
- Discussing the course you are taking, if your research is an assignment on that course.
- Discussing the methodology of your research in detail.
- Not mentioning a theoretical model.
- Not mentioning any aims.
- Not mentioning any objectives.
- Not mentioning any research questions.
- Mistaking an objective for an aim or a research question.
- Picking your research area first and then doing a scoping review.
- Referring to your research in the past tense.
- Talking about every step of the research as an objective.

▶ CHAPTER 2: ANSWERS

Exercise 1: MCT

Q1: Ans = A (See: Introduce the research context, p. 14 ↔ Outline the theoretical model, p. 15 ↔ Any mention of your methodology should be brief, p. 21)

Q2: Ans = A (See: Introduce the research context, p. 14 ↔ The report should be about the research not about the course you are taking, p. 20)

Q3: Ans = C (See: Identify the research area, p. 14 ↔ Your research area should not be too broad, p. 21)

Q4: Ans = D (See: Outline the theoretical model, p. 15 ↔ What is a theoretical model (and why do I need one)? p. 29)

Q5: Ans = C (See: Aims and objectives, p. 16 ↔ Research questions, p. 18)

Q6: Ans = B (See: Research questions, p. 18)

Q7: Ans = D (See: Research questions, p. 18 ↔ What is a theoretical model (and why do I need one)? p. 29)

Q8: Ans = A (See: Stating your hypotheses, p. 19)

Q9: Ans = D (See: Your research questions will decide your methodology, p. 25)

Q10: Ans = B (See: Does my research need to be original? p. 26)

Exercise 2: How serious are these mistakes?

Serious errors

(Not mentioning any aims ↔ Choosing research aims which aspire to achieve nothing more than answering the research questions ↔ Carrying out research which is entirely replicating a piece of previous research ↔ Picking your research area first and then doing a scoping review)

All of these are serious errors either because they completely undermine the central purpose of an introduction, which is to establish the nature and purpose of the research, or because they reveal what may be a fatal flaw to your research design. Without aims that connect your research to a wider issue, your research has no purpose, which means that no matter how effectively you carry it out, the research is pointless. The same would be true if you failed to mention any research context. Research which is just copying a piece of previous research with nothing new added suffers from the same flaw. While it's not guaranteed that picking a research area before reading any literature will produce flawed research, you greatly increase the chances of introducing flaws. This might be in the form of research which is similarly re-inventing the wheel or it could be research where you are unable to find relevant sources and so unable to construct the theoretical model needed to make sense of your findings.

(See: Introduce the research context, p. 14 ↔ Aims and objectives, p. 16 ↔ Scope the literature first, then pick a research area, p. 23 ↔ Does my research need to be original? p. 26)

Moderate errors

(Discussing the methodology of your research in detail ↔ Talking about every step of the research as an objective ↔ Discussing the course you are taking, if your research is an assignment on that course ↔ Not mentioning a theoretical model ↔ Not mentioning any research questions)

All of these are moderate errors owing to the fact that, while they do make your work much less effective, they do not fatally undermine it the way the serious errors do. The first three, relating to methodology, objectives and course details are all introducing material into the introduction that isn't necessary. This will either bore your audience, bury the more important information from sight or leave you lacking the space or word count you need to discuss more important information later on in the report. By contrast, the latter two issues, concerning models and questions, are about leaving out things that should be in the intro-duction. The absence of a theoretical model or research questions will make it harder to understand your aims. That being said, it's not as serious to leave them out as it was to leave the aims out because while the absence of the model or questions may make it harder to understand the purpose of the research, the absence of the aims makes it virtually impossible to understand the purpose. Also, you will have another chance to discuss both the model and the research questions in the literature review section, which means you can compensate for leaving them out of the introduction. Nevertheless, it is still a better choice to include both the model and the research questions in your introduction.

(See: Outline the theoretical model, p. 15 ↔ Aims and objectives, p. 16 ↔ Research questions, p. 18 ↔ The report should be about the research not about the course you are taking, p. 20 ↔ Any mention of your methodology should be brief, p. 21)

Minor errors

(Mistaking an objective for an aim or a research question ↔ Referring to your research in the past tense ↔ Not mentioning any objectives)

All of these are minor errors in the sense that, although they have a negative im-pact on the effectiveness of your introduction, the extent of their impact is much more limited than the moderate errors. As long as you have aims, objectives and research questions in your introduction, then using the wrong label to refer to each of them might be slightly confusing but only briefly. If you have writ-ten each of them correctly, your audience should be able to untangle the error without much effort. Similarly, the use of the past tense to refer to your research rather than the future tense is more of a technicality than anything else. Many readers might not even notice you've done it. The last error about "not mention-ing any objectives" is something of a red herring. If your research has a standard design, you may quite legitimately have no objectives which need mentioning. It would only be an issue if your design was very different from standard, and even in that case only if not mentioning an objective makes it harder to understand the aims. Overall then, these are things you should generally try to avoid doing, but you should not worry too much about it if you accidentally do one.

(See: Aims and objectives, p. 16 ↔ In the introduction, your research is still in the future, p. 20 ↔ Aims and objectives, p. 16)

3 The literature review

The literature review is the section where you review the claims and findings made within the literature which is exploring topics that are closely related to the research area of your research. You do this by showing how the claims, findings and unresolved questions to be found in that literature have inspired your research. By the end of your literature review, your audience should have a clear idea of what key questions in the literature remain unresolved and how your research proposes to resolve them.

▸ BEFORE YOU BEGIN THIS CHAPTER...

Before you are ready to begin writing your literature review, there are a number of steps in the research process you will need to complete first.

- Agree a research area, aims and objectives with your supervisor.
- Decide on the scope of your review (which types of sources, which years).
- Identify your search parameters (key words).
- Specify the time limit for your review.
- Conduct the literature review itself.
- Take notes on each relevant source located.

Once you have completed all of these steps you are ready to begin writing this section of the report.

DOI: 10.4324/9781003107965-3

▶ THE BASICS

In a literature review, you spend the majority of your time discussing other people's 'literature', which is their published work. You are trying to give your audience an overview of any literature which has looked at the same area as your research. There are a number of things your audience needs to know about the literature: the claims and arguments made, the results found and the questions asked. By telling your audience what has already been claimed or found by other researchers as well as what remains unknown, you set the scene for your research which is setting out to claim or find something new.

One of the first things many report writers want to know about this process is what counts as 'literature'? While the word 'literature' brings to mind old books and manuscripts on dusty shelves, these days a literature review also includes reviewing websites, textbooks, monographs (single author books), journal articles and more. Because the term 'literature' is so connected with books, many researchers prefer the term 'source' or 'sources' to refer to all of these different sources of information. However, in practice, you will find the terms 'literature' and 'sources' both mean the same thing and are interchangeable. As such, term 'source' or 'piece of literature' both mean one thing you have read, whereas the terms 'sources' or 'literature' both mean multiple things you have read.

However, whether you refer to them as literature or sources, the real challenge is not going to be what you call them, but how you select them, what you say about them and how you present it all in you review.

Structuring your review

Before you begin searching through the literature and deciding which sources to include in your review, you should first give some thought to how you will structure the literature review section when you write it. Planning the structure of your literature review section first will help you to focus your search for literature, making it quicker and more efficient.

The structure of the literature review section works best if it is arranged into sub-sections. The first sub-section contains an overview of all the other sub-sections, explaining the focus for each one. Each of the sub-sections after the first focuses on literature relating to one concept or relationship that you mentioned in your theoretical model (See: Outline the theoretical model, p. 15). Then, in the final sub-section of the literature review, you show how some of the claims, findings and unresolved questions found in that literature are the basis for your research questions.

One benefit from breaking your literature review down into sub-sections is that it turns it from one big literature review into several smaller more focused reviews. Each sub-section acts like its own miniature literature search, reviewing only the literature that is most relevant to the concept or relationship which is the focus of the sub-section. Combining all this related research within a sub-section allows you to compare and contrast the claims and findings of these various sources and identify any unresolved questions connected to that concept. At the end of each sub-section, you should offer a conclusion on the research you have reviewed within that sub-section. This conclusion should highlight what you think is the most important finding, concept or unresolved question among the literature you have discussed in that sub-section (See: Identifying the foundations and unresolved questions, p. 41). You will come back to some of these conclusion points again in the final sub-section of the literature review section (See: Framing your research, p. 43).

This is why you should plan the structure of your review first, as it helps to break down your literature review into series of mini-searches, with each search trying to locate sources related to the concept or relationship from one of these sub-sections.

Arthur is looking at people's attitudes towards workplace safety. He is interested in finding out if the attitudes are influenced by concepts such as age, seniority in the company and experience of workplace accidents. In his theoretical model he suggests that each of these concepts has a separate relationship to attitudes to safety. However, he also suggests they have a combined relationship which is greater than the sum of the parts. As such, the structure of his literature review would have a sub-section for each of the concepts and its relationship with attitudes to safety, followed by a sub-section which looks at their combined relationship with attitudes to safety, He will need to do a separate search for each of these sub-sections, starting with a search for literature on age and attitudes to safety, and then seniority and attitudes to safety, and so on.

One final note on the structure of the review is that within each of these subsections, you should always aim to review more than one source related to the concept or relationship which is the focus of the sub-section. Exploring multiple sources allows you to be confident that you are presenting your audience with a more complete and balanced picture of the literature in that area, something known as critical discussion (See: Criticality, p. 214). You create this sense of a 'more complete picture' by showing your audience how the different sources each reveal a different part of that 'picture'. For that reason, with each source you discuss you should be telling your audience what that source adds above and beyond what they already know from the other sources discussed within that sub-section.

Selecting your sources

When you are carrying out each of these smaller searches for the different sub-sections of your review, the challenge will be sifting through all the sources you find and deciding which ones to mention in your report. You want to make sure you mention those sources which are most relevant to that sub-section. The amount of 'relevance' that a source has can be determined in several ways. One way to determine relevance is based on the elements that the source has in common with your research. The source may look at the concept or relationship which is the focus of the sub-section, but does it involve the same wider context as your research (for example, looking at the same real-world setting) or was it asking similar research questions? A rule-of-thumb is that the greater the number of elements in common, the more relevant this source is to your research. Another way to determine relevance of a source is to consider how important that source is to all the literature which explores the concept or relationship. A source is only likely to become widely mentioned by other sources if its findings or concepts are considered to be reliable or important. A source like that is relevant to any research which explores that concept or relationship, including yours.

One of the sub-sections for Arthur's literature reviews is focusing on the relationship between age and attitudes to safety in the workplace, which was mentioned in his theoretical model. He needs to prioritise each of the sources he has found, depending on how relevant it is to that relationship. The lowest priority would be sources which mention age or attitudes toward workplace safety, but do not look at the relationship between them. Arthur may not mention any of these sources at all. The medium priority sources would be the less-well-known sources that mention the relationship between age and attitudes to safety in any context other than the workplace. Arthur may mention a few of these, if he cannot find anything better. The highest priority will be for widely mentioned sources which look at that relationship or any source which looks at that relationship specifically in the workplace. They may be harder to find, but Arthur will definitely want to include any of these high priority sources that he can find. If he can find enough of them he may not need any of the medium priority sources at all.

Why should I only use published sources?

Another basic rule about selecting sources, in addition to their relevance, is that they should all be identifiable, published sources. In any piece of academic writing, whenever you make a claim you need to combine that claim with some evidence which supports it, also known as marking an academic 'argument' (See: Argument, p. 119). When doing this, it is important to identify the source of your evidence, as your audience will want to know where your information is coming from. This is true in the real world as well as in reports. If one of your friends announced some astonishing fact (for example, that owning a cat makes you less likely to get cancer!) you would want to know where they had heard that fact.

Being able to identify our sources is important because we often judge the credibility of a claim based on the source of that claim. In real life, we often get away with having a very vague source (for example, your friend thinks they read about cats curing cancer somewhere on the internet) but that won't do for a research report. In a report, you need to clearly identify all your sources. Without a clearly identified source, your audience has no idea if the claims or findings based on that source have any credibility.

An important part of identifying a source is to indicate where that source was published, preferably somewhere it can be accessed by your audience if they wish to evaluate or read it for themselves (See: References: The basics, p. 151). It is for this reason that unpublished or unidentified sources are not considered to be appropriate sources, as there is no way for your audience to read or assess their credibility. This includes unpublished sources such as lecture or seminar notes. If a source was not published, or you can't find the publisher for a source, then you should not include any claims or findings in your literature review which are based on that source.

Of course, that raises the question as to whether you need a source to support every single thing you say. Can I just say a week is seven days long, or do I need a source on that claim? What about my own opinion on things, how do I include that? Both those questions fall outside the scope of this chapter but are discussed elsewhere in this book (See: Personal opinion vs informed opinion, p. 211).

Identifying the foundations and unresolved questions

The whole point of reviewing this literature is to identify the 'foundations' and 'unresolved questions' connected to your research area. The 'foundations' are the key claims, concepts or findings mentioned in the conclusions of the sub-sections in your review. They are referred to as foundations because your research will be using them as a starting point and 'building on top of them'. In order to spot a finding or a concept which is foundational in a selection of literature that you are reviewing, you should look for findings or concepts that are widely mentioned or have influenced a lot of other researchers. The purpose of telling your audience about these foundations is to help them gain a clear picture regarding what is already known about your research area and theoretical model. Filling in as much of the picture as you can with what is already known will reveal the 'gaps', those things about the research area and theoretical model that remain unknown, 'gaps' which you plan to fill in with the findings of your research.

Walter is researching how reading romantic fiction can shape our beliefs about relationships and our behaviour in real-life romantic relationships. In particular, his research focuses on the impact of romantic fiction which has been recommended to us by a friend.

In his literature review there are two sub-sections, one looking at the origin of our beliefs about relationships and the other looking at the things that affect our behaviour in romantic relationships. In the first sub-section he starts off by reviewing sources which discuss research on the origin of our beliefs about relationships. All he mentions about this research is the key finding, that people in close relationships (such as friends and family) act as role models, shaping our beliefs about appropriate behaviour in relationships. He also discusses some research which explores how our beliefs can be influenced by the media we consume, again focusing on one claim from that research, that the media we share with our friends can shape our beliefs. Finally, Walter mentions a specific piece of research which found that media shared by friends can have a major impact on beliefs and behaviour about recycling. This finding is one of the foundations for Walter's research as it shows that media shared by friends can influence both beliefs and behaviour, a finding that Walter will try to 'build on' by applying to a different kind of media and behaviour in his research.

In addition to laying the foundations for your research, the other details you would want from the conclusions of those sub-section are the 'unresolved questions', namely those issues or questions which remain unresolved or unclear. As well as any question which has been pointed out in the literature as being unresolved, this also includes questions that no one has tried to answer, or any question where the answer provided within the literature appears incomplete. Finding these unresolved questions is important since they will function as the basis for your research questions. In essence, each of your research questions can be considered as an attempt to answer one or more unresolved questions arising from the literature.

Sometimes a source will hand you an unresolved question 'on a silver platter' in the form of a suggestion for future research. You are more likely to find these in the discussion section of a research article. After reporting the findings of their own research, it is not uncommon for researchers to propose ideas for future research that could build on what they have found. You may want to do this yourself in your discussion (See: Future research, p. 123). Other researcher's proposals for future research make your life easy since they highlight the unresolved question by suggesting it needs further research. On top of this, they may also suggest previous research that is relevant to that question and they may even suggest a suitable methodology.

Not all unresolved questions are so easy to find. Sometimes you will need to spot unresolved questions based on certain phrases that the authors use. One thing to look out for is any place where the author speculates about something, a speculation being a claim which they believe to be true but for which they don't have any conclusive evidence. Anywhere they say that something "could be", "might be" or "maybe" true (or other similar phrases) are potential examples of an author speculating. Another way to locate unresolved questions is to consider that many research findings give rise to new questions which are unresolved. Sometimes these new questions are stated in the source, other times they will only occur to you as you read it. If they are stated in the source the previous researcher may speculate as to the answer, but not offer any evidence to support those speculations. For example, a finding which establishes that something is happening, such as that one event is causing another, raises new questions as to why it happens. Alternatively, findings that summarise people's experiences and so establish what those people think is happening raise new questions whether their perceptions are true. For these reasons, any previous research finding is worth examining to see if it has given rise to a new and unresolved question.

Framing your research

In the final sub-section of your literature review section, you summarise some of the foundations and unresolved questions from the literature and then link them to your research questions. The point of doing this is to demonstrate to your audience how your research will contribute to the overall research in this area by showing how you will help to address those unresolved questions. Similarly, you can highlight a finding, claim or concept from those foundations if one of your research questions is attempting to critically evaluate or expand on that finding, claim or concept. You do not need to summarise all the foundations or unresolved questions that you have mentioned in all of the sub-sections, only those that are related to your research questions. You also don't need to go into the methodology of your research at this point, that can wait for the methodology section.

[In Walter's final sub-section] *In conclusion we can see that our expectations regarding the romantic behaviour of others can be influenced by the reading of romantic fiction (Medina, 2013) and beliefs about relationships (Gilbert, 2018). What is not clear is whether the romantic fiction is influencing our expectations by first affecting our beliefs about relationships. As such my first research question asks whether there is a link between the amount of romantic fiction being read and the beliefs about relationships.*

▶ COMMON MISTAKES

Your research is still in the future

Similar to the introduction, the literature review is written from the perspective of the research being in the future. This is because the literature review is thought of as something you do before you carry out your own research. That is an easy thing for first-time researchers to get confused about since, in reality, the literature review may be something a researcher starts before the research takes place but continues to work on throughout the research process. Nonetheless, no matter when you start or finish it, you should always use the future tense throughout when talking about your research in this section of the report.

Write a literature review in sub-sections, not one big 'shopping list'

One of the more common flaws in a literature review written by a first-time report writer is a review that is presented as one long unbroken list of literature, sometimes referred to as a 'shopping list'. The problem here is a lack of structure. In the worst cases, a literature review of this type will have little or no structure at all, with the literature presented in no particular order, sources included for no obvious reason and each source discussed separately from the others. The problem with this approach is that it reads poorly and is hard to follow. On top of this, it may not be clear why those particular sources have been included and so the whole list can feel irrelevant. Any sources that are relevant are hard to remember because they get lost in the 'list'.

Structuring the literature review into sub-sections and grouping together related sources within each of those sub-section are the most basic steps needed to avoid this issue. However, there also needs to be a sense of structure within the sub-sections as well. At the start of each sub-section, there should be a brief explanation as to what the focus of that section is, which then clarifies what the sources in that section have in common. Then, at the end of each sub-section, there should be a conclusion. This conclusion could be highlighting a foundational claim, concept or finding, an unresolved question or all of the above. Either way, it reduces the sub-section to a key point or two which are much more easily remembered. Finally, a conclusion may also include a linking sentence to help link this sub-section to the next one, which helps the audience to see how each sub-section relates to the next one (See: Signpost words, p. 207).

Don't pad out your review just to show off your reading

Within each sub-section of your review, you need to consider why you are including any source that you mention to that sub-section. More is not always better and adding too many sources with no plan or purpose can be repetitive and will cause your audience to lose sight of the important points you are making with your review. Therefore, the first question you need to consider before you mention any source is this; does this source contain any foundational detail or unresolved question which your audience needs to know in order to understand your research? If not, then you need to reconsider whether you need to include it. Simply 'showing off' that you have read many sources is not going to impress anyone, especially if the sources seem irrelevant to your research. Any source that passes the relevance test also needs to add something new in addition to what has been contributed by the sources already mentioned. Again, if it adds nothing new then it probably does not need to be included. Finally, if several sources are adding roughly the same thing to the review, you should avoid mentioning them one at a time, since that can get repetitious. Instead, you should first consider what the important or noteworthy thing is that the sources have in common; you then mention that one thing and cite all those sources, collectively, as the source for that noteworthy concept, finding or claim. This way you get to demonstrate the breadth of your reading without boring your audience.

A literature review is not an essay

Another common mistake is to write your literature review as if it were an essay. Even worse, this kind of literature review usually reads like a *bad* essay entitled "Here is everything I know about *Topic X*". The reason for the confusion is that an essay and a literature review have a lot in common. Both are exploring an area, both draw on literature to make their points, both can be divided up into sub-sections with each sub-section focusing on part of the whole and both typically finish with a conclusion.

However, there is one critical difference between an essay and a literature review. An essay starts off with a question (the essay question) and the purpose of the essay is to provide an answer to that question from the sources reviewed. By contrast, a literature review starts with a research area or real-world issue and the purposes of the review is to generate questions, first the unresolved questions and then your research questions, from the sources reviewed. In a nutshell then, an essay starts with an unresolved question and ends with an answer, whereas a literature review starts with no question and ends with unresolved research questions. The reason you want unresolved research questions at the end of your literature review is to justify the need for your research to answer them. If you write your literature review like an essay, using the literature to come up with answers to all the questions you pose, then you have succeeded at nothing but making your research unnecessary. That may be a good way to write an essay, but a terrible way to write a literature review.

Research questions emerge from the literature review, not the other way around

Some first-time report writers make the mistake of attempting to develop their research questions first and then search for the literature to support those questions afterwards. This is a similar mistake to those who pick their research area without doing a scoping review of the literature first, and in both cases, it is a poor strategy (See: Scope the literature first, then pick a research area, p. 23). The flaw in the strategy is that, by deciding what your research questions are without knowing anything about the literature, you are taking a complete 'shot in the dark'. Relevant literature may be rare and take you much longer to find, and that is assuming it even exists. It is much safer and more efficient to review the literature first, using literature you know exists and has already been found to then inspire your research questions.

The faulty approach of inventing research questions before the review may be caused, in part, by the fact that the research questions are often included in the introduction section of the report, which comes before the literature review section. This gives a false impression that the research questions were invented before the literature review took place. As such, the other lesson to be learnt here is that the sections of the report are not always written in the order in which they appear in the report.

Too much methodology from previous research

A common feature of textbooks, when discussing previous research, is to tell us how that research was carried out. Since the purpose of a textbook is to explain things, this approach makes sense. Explaining how the previous research was conducted is a great way to teach people about research methods as well as telling them about the findings of that research. But a literature review is not a textbook and you are not trying to teach your audience about research methods or anything else. You are trying to establish the foundations for your research, showing your audience what is already known, and identify any unresolved questions. In this situation, the methods that the previous researchers used in their research are usually not important.

In your literature review, you would only include details about the participants or the methods used by previous research, if those details are relevant to your research questions in some way. For example, if you believed that a key finding in some piece of previous research was affected by their methodology, your research question might be asking if changing that methodology will result in a different finding.

> [In Walter's final sub-section] *There has been a good deal of research which has found no link between the reading of romantic fiction and expectations about the romantic behaviour of others (Little, 2000). However, much of this research has categorised a book as 'romantic fiction' even if the romance is only included in a sub-plot and not the main plot. As such, my second research question asks if the presence of romance in the main plot or sub-plot will affect the link between reading romantic fiction and our beliefs about relationships.*

Even if it is necessary to discuss the participants or method of a piece of previous research, you should keep it short. A sentence or two highlighting the issue with their method is usually enough and, as said before, only in those rare cases where the issue relates to your research questions. The rest of the time, your audience does not normally need to know who took part in the previous research you are reviewing or how that research was done.

▶ REFINEMENTS

Time or space = importance

Whether they realise it consciously or not, in the mind of your audience the amount of time or space you spend discussing any source, concept, claim or finding is an indicator of the importance of that source or finding to your research. If you spend a lot of time discussing the findings from a source, your audience will expect those findings to be a prominent feature of your research and vice versa. If you break this rule, for example only making a brief mention of something which later turns out to be critical, your audience will feel lost and annoyed.

They will feel lost because they have been 'ambushed' by a critical finding or concept that they have never heard of before and the annoyance comes from the fact that you wasted their time talking about other things which now appear to be less important. It would be like a murder mystery novel, with lots of suspects, but at the end the great detective reveals that the murderer was... a minor character mentioned only once on page six.

For this reason, you need to make sure you follow the rule of time-and-space-equalling-importance throughout your literature review. Thus, a source which discusses research that is in the same general area as your research but not closely related to any of your research questions should only get only a brief mention. A brief mention, in this case, may mean that you only mention one claim or finding from that source. By comparison, sources that are more closely related to your research questions would get more time/space devoted to them. This extra time/space may translate into mentioning multiple findings or claims from each source or you may look at multiple sources with similar findings or claims, exploring some of the developments or debates in this part of the literature.

You should still follow the previous guidance about avoiding discussions of methodology of previous research unless necessary. You should also avoid 'padding out' your discussion of an important source with lengthy and unnecessary explanation or description. The extra time/space needs to be filled with meaningful content, which is to say, a critical discussion of the literature on that topic (See: Criticality, p. 214). Naturally, this presents you with the challenge of finding multiple sources which share a focus on the concept, claim or finding in question so as to give it the discussion it deserves. However, if a concept, claim or finding really is that closely related to your research questions, then locating as much literature as you can on that concept or finding should be something you should want to do anyway.

The funnel

If you were to imagine that a literature review had a shape, that shape would be a funnel. At the top, near the start of the literature review, the focus is broad but as you move down, the further into the literature review you get, the narrower the focus gets. By the time you reach the end of the literature review the focus is concentrated on a very small number of concepts, findings or claims which are directly related to your research questions.

This applies both between and within the sub-sections of your review. What that means is when you consider the focuses of all of the different sub-sections of your literature review, you should arrange them in order of relevance. In other words, the sub-section which is least connected to your research questions goes first and the sub-section that is most closely connected goes last. If two sub-sections are equally relevant then consider whether one of them 'sets the stage' for the other; does one sub-section discuss concepts which are more basic and need to be understood first before you discuss the other? If so, the one with the more basic concepts goes first.

In this way, you go from general to specific when arranging the sub-sections, and the same is true of the order in which you discuss the sources within each sub-section. In each sub-section, you need to decide which of your sources will be the 'starting point' for the review in that sub-section. This initial source is the one that introduces the issue the sub-section is focusing on. Maybe it was the first piece of research in that area of research or the most influential one. You also need to pick another source which acts as the 'end point' for that sub-section. Usually the final source contains a claim or finding which is directly relevant to your research questions.

Once you have your start point and end point you then need to consider what other sources you mention in between. The sources mentioned in between act as 'stepping stones', helping the audience to follow the progress of the research in this area from start to end. Usually the start will be very general or basic and the end will be more specific, so the stepping stones show how we got from one to the other. For each source you add in the middle you should consider whether the source is necessary. Does it add something of value over what has already been added by the previous sources?

You also need to consider whether any of the sources in the middle add new details which do not lead on towards the final source you are aiming for. If that happens you need to consider why you are adding that middle source, does it add something which is necessary for the audience to know even if it is not obviously connected to the final source in that section? You should always consider the possibility that a middle source may go off on a tangent which does not add anything of value, in which case you should leave that source out of the review.

Brian is researching the impact of sleep on memory. Brian's theoretical model proposed that there is a relationship between the concepts of sleep deprivation and the mental resources involved in recall. As such, his literature review will have two sub-sections, namely sleep and memory. Since he is looking at the impact of sleep on memory, he decides to put the sub-section on sleep first. In the sub-section on sleep he will start off by discussing some of the most influential theories about the purpose of sleep. He will keep this discussion brief because the purpose of sleep is a very general topic. Having established why we sleep Brain can now talk about those times we can't sleep. This means he can now focus on sleep deprivation and the effects it has. There will be more detail at this level, looking at a few sources on the impact of sleep deprivation. The last of these sources mentioned will be ones that show sleep deprivation has an impact on problem solving. These are left until last because they mention the concept of 'recall' which means they are most closely related to the research questions which ask about sleep deprivation, mental resources and recall. Now that he has established the link between sleep and recall, he needs to tell us a bit more about recall, which is part of memory. As such, the second sub-section in Brian's literature review will be about memory. This will be a similar structure to the first sub-section, starting off with a brief discussion of the most general theories regarding memory, but finishing with a more detailed discussion on the role of mental resources in recall, because again the concept of mental 'resources' is most closely related to the research questions for the current research.

Use high quality sources

The quality of your sources is important, as the 'quality' of a source is usually a reflection of its credibility. You want your sources to be high quality, as you will be basing your research on their findings and if your sources lack credibility so will your research. As such, it is worth considering the quality of the more commonly used sources in a typical literature review.

The most desirable sources are usually journal articles and there are three main reasons that they considered the highest quality sources available. The first reason is that a journal article will have been through a peer review process, overseen by an editor. This process involves other experienced academics, the 'peers' in this case, who read the article and check that it is accurate before it gets published. The second reason is that recently published journal articles tend to be the most up-to-date publications, containing cutting-edge theories and the latest findings. Finally, it is a requirement in any journal that you must cite your sources and provide a full list of references, similar to the references section in a research report (See: References: The basics, p. 151). This allows the audience for that article to identify the sources on which the article is based and to evaluate the quality those sources for themselves.

Next in line, in terms of quality, are books. There are different kinds of books ranging from textbooks, which are teaching materials aimed at students, to monographs and edited volumes, which are research-focused books written by one person or several people, respectively. No matter which kind of book, they are all peer reviewed and edited prior to publication, which makes them credible sources. However, the level of scrutiny in the peer review process for a book is not as detailed as for a journal article, which lowers their quality rating a little. Also, books tend to be less up-to-date than journal articles, even if the book is published at the same time as the article, mainly due to the fact that books take longer to write. Another reason why textbooks, specifically, may not be as up-to-date is due to the fact that they normally focus on the more mainstream theories, overlooking the more recent theories which have not yet become widely known or accepted. This is less of an issue with a monograph or an edited volume, which can contain some of the latest concepts and findings in that area. In terms of identifying their sources, all books are usually aiming for the same standard as journals with regular citations and full lists of references. Overall then, books may be slightly lower quality than journal articles but are still considered high quality sources.

Once we move beyond journal articles and books, most other sources are quite a bit lower in quality and thus credibility. Sources at this level are things like websites, newspapers, TV shows, video blogs and other media. Websites are usually considered to be low quality since they rarely use any kind of peer review to check that their contents are accurate. Many newspapers, magazines and television shows are as bad as websites in terms of checking their facts, although some news media sources can be a little bit higher quality through the use of 'fact checking', which involves making sure that any claims made in the source have been checked against another source. This may sound like peer review, but the fact-checkers are not experts on the topics being discussed, which means it is not considered to be at the same standard as actual peer review. Also, most media sources are only repeating a small fraction of information taken from somewhere else which means it is the original source you should be interested in and not the watered-down version the media are passing on. Finding that original source can be difficult owing to the other reason that websites and media sources are considered low quality, which is their poor referencing. Low quality sources are inconsistent in identifying the sources behind the claims or findings they report, which makes it hard to determine the quality of the evidence behind those claims or findings. For all these reasons websites and media sources are considered low quality and so should be avoided as sources in a literature review.

One final point on sources is that first-time report writers can sometimes get confused as to the difference between websites, which are low quality sources and electronic journals (e-journals) which are accessed through the web, but are high quality sources. If you are in doubt as to which kind of site you are looking at, an e-journal will have details about its peer review procedures on the site and the sources provided through the site will be properly referenced.

Defining key terms

For most students, the only person likely to read the report that they are writing is the person who will mark it. Even so, you should write any report as if it was going to be much more widely read by people from different backgrounds (See: What is a report and why do we write them? p. 1). Taking this approach is good practice for later on in your career where the reports you write will be intended for a much wider audience. However, this means that you may need to define some of the terminology you are using as you cannot take for granted that your audience will already know all the technical terms you mention.

The need to define a term is not determined by how often it is used in your report, but rather how important that term is to your research. An important term is any term your audience needs to know in order to properly understand your research, and you will need to ask yourself whether your audience will know what the term means. This is a question that a lot of first-time report writers have difficulty answering, usually because their lack of experience means they are less sure which are commonly known terms and which are not. One rule-of-thumb you can use to help you make this decision is to ask yourself how often this term is used in sources in this research area. If it is a term that crops up constantly in almost any source in this area then your audience is likely to be already familiar with the term which means you probably don't need to define it. Along similar lines, another rule-of-thumb is that you don't normally need to define any words or concepts which are everyday terms that would be familiar to a non-academic audience.

There are a few exceptions to these rules. The first is when some part of the definition of that term really matters to your research. One example of this is where you plan to challenge some aspect of the standard definition for a term. In such a case you do need to explain what the standard definition is, even for a term your audience is familiar with, so you can explain which part of that definition you are challenging. The other exception to the rule of "not defining everyday terms" is when the term means something different in academia than it does in everyday use. Take for example the concept of 'arousal'. In psychology 'arousal' refers to any state of heightened activity in the body including fear, surprise, excitement and sexual attraction. In everyday use, the term 'aroused' refers almost exclusively to sexual attraction. Terms like this, with a broader or narrower meaning in academia, compared to their everyday meaning will need to be defined.

Maria is doing research on the relationship between the personality traits introversion/ extroversion, a concept known as 'locus of control', and obesity. The terms 'personality' and 'obesity' are everyday terms and do not need to be defined. 'Locus of control' is a psychological term not used in everyday conversation and so it will need to be defined.

'Introversion' and 'extroversion' are terms which are used both inside psychology and in everyday speech. However, the meaning for these terms is more specific in psychology and they are linked to a particular theory of personality. Consequently, Maria will need to define those terms as well.

▶ ADVANCED

Debates in the literature

It is a common occurrence that different sources will report findings or make claims which contradict or compete with each other. Sometimes the disagreement will be over whether something does or does not have an impact on the situation being researched. Other times they may disagree as to which out of a number of different factors is the most important factor in that situation. They may even agree that something is happening but disagree as to why it happens. Occasionally the researchers will be aware of the competing claims made by others and even address them, but other times each researcher will only present their own perspective and seem unaware of the alternative viewpoints.

It is a widespread practice in academic writing that you should present both sides of a debate such as this (See: Criticality, p. 214). It shows a breadth in your reading and awareness that there is more than one viewpoint on an issue, both of which are good qualities for a literature review to have. That being said, simply acknowledging that there is a debate should be seen as only the first step, and if you wish to write at an advanced level you should go further and make some effort to address this debate.

After you present both sides of the debate, your options for addressing it are either to attempt reconciliation between the two sides or to make the argument for one side having a stronger case than the other. Reconciling the differing viewpoints could be done at a methodological or conceptual level. Methodologically, if the two sides are both using empirical research you may be able to identify differences in the way they carried out their research which explain the different results. This might include different participants, measurements or conditions as well as other potential confounding variables not controlled by either side. What you are looking for is a factor which was overlooked by all the researchers but which affected their results. In effect then, you are then suggesting that if that factor had been taken into account they would have found similar results.

To reconcile the two sides conceptually you could look at the fundamental assumptions made by each side, how they approached critical definitions or how they framed the issue. Once found, such conceptual differences help to resolve the debate by demonstrating that the two sides are not actually in disagreement. Instead, you could show that the disagreement is the product of a misunderstanding or a fundamental difference in perspectives on this issue. What you are doing is suggesting that the two sides are mistaken in thinking they are researching the same thing when in fact they are researching theoretically distinct concepts or situations.

If you cannot see a way to reconcile the different sides, the other option is to adjudicate, by when I mean to see if you could find a reason to favour one side over the other. The most common reason why you might favour one side over the other is that a majority of sources support that side. Of course, it is important to consider why these sources support that side, otherwise you can end up with mindless conformity or dogmatism, with everyone taking one side because everyone else is doing it. A good researcher should always be a sceptic and wish to consider for themselves the evidence and arguments behind even the most widely supported side in any debate. Conversely, if you end up adjudicating in favour of the side that has a minority support among the researchers in this area, you will need to offer a valid reason why you believe the majority is mistaken on this issue.

Whether you reconcile or adjudicate, it can strengthen the position you take on that debate considerably if you are able to use your research to support your position. For example, if you claimed that the two sides of the debate got different results for a methodological reason, you have an opportunity to test that reason in the design for your research to demonstrate that changing the method changes the result. You don't have to do this for every debate in the literature that you reconcile, but you could view each such debate as an opportunity to make your research stronger by including at test of your reconciliation claim or reason for adjudication in your design.

Jacob is researching people's choices regarding the timing for their Christmas shopping. He found a debate in the literature over the impact that budgeting has on this behaviour. Some research has found that a budget-conscious shopper will shop earlier to get good prices while other research says that budgeting for Christmas has no impact on when you shop. Jacob believes that budgeting does cause early shopping and that the previous research which did not find this made the mistake of assuming people only have one budget for all purchases at Christmas. He thinks people have a budget for presents, which is separate from their budget for other Christmas related purchases. To support his case, he is going to measure both kinds of budget, general Christmas budget and their budget just for presents, to examine how both of them relate to when people buy presents, He

*expects that if he analyses the impact of the two budgets separately, he can reproduce
both sets of results for the previous research on both sides.*

Beyond the scope of the current research

Sometimes there will be concepts or findings which are related to the research
area for your research, but which you do not want to include in your theoretical
model. There are lots of reasons why this might be the case, ranging from practical issues (the concept is difficult to measure), methodological issues (measuring
that concept would require more time, participants or materials than you have
available to you) or even personal reasons (you have no interest in that concept).
Whatever the reason, if there is a concept that has been found to be relevant in a
lot of the literature but you do not wish to include it in your research, then you
have two options.

The first option is to simply leave that concept out of your literature review and
not mention it. After all, there are so many concepts in any area of research and
not enough space or time in your report to discuss them all. One potential issue
with this approach is that you run the risk that your audience may be aware of
the missing concept or findings and note their absence. If it is not mentioned,
your audience may jump to the conclusion that you don't know about the concept or the sources connecting it to research area for your research. This can raise
doubts about how comprehensive the literature review of your chosen research
area has been and how much control you have over potentially confounding
variables in your research.

The second option is to create a small sub-section in your literature review
where you discuss these kinds of concepts and findings. The idea is to show
that you are aware of the concept, and the literature which says that concept is
important, but that you have made a conscious decision not to include it and
give a reason why. The way you refer to these concepts or findings is that they
are "beyond the scope of the current research" which is a nice way of saying, "I
know about these. I am not including them for a good reason". You should keep
this sub-section short since it defeats the purpose of leaving these concepts out
if you spent a long time discussing them. Also, even if you include a sub-section
like this, you may still not have enough space/time to discuss all the concepts
that you could have been included here. In the end, it always comes down to
personal judgement regarding which concepts you mention in this sub-section.
It can also be a good complement to this sub-section if you then mention any of
these concepts in your design sub-section of your method and explain how you
have controlled for them (See: Controlling confounding variables, p. 78). After

all, if they are important concepts and you are not researching them, you want to make sure they do not end up as confounds.

▶ CHAPTER 3: EXERCISES

Exercise 1: MCT

1) The purpose of the literature review is...
   A. to explain how you are going to carry out your research.
   B. to identify the unresolved questions that your research will address.
   C. to explain how you came up with the idea for your research.
   D. to answer the research questions that you posed in the introduction section.

2) In your literature review you should start with the _____ sources and then, as the review progresses the sources you discuss become more and more _____ until you finish up with the _____ sources.
   A. oldest, recent, latest
   B. longest, concise, shortest
   C. least related, relevant, most related
   D. None of the above

3) The amount of space and time you spend discussing a source should be determined by...
   A. how important the concepts mentioned in that source are to the history of research in that research area.
   B. how familiar your audience is with the concepts mentioned in that source.
   C. how relevant the concepts mentioned in that source are to your research questions.
   D. how well known the researcher is that came up with the concepts mentioned in that source.

4) Which of the following statements about when you should include definitions of terminology is TRUE?
   A. You need to define any term that is important to your research.
   B. You need to define a term that means something different in academia compared to outside it.
   C. You do not need to define a term if it is only mentioned a few times in your report.
   D. None of the above.

5) The main difference between a literature review and an essay is that an essay
_____whereas a literature review _____.
   A. tries to answer the question is poses, is a search for unresolved questions
   B. talks about the future, talks about the past
   C. requires the writer to generate their own answers, uses the answers provided by others
   D. discusses an area in general, focuses in on a specific part of that area

6) Which of the following should NOT be included in a literature review section?
   A. A review of the concepts that you will not be including in your research.
   B. A point based on your lecture or seminar notes.
   C. A question which you do not answer.
   D. All of the above.

7) Journal articles and textbooks are considered to be better quality sources than websites or newspaper articles because...
   A. the accuracy of newspaper articles and websites has not been peer reviewed.
   B. journals and textbooks are more likely to identify their sources through references.
   C. many websites and newspapers pass on only a small fraction of other people's findings.
   D. All of the above.

8) When a literature review looks like a long list of previous research it is an issue to do with _____. If you can ensure that you _____ then you can usually avoid this happening.
   A. relevance, read more widely so you can provide critical discussion
   B. relevance, always refer to your research in the future tense
   C. structure, discuss each source in a separate paragraph devoted to that one source
   D. structure, gather related sources together into sections

9) For the majority of previous research that you cover in your literature review which key details about each piece of research are essential for you to mention?
   A. Concepts they mentioned, what they measured and what they found.
   B. Who took part, what they measured and what they found.
   C. Claims they made, who took part and concepts they mentioned.
   D. Claims they made, concepts they mentioned, what they found.

10) In the final sub-section of the literature review, it is a good idea to...

    A. link your research questions to key unresolved questions from the literature.

    B. offer a conclusion which answers the central question behind the review.

    C. summarise all of the key claims and findings from the literature you have reviewed.

    D. outline the methodology you will use to answer the research questions in your research.

Exercise 2: How serious are these mistakes?

A common problem faced by many first-time report writers is judging the relative importance of all the different rules and requirements involved in report writing. How important is it to identify a source for every concept, finding or claim I mention? How serious is it to make a referencing error? With this in mind you will find, in alphabetical order, 10 common mistakes made by first-time report writers. You need to put each of them in one of three categories of importance: serious errors, moderate errors and minor errors.

- Deciding on your research questions before your review the literature.
- Going into lots of detail about the methodology of your research or the previous research.
- Including sources that are not relevant to your research.
- Not answering the question asked.
- Not breaking up your literature review into sections.
- Not identifying a published source for each concept, finding or claim mentioned.
- Not linking your research questions to the literature.
- Referencing errors.
- Talking about your research in the past tense.
- Using low quality sources.

▶ CHAPTER 3: ANSWERS

Exercise I: MCT

Q1: Ans = B (See: The basics, p. 38 ↔ Identifying the foundations and unresolved questions in your research area, p. 41 ↔ A literature review is not an essay, p. 45)

Q2: Ans = C (See: Selecting your sources, p. 40 ↔ The funnel, p. 48)

Q3: Ans = C (See: Time or Space = Importance, p. 47)

Q4: Ans = B (See: Defining key terms, p. 52)

Q5: Ans = A (See: A literature review is not an essay, p. 45)

Q6: Ans = B (See: Why should I only use published sources? p. 40 ↔ Debates in the literature, p. 53 ↔ Beyond the scope of the current research, p. 55)

Q7: Ans = D (See: Use high quality sources, p. 50)

Q8: Ans = D (See: Structuring your review, p. 38 ↔ Your research is still in the future, p. 44 ↔ Write a literature review in sub–sections, not one big 'shopping list', p. 44)

Q9: Ans = D (See: Identifying the foundations and unresolved questions in your research area, p. 41 ↔ Too much methodology from previous research, p. 46)

Q10: Ans = A (See: Framing your research, p. 43 ↔ A literature review is not an essay, p. 45)

Exercise 2: How serious are these mistakes?

Serious errors

(Not identifying a published source for each concept, finding or claim mentioned ↔ Not breaking up your literature review into sections ↔ Not linking your research questions to the literature.)

All of these are serious errors, either because they sabotage the central purpose of a literature review, which is to establish the foundations and identify unresolved questions which are relevant to your research, or because they reveal serious flaws in your research design. Not linking your research questions to the literature is the most serious of the three, as the foundations and unresolved questions you work so hard to locate within the literature are redundant if they are not the inspiration for your research questions. Similarly, if you do not identify published sources for your claims or findings, then it is not a valid literature review because you have not identified the literature that you are reviewing. Compared to those first two issues, writing the literature review as one long unbroken list may not look as bad. After all, you could still be identifying published literature and linking it to the research questions somewhere inside that large list. However, if you do not break your review up into sections then it is unlikely your audience will remember much of that literature and so the majority of your efforts will have been wasted.

(See: Identifying the foundations and unresolved questions in your research area, p. 41 ↔ Structuring your review, p. 38 ↔ Why should I only use published sources? p. 40 ↔ Write a literature review in sub–sections, not one big 'shopping list', p. 44' ↔ Framing your research, p. 43)

Moderate errors

(Deciding on your research questions before your review the literature. ↔ Going into lots of detail about the methodology of your research or the previous research. ↔ Using low quality sources.)

All of these are moderate errors owing to the fact that, while they do make your work much less effective, they do not fatally undermine it the way the serious errors do. Of the three errors, using low quality sources is the more serious since it undermines a key purpose of the literature review which is to construct a credible foundation for your research. Using low quality sources not only undermines the credibility of your research, it can also cast doubt on the comprehensiveness of the literature review on the grounds that you are unlikely to choose to include low quality sources if you had accessed a suitably wide selection of the literature. Including too many details about methodology, yours or the previous research's, is less about including something bad than it is about including something unnecessary, which wastes precious space and means you have less time/space to discuss the important details. Finally, while deciding your research questions before your review is not guaranteed to end badly, it is taking a large and unnecessary risk which could cost you a lot of time you cannot afford, searching for literature which may be hard to find or many not even exist.

(See: Framing your research, p. 43 ↔ Too much methodology from previous research, p. 46 ↔ Use high quality sources, p. 50 ↔ Research questions emerge from the literature review, not the other way around, p. 46)

Minor errors

(Referencing errors ↔ Talking about your research in the past tense ↔ Including sources that are not relevant to your research ↔ Not answering the question asked.)

All of these are minor errors in the sense that, although they have a negative impact on the effectiveness of your literature review, the extent of their impact is much more limited than the moderate errors. Referencing is something you should be aiming to do without error, not because of its importance, but rather because it is one of the few places where there are exact rules to follow. Most of the time referencing errors are trivial, but if they become too commonplace they can distract you reader and may even make it harder to recognise which sources are being used. Including less relevant sources is another minor error but even small amounts of it still wastes space. It can be hard for a first-time report writer to judge where the 'line' is, in terms of judging what is or is not relevant to their research, but practice will help. Finally, using the wrong tense is the least important of these issues. At worst it is likely to suggest a lack of attention to detail which, although minor, is not a good impression to make on your audience. Overall then, these are mistakes you should generally try to avoid making, but you should not worry too much about it if you do end up making one.

The last error about "not answering the question" is a red herring. There is no question for you to be answering in a literature review. If you find yourself thinking "have I answered the question?" then you are still in 'essay mode' which is the wrong way to approach this section. You avoid this "error" by realising a literature review is not an essay.

(See: Your research is still in the future, p. 44 ↔ Selecting your sources, p. 40 ↔ A literature review is not an essay, p. 45)

4

The method

The method is the section where you explain to your audience how your research was carried out. You do this by telling them what your research was designed to do, who took part, which equipment was used, what people were asked to do and what steps you took to ensure it was all done ethically. By the end of the method section, you should have provided enough detail that your audience not only understands exactly what was done in your research, but they could also re-create it if they wished to.

▶ BEFORE YOU BEGIN THIS CHAPTER...

Before you are ready to begin writing your method, there are a number of steps in the research process you will need to complete first.

- Identify your theoretical model.
- Decide on your research questions.
- Identify the methodology needed to answer each research question.
- Review previous research to identify any suitable existing materials or methodologies that you can use.
- Develop or acquire any measures or equipment needed to complete your data collection.
- Secure ethical clearance for your proposed methodology.
- If your research requires human participants then, after receiving permission from any gatekeepers first, you should identify and approach the participants who will make up your sample and secure their informed consent.
- Collect your data.

DOI: 10.4324/9781003107965-4

Once you have completed all of these steps, you are ready to begin writing this section of the report.

▶ THE BASICS

The method section is the 'recipe' for your research, and it has two purposes. The first is to explain to other people how the research was done so that they know it was done well. The second is to provide them with the means to re-create what you have done to allow them to see if they get the same results (known as 'replication').

There are five sub-sections to the method section: design, participants, materials, procedure and ethics. It is a good idea to use sub-headings to show the name of each of the sub-sections. This helps your audience to know what to expect in each sub-section. It also helps you to ensure that you are putting the right information in the right place.

Each sub-section has a different job to do. The design sub-section tells your audience what type of research design you are using and why you are using it. The participants sub-section tells them who took part. The materials sub-section describes what methods or materials were used to gather the data. The procedure sub-section tells them how that data was gathered. Finally, the ethics sub-section outlines any steps that were taken to protect the rights of the participants. Let us dive into each one of those sections in more detail.

Design

In the design sub-section, you provide an outline of the methodology you plan to use and link the various elements of that methodology to the research questions. The aim here is to demonstrate how your methodology will answer those research questions as well as justifying why it is the most appropriate method for doing that.

It is worth noting that the design sub-section doesn't always appear in every report you will read. Often published articles don't require an identifiable design sub-section, and the same can be true of the assignment guidelines for some undergraduate or postgraduate report assignments. However, even if they don't require you to provide a design sub-section, these reports and articles will still need to contain information about the design, it simply ends up being distributed across other sub-sections such as the materials or procedure instead. As such, it is still worth knowing what goes in the design sub-section (and why) so you can do a good job of including the design information, no matter where in the method you end up mentioning it.

The key features of your design will have been decided by the research questions you posed in your introduction (See: Research questions, p. 18). This is because each research question requires a certain kind of data to answer it; this can end up determining not only the data you will be collecting but also how you go about collecting it and who you collect it from (See: Your research questions will decide your methodology, p. 25). As such, the first part of the design contains a summary of all the different data that research questions require. For each type of data, you will need to identify the data collection methods you will be using to collect that data. You don't need to go into much detail about each data collection method here, you will do that in the materials sub-section; here you just need to identify the general type of method being used in each case (for example, a questionnaire, a structured interview, an observation and so on).

Once the data types and collection methods have been identified, you may need to justify some of the choices made within those approaches. For example, in a quantitative design, you may need to explain why you decided to operationalise the concepts you are measuring in the way you did. 'Operationalising' is the term used to describe how you chose to measure a concept, in essence which measurable event or behaviour you are going to count as an example of this concept in action.

> *Ciara is looking at the impact that nervousness in a job interview can have on the ratings that the interviewers give.*

> [In Ciara's Design] *Looking at concept of 'nervousness', there are a number of ways I can operationalise this. These include observational methods such as counting nervous fidgets, biometric methods such as measuring their heart-rate or a self-report measure like a questionnaire which asks them to rate how nervous they feel. I decided to use the heart-rate monitor as I believe it will give the most accurate measure of nervousness since it can't be affected by the interviewee trying to look less nervous.*

Other examples of design decisions which may need justification are those occasions where the method or sample has not been decided by the research question and so you have to make a choice. If you choose one of several different potential methods or groups, any of which could have met the requirements of the research question, then that may be a decision worth justifying. Whether or not it *is* worth justifying depends on whether that decision produced a different out-come for the research. A 'different' outcome, in this context, can mean better or worse such as one method producing more accurate data than the other. As such, if you pick a method because it produces better data than the alternatives, then that reason for picking it is worth mentioning. However, 'different' doesn't has to be about being better, it can also just mean *different*, such as getting a different perspective on an issue depending on who you talk to. If you picked a method or group because you wanted the unique perspective that choice will give your research, then that reason for picking it is also worth mentioning. To recap then, if you made a choice in your design which wasn't forced upon you by a research question, and the choice could have affected the outcome of the research, then that is a choice you need to justify.

It helps if the arguments you make in defence of your design can be supported by cited references. Textbooks on research methods are one possible source for such citations, since they will often debate the merits of different research methods, but only if you can relate their point to your specific research and methodology. It is also acceptable to cite another piece of research that used the same method as a justification for using that method in your research. This type of justification is stronger if that previous research offered a rationale for using that method which you can mention along with the citation itself. Not all your defences need to be theoretical though. It is acceptable to cite practical reasons for design choices. Research takes place in the real world with time limits, financial costs, uncoop-erative people and plain-old bad luck. If there were practical reasons for some of your design choices, then say so.

Participants

The participants sub-section is where you identify the people who took part in your research. Your participants are sometimes known by another collec-tive name, your 'sample'. This refers to the fact that this small group of peo-ple is standing-in for a much larger group. The larger group, known as the 'population', is usually too large for it to be practical to include all of them. Thankfully, you don't need to. As long as your sample is made up of the same type of people as your population, then you can research the smaller sample and whatever you find can usually be considered to be true for the larger population.

There are a few things that you will want to tell your audience about your par-ticipants, some of which may relate to the concepts you are studying in your research, and the rest is general information which you would mention in any research. Included in the general information would be the number of people that participated, where they are from and how you recruited them. Beyond that, you should mention any details about the participants which might be relevant to any of your research questions. You should only share details about your participants if those details are relevant to your research.

[In Ciara's Participants] *My participants were fifty adults from the UK, all of whom are clients in a local recruitment agency and are seeking employment. They were recruited through a notice requesting volunteers hung in the agency waiting room.*

If some of the details that you share about each participant have the effect of dividing up your sample into different groups, then it may be helpful to show how many participants were in each group. Usually, the easiest way to present this kind of information is in a table.

Ciara's research questions also consider if the interviewee's age, level of education and number of years of previous employment might affect both their nervousness and ratings. She grouped them into ranges for both their age and years of employment,

[In Ciara's Participants]

TABLE I Number of participants in each of the age, level of education and years of employment groups

Age	18–24	25–40	40+		Total
	10	34	6		50
Highest level of education	A-Level	Undergrad	Post-grad	Doctoral or post-doc	
	8	28	12	2	50
Years of employment	0–3	4–6	7–10	11+	
	13	9	27	1	50

While a table like this is well suited for research with larger samples, at the other end of the spectrum with very small groups of participants (for example, ten participants or fewer) it can make more sense to introduce them as individuals rather than describe them as a group. When using this approach, you would usually assign each participant a pseudonym (false name) so as to allow you to refer to them individually without revealing their identity and so compromising anonymity (See: Ethics, p. 71).

Saeed is looking at the techniques used by professional athletes to regain confidence following a major set-back. He has interviewed three people who have experienced this particular life-event and has assigned each participant a pseudonym based on the first three letters of the alphabet.

[In Saeed's Participants] *There were three participants in this research, who for anonymity's sake will be referred to using pseudonyms. Adam is a rugby player whose missed tackle cost his team a critical match. Brian is tennis player who was knocked out of his most recent tournament without winning a single game. Finally, Carol is a canoeist whose hopes of making her nation's Olympic team were dashed owing to a minor illness.*

One final detail you may need to mention in this sub-section relates to any steps that were necessary to gain access to a specific sample. These steps usually involve approaching 'gatekeepers', the term used to describe any group or individual whose permission was necessary to gain access to the sample. It is not necessary to go into any great length about this process of gaining access, a sentence or two identifying which gatekeepers granted you access should be enough. These details are important because, not only do they demonstrate that your research was ethical, they are necessary information for anyone who wishes to access a similar sample for the purposes of replicating your research.

Materials

In the materials sub-section you discuss the nature and origins of any methods, measures or equipment that you used to collect your data. The term 'material' can be used to refer to many things, such as questionnaires, tests, observation techniques or computer programs. It is typical to break this sub-section up into paragraphs with each paragraph focusing on one of the materials. No matter what type of material it is, you will need to provide the same information about it: its origins, how it functions and any evidence of reliability or validity.

Whether you are using materials that you developed as part of your research or some existing materials that were developed as part of a previous piece of research, you need to identify where they came from. If any of your materials were developed as part of previous research, then you cite the reference for that previous research. Alternatively, if any of your materials were developed by you as part of your research, then you need to give a very brief description of that development; the people involved in developing those materials, any instructions they were given and the steps they followed while developing them.

Having described the origin of the material, the next step is to outline how it works. For materials like a questionnaire or interview, you will need to identify the number of questions and what type of response options the questions offered (such as open response, multiple choice, yes/no and Likert scale). If there are several different types of questions, you should indicate how many of each type. To help your audience get a clear idea of the questions you are describing, you should also include one example of each of the question types in the paragraph. For materials like a test or a piece of software, you need to give some idea of how the test or software works, what the participant sees, what they are being asked to do and so on. For materials like an observation method, you should explain what is being observed and any agreed list of behaviours the observers were looking for. If any of these materials are quantitative measures, which produce a score, you should also explain what the score means and how it is calculated. For some quantitative measures there is more than one score produced. For example, some surveys have separates sections, and the results from individual questions within each are combined to produce a total score for that section. In these cases, you need to explain how each total is calculated as well as what the total means. Whenever you need to explain what a score means, the best way to do it is to explain what a high score would mean and what a low score would mean.

The final detail you should include about any of the materials, if you can, is evidence of its reliability or validity. Reliability refers to how consistent the material is: is it accurate and unambiguous? For example, if a test shows I have a good memory today then, assuming my memory does not change much from day to day, the same test should also show that I have a good memory tomorrow. Validity refers to how sure you are that your materials measure or test the things they are claiming to measure or test. You could be confident that a questionnaire with high validity is measuring exactly what it says it is and not a similar or related concept. Evidence of reliability and validity are more commonly available for quantitative materials, owing to the fact that there are statistical tests which claim to measure those qualities. If you have conducted those kinds of statistical tests in a pilot study (See: Pilot studies, p. 77), or if a piece of previous research has conducted them, then you should mention the test results here. However, evidence for the reliability or validity of any material can come from the widespread use of that material in other research. In such cases, citing key examples of important or recent previous research which has successfully used this material can also function as evidence of the material's reliability or validity.

The interviewers in Ciara's research are using a questionnaire to rate each interviewee on their suitability for a hypothetical job opportunity. Ciara needs to identify the origin of this questionnaire, how it functions and evidence of its reliability.

[In Ciara's Materials] *The questionnaire used to rate the suitability of each participant for the hypothetical position was the Employment Suitability Measure (ESM) by Boyd (2000). The ESM contains twenty statements which describe the employment related characteristics of the person being interviewed. The person completing the measure is asked to indicate the degree to which each statement describes the person they are interviewing. A typical statement is "This person is reliable". Responses to each statement are measured using a 4-point Likert scale ranging from 1, indicating that the statement described them very poorly, to 4 indicating the statement described them very well. All responses were summed to produce an employment suitability total for that individual, with a high score indicating they were very suitable for the job. The ESM has been widely used in a variety of research on employability including Larson (2019) and Fitzpatrick (2020).*

Where possible, you should try and include a sample copy of each type of material you used in the appendices, making sure to include a link to the relevant appendix when you are describing each of those materials in this sub-section (See: Appendices: The basics, p. 159). An unused copy of a questionnaire, a screenshot of any online materials or photos of any special equipment can all be put in an appendix to help your audience to better understand those materials. When including examples of materials in an appendix, include unused examples of questionnaires so you don't reveal any personal data and, for larger materials, including some of the material may be enough without needing to show it all (See: Be careful about confidentiality issues with your appendices, p. 161 and Be selective about what you put in an appendix, p. 160.)

Procedure

In the procedure sub-section you explain what happened during data collection. You do this in three parts: how you briefed the participants, how the data was collected and any steps taken after the data collection. All of these tend to be brief explanations and, as such, the procedure sub-section tends to be relatively short and simple.

A 'briefing' is where you explain something and so, when describing your briefing to the participants, you should mention how the research was explained to them, including any instructions that were provided. If possible, you should include a copy of those instructions in an appendix, making sure to include a link to that appendix in this sub-section (See: Appendices: The basics, p. 159). If the participants were briefed in multiple separate groups you only need to describe one example of how a typical group was briefed.

When describing the data collection itself, it is often enough to simply identify which materials were used and what the participants were asked to do. If there are any specific details that matter, such as the order in which the materials were used or any special conditions governing how they were used, they should be mentioned here.

When describing the steps that occurred after data collection, it is typical to mention how the participants were thanked and any de-briefing that took place. 'De-briefing' is the term used to describe a more complete explanation of the aims and research questions for your research, which is given to the participants after they have completed their part in the research. De-briefs are necessary for any research where you don't wish to tell the participant everything about the aims of the research in the briefing before they take part, just in case it affects their behaviour during the data collection. Not all research needs a de-brief.

[In Ciara's Procedure] *The participants in this research were the people who responded to the poster in the agency waiting room. Using email, I outlined the aims of the research and invited them to participate. Those who agreed were asked to attend a mock interview for a hypothetical job. Before going in to the interview, they had a heart-rate monitor placed on their wrist. They then completed a thirty-minute mock interview by a panel of three interviewers. At the end of the interview, the lead interviewer completed the Employment Suitability Measure (ESM), including the average heart-rate score provided by the heart-rate monitor. Following the interview, the participants had a short meeting with me where I thanked them for their participation, de-briefed them on the research and invited them to ask any questions.*

Ethics

The ethics sub-section covers any steps you took to ensure that your research conformed to ethical guidelines. Similar to the design, this is another sub-section that doesn't appear in every report. In many published articles, it is simply taken for granted that the research was done ethically, or it is covered in a single line stating that ethical clearance was received, which implies that all ethical precautions were taken. In student research reports, however, there is usually an expectation that the ethical precautions taken in the research will be discussed in the report.

While some ethical issues will be specific to your research, others such as informed consent, confidentiality and the right to withdraw, apply to any research that involves human participants. As such, if your research had human participants then this sub-section is needed so you can mention how you managed these three ethical issues.

Regarding informed consent, you will need to explain how you provided all the information that your participants needed to know about your research before they could agree to participate. You should include a copy of the participant information sheet and consent form in an appendix, making sure to include a link to that appendix in this sub-section (See: Appendices: The basics, p. 159).

Regarding confidentiality, you will need to explain how you arranged for participation in your research to either be anonymous or remain confidential. If you are unsure of the difference, with confidentiality only the researcher knows which participant generated which data, but with anonymity even the researcher does not know which participant generated which data.

Regarding the right to withdraw, you will need to mention how you explained this in your guidance to participants before they took part, so they were aware that they could withdraw from the research at any time. You should also show how you provided them with contact details, so they could withdraw their data after the fact. If you included these directions on your participant information sheet, then that information sheet should be included in an appendix, making sure to include a link that appendix in this sub-section (See: Appendices: The basics, p. 159).

In addition to these standard ethical precautions, if you were dealing with vulnerable participants or a sensitive research topic, then you will need to mention what steps you took to deal with them ethically. Examples of this might include special guidance or conditions you set up beforehand to support the participants during the research. Alternatively, it might come in the form of additional elements you added to your de-brief, such as contact details for organisations who offer support to anyone affected by the issues your research was exploring.

[In Ciara's Ethics] *During recruitment, I provided potential participants with a participant information sheet (included in Appendix A). This sheet explained that the research was looking at people's performance in interviews, outlined the mock interview process and discussed the mechanisms for anonymity and withdrawal. Anonymity was achieved by having the heart-rate and interview ratings recorded by the lead interviewer, without recording the name of the participants. After the mock interview, participants were de-briefed, offering a more complete explanation on the topic of nervousness and its impact on performance. Finally, participants were notified of training courses offered by the placement agency on interview technique.*

▶ COMMON MISTAKES

Design: Justify your research, don't just recite the research methods textbook

Often, when asked to justify the use of any part of their methodology, a first-time report writer can end up repeating a condensed section of their research methods textbook. These 'textbook justifications' are usually chock full of generic statements and clichés. This includes justifying qualitative methods because they produce "richer data" and are the only way to "really understand" something or justifying quantitative methods because they are "objective" and produce "broader data". Another cliché is to justify a qualitative method by pointing out the general limitations of all quantitative methodologies or vice versa. The problem with all of these justifications is not that they are untrue, but rather that they are so widely known that they go without saying, so you don't need to give up valuable space listing them.

Instead of spouting clichés, you should remember that most of your methodology needs no justification. This is because it is usually the research question that determines the methodology (See: Your research questions will decide your methodology, p. 25). As such, most of the time, once it is clear which method is linked to each of the research the questions, your audience will see how the question determined the method, leaving no need for justification beyond that. The only exceptions are when there was a choice made which wasn't a requirement of the research question. If you had such a choice, then you do need to justify your decision, but it is important to relate that justification to the specifics of your research. It could be some theoretical reason why that methodology was necessary for the topic you are researching, or a practical reason relating to your participants or even your personal situation as the researcher. As long as you are justifying the chosen methodology in terms of your specific research, then you are on the right track.

> *Saeed's research, which looks at athletes recovering from a major set-back, is using a qualitative methodology. This was largely determined by research questions, which seek to understand the participant's experience and so the choice of a qualitative approach does not need justification. The one choice he did make, and so will need to justify, was to use an interview rather than a survey, both of which could be used to ask qualitative questions.*

> [In Saeed's Design] *In this research I explored the athletes' experiences of recovering from a professional set-back, and how they framed the set-back to themselves. Data was collected on both these topics using a structured interview. An interview was chosen as it*

is more effective at building trust, which Barnum (1956) argues is critical in getting more honest and open responses when researching a sensitive issue. This made it the right choice for researching the sensitive experiences related to a personal setback.

Participants: Too much information

First-time report writers tend to overshare when it comes to participant details, mentioning details in the participants sub-section that are not related to any research questions and so have been collected and shared for no clear reason. Common examples of these include the age or gender of the participants, which are often shared for no other reason than the fact that the report writers have seen those details shared in other reports (who, in turn, are probably copying others and so on).

As well as taking up valuable space with information that has no clear use, sharing too much information about your participants undermines the anonymity protections in your research by making it slightly easier to figure out who took part. The same is true when you are too specific about where you recruited your participants. To avoid oversharing, the question to ask yourself regarding any detail you could share about your participants is whether the audience need to know this detail to understand the findings of your research. If the answer is 'yes', then you should share that detail about your participants, but if the answer is 'no' then don't share it.

Participants: Random sampling

A common mistake made by first-time report writers is to describe their sampling method as random sampling. This happens because most first-time researchers will take anyone they can get as participants, and since this approach feels like it has no plan or pattern, it appears to them to be random sampling, but it is not. In reality, the recruitment method employed by most researchers falls into one of three categories: opportunity sampling, criterion sampling and snowball sampling. To help you identify which type of sampling you are using, we will look at each of them in turn.

Opportunity sampling describes the approach to recruitment where you recruit anyone you can, with no particular plan or preference. For example, if you posted a notice about your research on social media and then accepted anyone who responded to it, that would be opportunity sampling. On the other hand, criterion sampling is almost the opposite of opportunity sampling. With criterion sampling, you are recruiting a specific group or type of person, usually because your research questions require them. For example, if you recruited only the members of a specific sports team so you can research the impact of the training system used by their coach, then that was criterion sampling. However, that fact that your participants belong to a specific group does not automatically mean that you are using criterion sampling; you should only claim to be using criterion sampling if their membership of this group matters to your research. For example, if you approached only the students in a class to take part in your research, but it didn't matter to your research that they were students, then that was an opportunity sample. Finally, snowball sampling is when you recruit a small number of participants yourself and then those participants help you to recruit others to take part as well. It is possible to use a combination of these sampling methods at the same time, although you will generally find that there is one sampling method you use more than the others and that is the one to mention when talking about sampling.

Materials: Everyday items are not materials

It is very easy to take the idea of listing all materials used in the research too far. In the same way that there is no need to define everyday words in the literature review (See: Defining key terms, p. 52), there is no need to list everyday items in the materials. Examples of items that would not need to be listed include things like a pen and paper, table and chairs, a watch to record the time and so on.

Materials: If you develop your own materials, tell us how you did it

You would think that any report writer who had spent all the time and effort needed to develop their own materials, such as creating the questions they used in their questionnaire, would want to brag/explain to their audience how they did it. However, one reason that many first-time report writers are rather vague, or even completely silent, about the process behind the creation of materials for their research, is because there wasn't much of a process.

It is not uncommon for first-time researchers to simply invent a list of questions by themselves and then use them in the research with no further development. If that doesn't sound very scientific or rigorous, that is because it is not, which may explain why they leave it out of the report. Trying to 'gloss over' weak methodology in this way won't change the fact that it is weak. The ideal solution to that problem is to use a more robust method to develop your materials (See: Pilot studies, p. 77), but no matter how simple or sophisticated your development processes were, you should still explain those processes in your materials sub-section. Leaving them out makes it look as though you are hiding something, and that is worse. You can keep it brief, and your audience doesn't need to know every twist and turn; you only need to tell them enough to allow them to develop their own materials in a similar manner.

[In Saeed's Materials] *In order to develop the questions I used in the interview, I began by identifying the issues relating to the two research questions that I wanted to explore through the interview process. This produced a total of eight issues, which I shared with two other academics. The three of us then worked independently to generate as many different questions as possible relating to those eight issues. All the questions were then pooled and duplicates were eliminated. Finally, with my two colleagues and I acting as judges, sixteen questions were selected, two relating to each topic, based on the combined votes of all three judges.*

Ethics: Don't believe that your research has no ethical issues

The importance of following strict ethical guidelines may feel like it only really applies when you are dealing with vulnerable participants or sensitive research topics. In reality, you need to worry about being ethical no matter what the topic or who is taking part in your research. Even when the topic of the research is completely harmless or your research is a coursework assignment and will never be seen by the wider public, you still need to offer your participants the same ethical protections as any other researcher. The importance of ethics is also easy to underestimate when the participants are friends or family. In those cases, it is important to keep in mind that your relationship outside of the research doesn't matter. As long as someone is providing you with data for your research, the only relationship that matters at that time is that you are their researcher, they are your participant and all participants deserve to be treated ethically.

Another place where ethics are easy to overlook is when the data come to you indirectly, by which I mean you are dealing with published sources of data rather than collecting the data yourself. This happens when you use official documents, archival records, online materials, social media, historical documents or other such data sources that were not created specifically for your research. Common excuses used to argue that there is no need for any ethical protections here include: telling yourself that the data is 'public information' or is being produced by group or organisation and so no individuals are ever being identified. While it is true that this kind of data may need slightly different steps to ensure it is used ethically, it does still deserve ethical consideration and protection. Informed consent, confidentiality and the right to withdraw can and should still be offered to the holders or owners of this kind of data. For example, you could contact the owner of a website before using data from that site in your research to get their informed consent.

Whether it is friends and family, or the owner of a data archive, you may find that getting the usual ethical permissions is not hard; in fact, it may be just a formality, but it is still worth doing. Your participants rely on you to go the extra mile to look after their rights, and even if the individuals who originally created the archival data may never know what you did to protect them, it is never a wasted effort.

▶ REFINEMENTS

Pilot studies

Your methodology is just a plan outlining how your data collection should work, but even the best laid plans don't run smoothly the first time. As such, before launching into full-scale data collection for your research, it is a good idea to carry out a test run first. This test run is known as a 'pilot study' and its purpose is to make sure that your methodology is sound. You could do this by checking how well things are working after the first few participants have taken part, but if you do that and find a mistake, it could mean all the data from those participants is flawed and unusable. This is why pilot studies should ideally be run using a few people who are not suited to be real participants in your research. By running a small-scale pilot study, you get to see if your materials work before you try using them with real participants, who may be a limited resource that you don't want to waste.

If you go to the bother of carrying out a pilot study, you should mention it in your report, since it is an important detail. Your audience needs to know about the steps required to produce reliable and valid materials. You should describe the pilot study as part of the materials sub-section. You should indicate what the pilot was testing, how many participants were used and what changes, if any, were made to the materials as a result. There is no need to go into much detail on any of this, a sentence or two on how the pilot was carried out and any changes made is enough. It is not a rule that there *must* be changes resulting from a pilot study though; finding that the materials were already as good as they could be is an entirely valid result.

If you do make changes to your materials as a result of a pilot study, it is up to you to decide which version of the materials you include in the appendices. Depending on how much space those materials take up, you could show both the version before changes and the version after changes. It is also acceptable to just show the 'after' version since that is the version you will have used in the actual data collection for your research. If you do run a pilot study, it helps if you then refer to the real data collection and analysis as the 'main study'. This helps to distinguish it from the pilot study, so your audience knows which data and which analysis you are talking about in your discussion section.

Controlling confounding variables

Not every variable that might affect your research area is of interest to your research. When constructing a theoretical model (See: Outline the theoretical model, p. 15) you will have focused on certain variables and will only care about their impact on, and relationships with, each other. But this raises the question as to what you should do about the variables which are not of interest to you right now, but which can still affect the outcome of your research, sometimes known as 'confounding variables'. The solution is to prevent any confounding variable from interfering with your research and its outcomes by 'controlling' these variables.

There are two kinds of control: statistical and methodological. Statistical control is only really possible in quantitative research, as it involves including any confounding variables in your statistical analysis in such a way as to mathematically remove the impact they have on all the other variables. Methodological control is where you design your research in such a way as to remove the potential impact of a confounding variable. For example, if you thought that a participant's age might affect the issue you wish to research, you could arrange for all your participants to be the same age. However you do it, the purpose of controlling a variable is to remove the impact of confounding variables on your research area, so you can research the things you are interested in with greater clarity.

If you are controlling any variables, you should identify them in the design sub-section. As well as identifying the variable, you should explain how you are controlling it and why. Explaining how you are controlling it means describing the type of control being used and how that control is being achieved. Explaining why will usually involve offering a reason or citing a source that identifies the variable being controlled as a confounding variable. You may end up mentioning control in the participants section as well, especially if you recruited certain participants specifically to help you achieve control on a particular variable.

Sample size vs. accessible population size

When you identify the number of participants in your research, it can be useful to give some indication as to the size of the accessible population they were sampled from. The accessible population is the total number of people that it was possible for you to approach, given the amount of time and resources that you had. This kind of information can be found in a number of different ways.

If you are approaching anyone you can find in an opportunity sample, you could identify the total number of people who were invited to participate alongside the number who actually agreed to participate. If you advertised your research in a public or online space, you could indicate the duration for which the advert was displayed. If you were recruiting from a specific group, you could mention the total number of people in that group, again alongside the number who actually participated. For example, if you were recruiting from a particular university course, you could mention the total number of people enrolled on the course alongside the number who participated in your research.

This kind of information is useful since it gives your audience an indication as to the representativeness of your sample. For example, if you only had 12 participants from a course on which 200 students are enrolled, it allows your audience to reflect on the representativeness of your sample when evaluating and generalising your findings. There will be a temptation to leave this information out if it might make your research look less impressive or less credible. That is understandable, but leaving it out for that reason undermines what should be a core principle of any research, which is to present the most accurate picture possible of the issue being studied. What good is any research if it only looks credible when you keep certain things about it a secret?

▶ ADVANCED

Using existing materials vs. developing your own

When it comes to selecting materials for your research, there is often a choice between, on the one hand, looking for an existing measure that has been developed by another researcher for their research and, on the other hand, developing your own.

Looking for an existing measure has its pros and cons. On the positive side, if you can locate an existing measure, then you will also be able to cite the research in which it was used as one of the foundations for your research in your literature review. (See: Identifying the foundations and unresolved questions, p. 41). Another potential positive with an existing measure is that researcher who developed the measure, or someone else who has used it, may have carried out some reliability analyses on it. You should report such reliability findings and cite the research in which those findings were published when you describe the measure in your materials sub-section (See: Materials, p. 68).

On the negative side, it can be time-consuming to find an existing measure that exactly matches the concept that you wish to research. Also, it is common enough for researchers to publish their research without including a copy of their materials or without any instructions on how to use or score them. One potential solution to this problem of an existing measure which is mentioned, but not included, in a published source is to contact the first author of that source. Typically, the name and the contact details of the first author of a journal article are included with the article itself. Even if the contact details are not included, the name of the author and the university they are affiliated to usually are included, which allows you to search for contact details online. Once you have contact details, you would be able to contact the main author and politely ask for a copy of their measure. While it is possible that the researcher purchased that measure and so won't be able to share it, this is the exception not the rule, as most researchers use measures which they either developed themselves or were given for free. Most academics are happy to help out others with their research. After all, they are researchers themselves, and it can only serve to enhance their reputation if they share their materials and thereby promote their research. Even those academics that don't want to, or can't, share their materials for some reason will still appreciate that you had the courtesy to ask and so there is nothing to lose by asking.

It may appear to be easier or quicker to develop your own measure when compared to the challenge of tracking down an existing measure. However, there are some hidden costs to developing your own measure. First, it now becomes essential to run a pilot study and conduct a reliability analysis. When using an existing measure, a pilot study and reliability test might be considered recommended-but-optional (See: The basics: materials, p. 68 and Pilot studies, p. 77), but they are an absolute requirement when using a newly developed measure for the first time. This can be time-consuming, especially if your research is only one of a number of assignments you are working on. In the long run, you can end up spending just as much time developing, testing and refining a brand-new measure as you would have spent trying to locate an existing one and so neither can be considered a guaranteed 'quick' option compared to the other.

If the need to carry out a pilot study and reliability analysis are some of the cons that come with developing your own measure, what about the pros? One positive thing about a measure which you have developed yourself is that you can be sure that it is designed specifically to measure the concept you want to measure in your research. Also, being diligent in your development of a new measure, such as using pilot studies and reliability tests to do it right, can be a great way to demonstrate your research skills to your audience. For this reason, if you do end up developing your own measure, you definitely should include details of its development in your materials sub-section. This should include an explanation as to why you chose to develop your measure and reasons for any important decisions made in its development. Finally, you should offer some description of any changes that were made as a result of any reliability tests, validity tests or the pilot study,

One final option worth considering is something of a compromise in this choice between old and new measures and involves you modifying an existing measure. This still counts as a new measure, in the sense that it will need a pilot study and reliability analysis just like any other new measure would need. The advantage that comes from such an adaptation is that using a tried-and-tested existing measure as your starting point means there is a much better chance that your adapted measure will retain a lot of the original measure's reliability and validity. This makes it less of a leap-of-faith when compared to developing your own measure from scratch.

Positionality

The traditional view of the researcher is one of an objective outsider disconnected from the events they are researching. The researcher uses carefully controlled laboratory conditions to avoid any unintended influence on the outcome of the research (See: Controlling confounding variables, p. 78). In social sciences, the researcher remains objective and disconnected by formalising their relationship with the participants (See: Procedure, p. 70) and controlling what the participants know about the research (See the concept of 'de-briefing' in Ethics, p. 71). Ultimately, the reason for avoiding any unintentional impact on the outcome of the research is to ensure the most reliable and valid measurements; to get the clearest understanding of the thing being studied as it 'really is'. The philosophy behind this approach is known as 'logical positivism', and though it is one of the dominant research paradigms, a 'paradigm' being a standard viewpoint or approach, it is not without its critics.

Some critics question whether it is possible to achieve the positivist ideal of an objective observer who has no unintended impact on the research or its outcomes. They would cite the Heisenberg uncertainty principle, which suggests that the act of measuring something changes it. While this principle was developed originally for use in particle physics, it has been embraced by philosophers of science who see it as a fundamental critique of pure objectivity. In the social sciences, they would argue that the act of researching something changes people's behaviour, a view which is supported by psychological research into potentially confounding experimental phenomena, such as demand characteristics, experimenter effects and the Hawthorne effect. Others would go further, suggesting that a researcher's beliefs will affect all aspects of the research, starting with the choice of research area and theoretical model, onwards through data collection and analysis, right up to the conclusions drawn at the very end in the report. Again, there is ample evidence in psychology to suggest that our beliefs do affect how we make decisions, solve problems and interpret what we see. Given this, critics would question whether a researcher could achieve anything close to the ideal of objectivity and disconnection enshrined in the positivist approach to research.

One solution is to consider the positivist approach, where empirical data is collected under controlled conditions, as only one of several valid approaches to research. An example of an alternative approach would be ethnographic research, where the researcher becomes 'embedded' in the social context they are researching. This can mean establishing social relationships with the people in that context and the researcher can even becoming an active participant in the situation being researched. For example, a researcher studying the impact of leadership style on productivity among seasonal workers in a farm might seek to become a seasonal worker themselves, working alongside the others. Other alternative approaches include participatory research, where no distinction is made between researcher and participants. Everyone is involved in directing the research, gathering the data and interpreting its findings, a process generally referred to as 'participant observation'. These alternatives to the positivist approach to research are often associated with a use of qualitative data and a research philosophy known as 'Interpretivism'. A researcher using an interpretivist approach typically takes the viewpoint that the researcher cannot be separated from the thing they are researching. As such, to understand the research and its findings it is necessary for the audience to know about the researcher or at least to know about those aspects of the researcher that are relevant to the research.

This information, the aspects of the researcher that are relevant to the research, can then be included in an additional sub-section of the method, with the title 'Positionality'. There are no formal rules as to what must be included in this sub-section, it is for the researcher to decide that through reflection.

Examples of the sort of details a researcher might share here include outlining their beliefs and expectations relating to the research area prior to the research, recognising any agenda or ulterior motives they had in choosing the research context, discussing their role within the research context and its potential impacts, and discussing their hopes and expectations in relation to the findings of the research. It's worth noting that even if positionality is acknowledged, that doesn't magically remove its impact on the research. That should not be seen as a negative or even a limitation, after all the removal of all unintended impact from the researcher is a goal of a positivist rather than an interpretivist approach. By acknowledging their positionality, the researcher seeks to recognise its impact so they can reflect on it when considering their research findings or the meaning of the research as a whole. By sharing this positionality with your audience in the method section, you are allowing them to do the same.

▶ CHAPTER 4: EXERCISES

Exercise 1: MCT

1) The goal of the method is…
   A. to say who took part in the research.
   B. to identify the tests and questionnaires used.
   C. to explain what was involved in taking part in the research.
   D. All of the above.

2) The _____ explains what the participants did during the data collection, the _____ identifies the things used to collect the data, while the _____ talks which methods of data collection are to be used and why.
   A. design, materials, procedure
   B. design, procedure, materials
   C. procedure, design, materials
   D. procedure, materials, design

3) The term 'operationalise' refers to deciding which…
   A. variables to include in your research so you can answer you research questions.
   B. event or behaviour you will use to represent a concept you want to measure.
   C. questions to include in your questionnaire or interview.
   D. which everyday objects qualify as research materials.

4) When talking about your participants you should always make sure to mention…
   A. as much detail as possible so your audience can get a sense of who they are.
   B. basic demographics such as age, gender and nationality.
   C. only those details which might affect the outcome of your research.
   D. any occasion when you used random sampling.

5) A material's _____ refers to how consistently and accurately that material measures something, whereas it's _____ refers to whether that material is actually measuring what it is supposed to be measuring. Evidence of both of these can come from statistical tests, but only if that material gathers _____ data.
   A. reliability, validity, quantitative
   B. validity, reliability, quantitative
   C. reliability, validity, qualitative
   D. validity, reliability, qualitative

6) In some published articles there is either no mention of ethics or that topic is covered by single sentence saying ethical clearance was received. Why is this?
   A. If you are not dealing with a sensitive topic then there are no ethical issues with your research that need reporting.
   B. If your sample does not come from a vulnerable population then there are no ethical issues with your research that need reporting.
   C. In professional research it is often assumed that the research follows all ethical precautions.
   D. All of the above.

7) Why should you always carry out a pilot study before conducting your actual data collection?
   A. Unless you have tested your methodology first, you will be unable to tell your participants what is involved in your data collection and so they cannot provide informed consent.
   B. A pilot study allows you to find out if there are any flaws in your materials or your research design so you don't lose data and participants to those flaws.
   C. A pilot study is necessary to establish that there is an issue in the research area that needs to be resolved or better understood, which then justifies the need for your research.
   D. It is a trick question, you only need to carry out a pilot study if you have developed your own measure, but not if you are using someone else's measure.

8) On the one hand, using an existing measure developed by another re-searcher does NOT mean that _____, whereas on the other hand developing your own measure does NOT mean that _____.
  A. you can compare your findings to theirs, you can be more confident that the measure is a good match for the issues you are researching.
  B. you can cite the previous research as part of your literature review, you can take an existing measure and modify it.
  C. you can cite the results from other researcher's checks on the validity or reliability, you will impress anyone with your research skills.
  D. you will have to pay to be allowed to use it, you will save yourself time compared to locating an existing measure.

9) Positionality is based on the idea that....
  A. certain things are so widely known to be true that they go without saying and so you don't need to waste any space explaining them to your audience.
  B. there are certain variables which are not included in the theoretical model and yet they still need to be controlled so they don't affect the outcome of the research.
  C. a researcher should always aim to be an objective outsider, disconnected from the events they are researching so as to avoid any unintentional impact on the outcome of the research.
  D. the beliefs of the researcher can influence their research and should be made known so they can be taken into account when interpreting the research.

10) When talking about your participants which of the following should you NOT mention?
  A. The number of people you approached to participate but who turned you down.
  B. Details about your participants which affect the outcome but aren't part of any of your research questions.
  C. Anything which might reveal their identity.
  D. None of the above.

Exercise 2: How serious are these mistakes?

A common problem faced by many first-time report writers is judging the relative importance of all the different rules and requirements involved in report writing. Are all the sub-sections of the method equally important? How bad is it to mention everyday objects in your materials? With this in mind you will find, in alphabetical order, 12 common mistakes made by first-time report writers when writing their method. You need to put each of them in one of three categories of importance: serious errors, moderate errors and minor errors.

- Including everyday items among your list of materials.
- Justifying quantitative methodology by critiquing qualitative methods or vice versa.
- Justifying your methodology in general without any mention of how that methodology meets the specific requirements of your research.
- Leaving out your design sub-section.
- Leaving out your ethics sub-section.
- Leaving out your materials sub-section.
- Leaving out your participants' sub-section.
- Leaving out your procedure sub-section.
- Not explaining how your self-made materials were developed.
- Not mentioning how many participants were approached but declined to participate.
- Referring to your sampling as 'random' when it's actually 'opportunity'.
- Using materials that were self-made without the use of a pilot study.

▶ CHAPTER 4: ANSWERS

Exercise 1: MCT

Q1: Ans = D (See: The basics, p. 64)

Q2: Ans = D (See: Design, p. 64 ↔ Materials, p. 68 ↔ Procedure, p. 70)

Q3: Ans = B (See: Design, p. 64 ↔ Everyday items are not materials, p. 75)

Q4: Ans = C (See: Participants, p. 66 ↔ Too much information, p. 74 ↔ Random sampling, p. 74)

Q5: Ans = A (See: Materials, p. 68)

Q6: Ans = C (See: Ethics, p. 71 ↔ Don't believe that your research has no ethical issues, p. 76)

Q7: Ans = B (See: Pilot studies, p. 77 ↔ Using existing materials vs. developing your own, p. 79)

Q8: Ans = D (See: Using existing materials vs. developing your own, p. 79 ↔ Materials, p. 68)

Q9: Ans = D (See: Positionality, p. 81 ↔ Controlling confounding variables, p. 78)

Q10: Ans = C (See: Participants, p. 66 ↔ Participants: Too much information, p. 74 ↔ Controlling confounding variables, p. 78 ↔ Sample size vs. accessible Population size, p. 79)

Exercise 2: How serious are these mistakes?

Serious errors

(Leaving out your participants sub-section ↔ Leaving out your materials sub-section ↔ Leaving out your procedure sub-section ↔ Using materials that were self-made without the use of a pilot study.)

All of these are serious errors, either because they completely undermine the central purpose of the method, which is to explain how the research was carried out, or because they reveal what may be a fatal flaw in your report or your research design. Knowing who took part, what they were asked to do and how the data were collected are the indispensable core elements of the methodology. Leave any one of them out, and it would be difficult to understand how the data in your research was produced, while also making it impossible to reproduce your research. On the other hand, while a failure to talk about a pilot study you have done is only a minor error (discussed later), the failure to do a pilot study in the first place is much more serious. Jumping straight into the data collection phase with an untested methodology leaves you wide open to flaws in your design which might make some or even all your data completely invalid.

(See: The basics, p. 64 ↔ Participants, p. 66 ↔ Materials, p. 68 ↔ Procedure, p. 70 ↔ Pilot studies, p. 77 ↔ Using existing materials vs. developing your own, p. 79.)

Moderate errors

(Justifying quantitative methodology by critiquing qualitative methods or vice versa ↔ Justifying quantitative methodology by critiquing a hypothetical alternative design which used qualitative methods or vice versa ↔ Leaving out your design sub-section ↔ Leaving out your ethics sub-section.)

All of these are moderate errors owing to the fact that, while they do make your work much less effective, they do not fatally undermine it the way the serious errors do. The first two involve making generic statements about the merits or flaws of a methodological approach without connecting it to your specific research. This will bore your audience and waste valuable space by telling them things they already know without shedding any light on any real methodological decisions you made in your research. The absence of a design sub-section will make it harder to see how the measures provided the data that the research questions needed, while also leaving gaps in your audience's understanding of the methodological decisions that weren't clearly driven by those research questions. The absence of an ethics sub-section raises the spectre that the research was unconcerned about, or even breached, the participants ethical rights. These are only being treated as less serious than the absence of the materials or participants sub-section because the absence of the design or ethics sub-sections have a less dramatic effect. Your audience may still be able to link the materials to the research questions if the materials section is detailed enough, and while the absence of an ethics section will leave doubts about the ethical precautions taken, it will still be assumed that your research was ethical in its execution. Nevertheless, it is still a better choice to include both the design and the ethics sub-sections in your method.

(See: Justify your research, don't just recite the research methods textbook, p. 73 ↔ Design, p. 64 ↔ Ethics, p. 71 ↔ Don't believe that your research has no ethical issues, p. 76.)

Minor errors

(Including everyday items among your list of materials. ↔ Not explaining how your self-made materials were developed. ↔ Not mentioning how many participants were approached but declined to participate ↔ Referring to your sampling as 'random' when it's actually 'opportunity'.)

All of these are minor errors in the sense that, although they have a negative impact on the effectiveness of your method, the extent of their impact is much more limited than the moderate errors. Listing everyday items as materials is a waste of space in your report, but thankfully not too much space. Leaving out how you developed your materials or how many people you approached are not so much flaws as missed opportunities to impress your audience with the rigour of your methodology. It's OK to claim the credit you deserve by letting your audience know these things, so long as you keep it brief. As for the confusion between 'opportunity' and 'random' sampling, that is just a mistake about a label, but not an important one. Overall then, these are mistakes you should generally try to avoid making, but you should not worry too much about it if you do end up making one.

(See: Everyday items are not materials, p. 75 ↔ If you develop your own materials, tell us how you did it, p. 75 ↔ Sample size vs. accessible Population size, p. 79 ↔ Random sampling, p. 74)

5

The results

The results is the section where you announce the findings of your research. You do this by walking your audience through all the analyses you carried out, discussing them one-analysis-at-a-time. For each analysis, you start by identifying which method of analysis was used and how it was carried out, followed by a discussion on the key findings, before finally using those findings to provide answers to the research questions. By the end of the results section, your audience should have a clear understanding of what you have discovered, how you made those discoveries and what the discoveries tell us about the issues which are the focus of the research questions.

▶ BEFORE YOU BEGIN THIS CHAPTER...

Before you are ready to begin writing your results there are a number of steps in the research process you will need to complete first.

- Collect your data.
- Identify the most suitable method of analysis for each type of data.
- Carry out any additional tests to verify the reliability of your measures and the suitability of your data. Make any changes necessary to your data or method of analysis based on the outcome of these tests.
- Analyse your data, including a review of summary data to elaborate on those findings if necessary.
- Locate the main results of each method of analysis and determine what answers to each of the research questions are indicated by those main results.

DOI: 10.4324/9781003107965-5

Once you have completed all of these steps you are ready to begin writing this section of the report.

▶ THE BASICS

Once you have collected the data, the next step is to analyse it. Contrary to what you may have heard, the facts do not speak for themselves; they need to be analysed and interpreted. This is what the results section is for; here you get to explain to your audience how the findings were produced and what they mean. The results section will typically be broken up into a number of sub-sections. In each sub-section, you will explain one of the methods of analysis you used, what the main findings of that analysis were and what answers to the research questions those findings provide.

While it is fair to say that announcing the findings is the most noteworthy part of this process, you shouldn't underestimate the importance of explaining the analysis or relating the findings to the research questions. Explaining the method of analysis is critical because it helps your audience to see where those findings came from. If you want your audience to believe that your findings are accurate, then you need to walk them through the method of analysis used to produce those findings. Relating the findings back to the research questions is also critical because it helps your audience to see what those findings reveal about the research area. We shouldn't forget that your findings are not just telling us what happened in your research, they are revealing something important about the real-world situation you are researching.

If the task of explaining the analysis or relating the findings sounds challenging to you, then you are not alone; a lot of first-time report writers find the results section a little daunting. That is hardly surprising; the results section is one of the most technically demanding parts of the report. Different methods of analysis need to be explained in different ways, and there is often specific terminology which must be used when you do that explaining. The good news is, if you use the same method of analysis in multiple pieces of research, you will tend to use the same terminology and even a similar structure each time you report the findings from that type of analysis. This means that the first time you report the findings from a new method of analysis is the toughest, but having done it once, you can effectively re-use the same structure again and again like a template. This can turn the results section from one of the toughest sections to write into just another section, no harder or easier than any other.

Finally, among all these concerns about terminology and technicalities, you shouldn't forget the bigger picture. The big pay-off you get in return for all the effort needed to master this section is that the results section is where you get to 'pull the rabbit out of the hat' and reveal something to your audience which is genuinely new and possibly unexpected. What you reveal to them in the results section may be the one thing they recall when everything else about your research has faded from their memory.

Structuring your analyses using sub-sections

It is worth noting that the technical nature of the results can make it as challenging for your audience to read as it is for you to write. An effective structure will help with that, and a key part of achieving an effective structure in the results section is to break it up into sub-sections. As a general rule, each sub-section of your results should focus on one method of analysis. Each sub-section should include all the elements needed to explain that method of analysis and its findings. These elements would include: the type of data used, the method of analysis chosen, the findings of that analysis, an elaboration of those findings and a discussion of the relevance of the findings.

> *John is conducting research which looks at the strategic choices people make when they play games. One of his research questions asks whether changing your playing style in response to the moves of your opponent helps you to achieve a higher score in the game. He will be analysing the difference in score between various groups of players who prefer different playing strategies, by using a statistical test known as an ANOVA. His second research question asks whether a player's confidence is related to their success in the game. He will be analysing the relationship between these two variables using a statistical test known as a Correlation. As such, John will divide his results section into two sub-sections, one of which will focus on the ANOVA and the other on the Correlation.*

Ideally, you should present each of these sub-sections in a separate paragraph, which would help to distinguish one sub-section from another. You can give each sub-section its own sub-heading if you wish, identifying which method of analysis that sub-section will focus on, but that part is optional. Whether you use paragraphs alone, paragraphs and sub-headings or some other method, it is important to have a structure which helps to distinguish between the different methods of the analysis you are talking about in the results section. By presenting each method of analysis within a clearly defined sub-section, it avoids confusion over which data or which finding is connected to each method of analysis.

One thing to watch out for, mainly in qualitative analyses, are those methods of analysis which produce several key findings, each of which can be discussed and related back to the research questions individually. Most first-time report writers encounter this situation when reporting a thematic analysis. You could discuss all the themes produced by a thematic analysis within a single sub-section, but it would be a very long sub-section, and that undermines the point of using sub-sections to break up your results and make them easier to follow. For this reason, with a method of analysis, such as a thematic analysis, which produces several key findings, it works better if each theme is discussed in a separate paragraph. Since all these themes are coming from the one method of analysis, you only need to mention the type of data and method of analysis used when discussing the first theme in the first paragraph. For all of the other themes in the other paragraphs, you can skip the type of data and method of analysis elements, which haven't changed, and instead focus on reporting, elaborating and considering the relevance of each theme.

> John's colleague Alicia is carrying out a separate piece of research, looking at a player's understanding of the impact that their strategy has on their success at the game. In her research question, Alicia is asking how the players make sense of the relationship between their successes and failures in the game and their strategy. She asked each player to write a post-match diary and has analysed their diary entries using a thematic analysis. The results of the analysis identified three themes: the mind of your opponent, coordination vs competition and the prisoners' dilemma. Alicia will only have one sub-section in her results, the thematic analysis sub-section, but it will contain three paragraphs, each focusing on one of these three themes.

Elements within an analysis sub-section

As was mentioned previously, each sub-section typically contains the following elements: the type of data included, the method of analysis used, the findings of the analysis, an elaboration on the findings and the relevance of the findings. We will now look at what goes into each of these elements in a little more detail.

Type of data

The first thing you should mention about each analysis are the types of data used in that analysis. Knowing which types of data were used will help your audience to make sense of the findings. While it is also helpful to identify the method of data collection used, you can keep it brief as a more detailed explanation of the materials and procedure were already provided in the method section. All you need to say about data collection here in the results is a one-line identification of the type of data collection method or the name of the measure used.

In John's research, his ANOVA analysis used two types of data, game scores and playing style.

[In John's sub-section on his ANOVA analysis] *The data used in this analysis was the game performance scores, measured using the Leikisman Asymmetrical Pay-offs Game (APG), and the players' playing style, measured using a playing style preferences checklist.*

Method of analysis

Having identified the data that was used in the analysis, the next step is to explain how that data was analysed. You do this by identifying the method of analysis as well as any relevant details about how the analysis was carried out. What counts as a relevant detail varies depending on the method analysis, but as a general rule, if it is possible to carry out the same analysis in a few different ways, you should specify which way was used. Also, in quantitative analyses each of the variables involved plays a different role in the analysis (for example, the dependent and independent variables), and so in these cases you need to identify which variables fit into each of the roles in the analysis.

As well as identifying the method of analysis and how it was carried out, you should also say what the analysis was looking for. Typically, each analysis is attempting to test a hypothesis or find an answer to one of the research questions. As such, you should paraphrase that hypothesis or research question, so as to give your audience some idea of what the analysis is looking for. This will help your audience to make sense of the findings when you discuss them.

[In John's sub-section on his ANOVA analysis] *The analysis used was a one-way ANOVA, in which the dependant variable was 'game score' and the independent variable was 'preferred playing style', which had three levels ('no changes', 'changed according to a plan', 'changed in response to the other player'). The point of the analysis was to determine if there was a significant difference in game scores between players who prefer different playing styles.*

Findings of the analysis

Having identified your method of analysis, the next step is to report the main results of that analysis. Even a simple analysis can produce many results, but only a small number of them will be relevant to your research questions, those results being the 'main' results. Your job as the researcher is to sift through all these results so as to identify those main results which will reveal what the key finding is for that analysis.

The main results you are looking for are likely to be different depending on the type of analysis you are using. The good news is that each type of analysis has a set of results that are widely recognised to be the main results for that type of analysis. For example, if you are using a t-test statistical analysis then the main results for that analysis will always be the 't value', 'df value' and 'p value' which are easily found among the results that the t-test produces. The table below shows the most common types of analysis, what the main results are in each case and what key finding those results will indicate.

Type of analysis		Set of main results			Key finding
T-test		t value	df (Degrees f freedom) value	p value (significance)	There is/isn't a difference between two groups
Correlation		r value	p value (significance)		There is/isn't a relationship between two variables
ANOVA	For the model	F value	df (Degrees of freedom) value for variable and error	p value (significance)	There is/isn't a difference between more than two groups
	For each pair of groups	Names of the two groups	p value (significance)		
Regression	For the model	F value	df (Degrees of freedom)	p value (significance)	One variable does/doesn't predict another
	For each predictor	b (Beta value)	p value (significance)		
Thematic analysis		Name of the theme	Explanation as to the nature of the theme		What does the theme reveal about the comments?

The set of main results shown for each type of analysis can be used to determine one key finding for that analysis. The key finding is an explanation of what the main results are telling us. As such, when reporting the findings of an analysis you would typically start off by telling your audience what the main results are and then follow that by stating what key finding is indicated by those results.

If your main results are numerical, these can be included in a sentence by placing them inside brackets and including a letter or symbol to indicate what the number means. If you have a hypothesis linked to this analysis (See: Stating your hypotheses, p. 19), then this is where you say if the main results either support that hypothesis or fail to support it. After stating the main results (and hypotheses, if necessary) you then explain what key finding is indicated by those main results. In practical terms, this means explaining what the main results are telling us using uncomplicated, everyday language, without any technical terminology, that anyone could understand.

[In John's sub-section on his correlation analysis] *The results of the correlation show a significant positive correlation between game score and confidence ($r = 0.87$, $p < 0.01$). This supports the second hypothesis which predicted that player confidence would be significantly positively associated with game performance. All of this indicates that players with higher game scores also have higher levels of confidence, and vice versa.*

[In Alicia's sub-section discussing her first theme] *The first theme I identified was labelled "the mind of your opponent". This theme represents the players' beliefs regarding what occurs when you attempt to 'know' what your opponent is thinking. This theme suggests that a number of player behaviours, including how they respond to their opponent's moves, may be driven by that player's belief about whether it is possible to know what someone else is thinking.*

Elaborations on the findings

Once you have reported your key finding, the next steps are to elaborate on those findings and discuss their relevance. The order in which you do these two things is up to you. You should decide which will make more sense to your audience, if you elaborate first and then discuss relevance or the other way around. One situation where you should definitely elaborate first is if the results of that elaboration are needed to answer any of the research questions, which are talked about when you discuss the relevance.

Elaboration means going into more depth, when discussing the key finding, by providing a more detailed explanation of what the finding means. This is usually done by providing additional data either in the form of summary data or sample responses, which can be used to either make the meaning of the key finding even clearer or to add something to your audience's understanding of that finding. However you go about elaborating on the key finding, you will need to make sure that you spell out to your audience what this additional data or example reveals about that finding. No matter how obvious it may seem to you what extra clarity or understanding the additional data is providing, you should never assume that it goes without saying.

When providing additional data in a quantitative analysis, often known as 'summary data' or 'descriptive data', there are a number of ways you can go about presenting it. A table or chart is usually the most effective way to display how groups differ in terms of their scores or responses, while a graph is better at showing the relationship between two variables or the change in a variable over time.

In John's ANOVA analysis, the key finding is that all three groups, which represent the three preferred playing styles, have significantly different mean (average) game scores from each other. John will now try to elaborate on those findings to help his audience to see what those differences tell us.

[In John's sub-section on his ANOVA analysis] *If we look at the average scores for players in the three groups, we can see that the scores in the 'no changes' group were considerably lower than both the other groups. We can also see that although the two groups which prefer changeable playing styles have more similar scores, the group changing in response to an opponent is the more successful of the two (See Table 1).*

TABLE I **Mean game scores across the three strategies**

Preferred strategy	No changes	Changed according to a plan	Changed in response to the other player
Mean score	12.8	17.8	19.3

All of this suggests that having a changeable playing style is the most import element of a successful strategy, and that making those changes in response to your opponent offers a smaller but still critical additional advantage.

When summarising data, the guiding principles should always be to keep it short and simple. Don't forget that you are trying to help your audience understand the findings better, and overloading them with tables and graphs wouldn't help. As such, you should try to avoid having multiple graphs or multiple tables when elaborating on a single analysis. If you find you want to present multiple graphs or tables, you should consider if it is possible to combine them into one larger graph/table. However, be careful not to overdo those combinations; the overall size of any one graph or table should never take up more than half of the page. Also, be mindful that too much information in a single graph or table can defeat the purpose of trying to make the findings clearer.

When providing additional data for a qualitative analysis, this is usually done in the form of a quote; typically, a response from a participant which is a particularly good example of the point that you are attempting to explain to your audience. The same principles of short and simple also apply here. One participant's quote should be enough; you don't need to show that lots of people agreed and said the same thing. After all, you are not using this quote to try and prove that something is true, the point of the quote is to help your audience to better understand the findings.

> In Alicia's thematic analysis, a key finding has been the emergence of the theme "the mind of your opponent", which focuses on people's beliefs on what happens when you attempt to 'know' what your opponent is thinking. She will now try to elaborate on those findings to help her audience to see what they mean.

> [In Alicia's sub-section discussing her first theme] When it comes to knowing the mind of your opponent, there appears to be a clear split between those players who believe such a thing is possible and those who don't. To the non-believer, it's not about trying to read your opponent's mind, it's about imagining what you would do in their situation. As player 52 put it, "You can never know for sure why he [the opponent] makes a move like that, but I guess I'd have been playing for a draw too if I were in their shoes".

Relevance of the findings

As well as elaborating on your findings, you need to discuss their relevance, which means linking them back them to the research questions you posed in your introduction. You do that by discussing what the findings of the analysis reveal about the issues that the research questions are asking about. Although it is possible that the findings may be relevant to more than one research question, the most likely scenario is that the findings from each method of analysis will have a greater relevance for one research question above all others. As such, you should focus on relating the findings of the analysis under discussion to that most relevant research question.

When it comes to relating the findings to a research question, although there is no exact formula for doing this, if you are doing it for the first time there are some prompts you can use to help get you thinking about possible connections. Take any key finding from the analysis, consider the research question you think that finding is related to and then consider the following prompts:

- What is the issue that research question is concerned with?
- How is the finding of the analysis connected to that issue?

- Does the finding give us a new perspective on that issue, a new way of looking at it?
- Does the finding reveal something about the issue we didn't already know?
- Does the finding answer any questions about that issue and/or raise any new questions?

> [In John's sub-section on his ANOVA analysis] *The first research question asked whether changing your playing style in response to the moves of your opponent helps you to achieve a higher score in the game. The results confirm that changing your playing style is more likely to produce a higher score, which suggests flexibility in your style is a key skill for successful game players. However, the fact that changing your playing style according to a pre-determined plan was less successful than changing in response to your opponent's moves, suggests that flexibility alone is not enough to explain success. It raises the possibility that 'effective play' may be more about locating a style of play that your opponent finds hard to defeat, than it is about locating the most efficient style possible.*

You may be tempted to explore the links between the findings of your research and the findings of previous research which looked at the same research area. However, you should only consider discussing such links in the results section if those links have some relevance to answering one of the research questions. Otherwise, that sort of general discussion about the wider implications of the findings from your research to the research area and the wider context can wait until the discussion section (See: Wider implications, p. 118 and Past Research, p. 119).

▶ COMMON MISTAKES

Trying to report too many findings

There is a tendency with first-time report writers to overdo it when they report their findings. They may include multiple quotes or graphs to support every single point being made or attempt to analyse every question in their questionnaire/ interview individually. This bad habit is made even worse if the data collection has not been carefully planned, resulting in a lot of data being collected for no clear purpose. The attempt to analyse all this data then produces lots of analyses also with no clear purpose. Sometimes this excess of analysis is a misguided attempt to show off how much data has been collected, or it can be a sign of desperation, a faint hope that the sheer quantity of analysis can compensate for any errors or a lack of depth in that analysis. In reality, presenting an overabundance of results is more likely to confuse or bore your audience than impress them, and it does more to advertise a lack of confidence rather than cover it up. Worse still, presenting too many analyses and findings will almost certainly 'bury' those few findings that do matter, producing a results section that will appear to have nothing interesting to say, but still take a lot of time saying it.

The secret to being memorable, when it comes to presenting your findings, is to be concise. A good results section is one where you tell your audience only those things they need to know, and everything is communicated in the most economical amount of space possible. This can be achieved in a number of ways. It starts long before you ever write your report, when you plan your data collection so that you only collect the data you need to answer your research questions (See: Design, p. 64). Furthermore, you should summarise your data before analysing it so that you are analysing totals or means which combine the responses from multiple questions rather than analysing every question individually. Never use multiple quotes, graphs or tables where one would do. Finally, you should apply the same rule that the amount of time spent discussing something should depend on its importance, that we talked about for the literature review section (See: Time or space = importance, p. 47). Analyses which don't find anything of interest should be dealt with quickly by acknowledging the type of data and method of analysis as usual, but reducing any discussion on the findings to a single statement that nothing of interest was found. You can move any details about the analysis which are not critical into an appendix, providing your audience with a link to that appendix if they wish to see them (See: Appendices: The basics, p. 159). This saving in space can then be used to report the analyses which produce more important findings in greater detail. The combined effect of all these steps will be a results section which spends the time it needs on the important findings, while keeping the section as a whole short and to the point.

Significance is an all-or-nothing quality

When it comes to reporting the main results of a quantitative analysis, often the most important result is the significance result. This significance result is compared against a target value (often 0.05 in most social sciences) and if the significance result is lower than the target value then the analysis is said to be significant. This means the analysis has found what it was looking for and the theoretical model has been supported. However, if the significance result if equal to, or higher than the target value, then you must conclude that the analysis is non-significant. This means the analysis did not find what it was looking for and the theoretical model has not been supported.

While a non-significant result should be no more or less desirable than a significant one, it is very common for researchers to prefer finding evidence which supports their theories than not to. This can lead to a lot of frustration with non-significant analyses, especially if the significance result is very close to the target value, while still being on the wrong side of the line. In those situations, there is a real temptation to try to highlight the closeness of the result, as if that demonstrates that the theory or claim which the analysis was testing was mostly right. First-time report writers can start using expressions such as "approaching significance" or "mostly significant" and then use them as an excuse to talk about the theoretical model as if it had been supported.

This is both poor statistics and poor research. The target value for significance is meant to be an absolute requirement. It is all-or-nothing; either you meet the requirement or you don't, there is nothing in between. You can think of testing for significance like entering a competition where there is only one winner. Either you win or you lose. If you lose, talking about "mostly winning" or "approaching a win" will just sound like face-saving ways of hiding the fact that you lost. In a report, talking about "almost significant" results creates the impression that either you don't understand statistics or can't admit when you are wrong. You need to adopt an all-or-nothing approach to significance. It helps if you embrace the idea that non-significant results are an essential part of the research process. Furthermore, not finding something, especially where many others have claimed you should find it, can be a really important challenge to preconceptions and a stimulus for reflection.

Dumping stats clutter into the results

The output files produced by most statistical software often contain pages of complex tables and figures for even the most straightforward statistical analysis. While this level of detail is necessary in the output file, as it enables you to understand the findings of your analysis, very little of it needs to be presented to the audience in the results section. As we saw when discussing the main findings, you can pluck out the individual scores that you need from the output and include those numbers directly in the text of the result section (See: Findings of the analysis, p. 93). When it comes to additional data, usually presented in tables or graphs in the output, instead of pasting the table or graph as it appears in the output file into your results section, you should try to re-create it from scratch using the appropriate feature of your word processing software. Most word processing software has features that allow you to create tables and simple graphs. The advantage of this approach is that a table or graph you have re-created in this way can be both simpler and clearer than the one that appears in the output file. This is because the re-created table/graph will only contain those details that you choose to carry over from the output, the details you need to make the point you trying to make with that additional data.

If you believe that your audience would benefit from a chance to see some of the details of the analysis that were not included in the results section, you can provide them with a more complete breakdown of the findings of that analysis in an appendix. If you choose to do this, make sure to include a link to that appendix in the sub-section of the results where you discuss that method of analysis (See: Appendices: The basics, p. 159). When creating such an appendix, you should still take the time to decide which additional elements from the output file your audience really needs to see (See: Be selective about what you put in an appendix, p. 160). Dumping the entire contents of the output file into an appendix will either look like you don't care or that you don't really understand your analysis and so don't know how to be more selective. You should also make the effort to present those outputs in a clearer and better formatted fashion than the statistical software will have done (See: Tidy up those statistical appendices, p. 161). Here again, re-creating the tables and graphs in such an appendix is always preferable to cutting and pasting them from the output file into your report.

Explain your findings, not your statistics

Many first-time report writers go a little too far in explaining their analysis, offering a level of explanation you might give to someone who had never even heard of that method of analysis before. Examples of unnecessary explanations include: offering a basic explanation on what an analysis of this type is designed to do; providing definitions for all of the terminology used in the analysis; detailing every step in the analysis (not just the ones that produce a finding); discussing why this type of analysis is the appropriate method of analysis for the research design.

Possibly this is a misguided attempt to show how well they understand their analysis, or a too literal interpretation of the guidance which states that you should explain how the analysis was carried out. Whatever the reason, these types of explanation are unnecessary in a report. You should act as if your audience is either already familiar with most of the common methods of analysis and the terminology associated with them or can educate themselves if they need a more detailed explanation of any method of analysis. As such, the only kind of explanation you will need to provide in the results section occurs when an analysis could be carried out in a number of different ways, requiring you to explain which of those ways you chose.

When John is discussing his ANOVA analysis, he does not need to explain the basic facts about the ANOVA, such as that an ANOVA is used to find differences between groups, or that an ANOVA is appropriate when comparing more than two groups. He also does not need to explain what terms like 'significance' mean, when using them to report the findings of the ANOVA. One example of something he would need to explain is that in the final step of the ANOVA he used the 'Bonferroni' analysis. This deserves a mention because there are many ways you can carry out that final step in the ANOVA, and so his audience needs to know in which way John chose to do it.

▶ REFINEMENTS

Mind your language

When you are reporting your findings or relating them back to the hypotheses and research questions, you need to choose your words very carefully. Certain words carry a very specific meaning when used to report findings and so you should make sure you only use those words when it is appropriate to do so, avoiding them otherwise.

For example, when it comes to quantitative findings, you should avoid using the words 'prove' and 'disprove' because they suggest that we now understand that issue completely and there is no need for any further research or analysis. Since the idea of any issue being completely understood runs contrary to the way most scientists' view research, this is not a claim you want to appear to be making (See: Why don't we say prove and disprove? p. 105). Instead, when reporting a finding which shows a significant difference or relationship, you should say that the finding 'demonstrates' or 'supports' the existence of such a difference or relationship. Likewise, if the findings were non-significant, you would say the findings were 'unable to demonstrate', 'did not support' or 'did not show' the difference or relationship you were looking for. The same rules apply when relating the findings to a hypothesis, in which case you should say that the findings 'support' or 'fail to support' the hypothesis, but not 'prove' or 'disprove' it.

When it comes to qualitative results, you should avoid saying that a finding is 'significant', which is a term you should reserve for reporting quantitative findings, opting instead for alternatives such as 'important' or 'noteworthy'. Similarly, you should avoid saying that findings from a qualitative analysis are evidence of a difference between groups, a relationship between variables or one thing causing another. Instead, the most you should say is that your findings 'suggest' a difference, relationship or cause, or that such a thing could be 'inferred' from your findings. This approach acknowledges the strengths and limitations of qualitative analysis: ideal at providing an insight into people's experiences, reasoning and perceptions, but not well equipped to test the accuracy of that reasoning or perception. Using terms like 'suggest' or 'infer' recognises that when a qualitative analysis identifies potential patterns in, or additions to, a theoretical model, those patterns or additions remain untested. Based on the findings of a qualitative analysis, there may appear to be clear signs of a difference between groups, or one thing causing another, but appearances can be deceptive. Thus, a quantitative analysis would be needed to determine whether there is any evidence to support the existence of this apparent difference or cause. Until you do such an analysis, you should only talk about what *appears* to be there or what the findings *suggest* may be there, but no more than that.

Know your analysis

As I have said before, the results section is one of the more technically demanding sections of the report. When explaining how a method of analysis was carried out or what its findings were, you will need to be careful to use the appropriate terminology and make sure that your explanation is complete and correct. Any gaps in your understanding of your method of analysis will be very noticeable. Even if you have carried out the analysis correctly, any mistakes in your reporting of that analysis can undermine its impact by causing your audience to wonder if you know what you are talking about. Worse still, a mistake in the analysis itself, or your understanding of that analysis, can lead you to report findings which are completely invalid. This, in turn, can deal your research a fatal blow by causing you to draw invalid conclusions based on invalid findings and thereby producing the wrong answers to your research questions. Since a large portion of the discussion section will be influenced by those wrong answers, the knock-on effect of mistakes in your analysis can be extensive.

Of course, not every mistake in your analysis will have such a dramatic impact, some will be minor and easily overlooked. Nevertheless, the possibility that a mistake can be so significant is enough reason to make fully understanding your analysis a priority. You don't need to become a world-leading expert. Instead, a good working understanding of each method of analysis you plan to use should be a basic requirement before using that method. This means not using any form of analysis you don't fully understand, and studying examples of any type of analysis you plan to use before you use them on your own data. Finding examples of that analysis, or someone who is more knowledgeable on that form of analysis to review your findings, would be ideal. While mistakes will happen, taking these precautions can help to ensure that any such mistakes are so tiny, that no one else but you will even notice them. (These tiny mistakes will still bug you though, trust me on that!)

Summary data, tables and graphs

When deciding how to present any piece of additional data as part of elaborating on a key finding, you should be asking yourself what role that data will play in that elaboration. On the one hand, its purpose may be to simplify understanding, helping the audience to make sense of the key finding more rapidly or with less effort. On the other hand, the aim may be to add a little complexity rather than remove it, adding another layer of detail to reveal something that wasn't obvious based on the key finding alone. Identifying the role for the additional data is very important because different methods of presenting that data have different strengths, and so matching the presentation method to the role helps you to make sure that one supports the other.

With quantitative data, you are often faced with the choice of using a table, chart or graph to present that data. As a rule, charts and graphs are better if you wish to simplify things, while tables are better at presenting complexity. As we discussed earlier, tables and bar charts are good at presenting differences between groups, while graphs are good at presenting the relationship between variables. Tables are also good when you need to combine a variety of data which was measured in different ways into a single presentation, or when you need to present a lot of data in one place.

When it comes to the appearance of the table, as we discussed earlier you should try to avoid a single table taking up more than half a page in the report. You should also avoid having any table that stretches over two pages of the report. If the table is appearing on two pages because it begins near the end of a page, then try adding a page-return above it so as to move it down to a new starting position at the top of a new page. You can also reduce the table size by reducing the font size or switching to single-line spacing inside the table. In a similar vein, you should avoid having graphs or charts which take up more than a third of the page. You should try to shrink the size of the graph or chart to avoid this, but always aim to keep the aspect ratio (the relationship between the height and width of an image) the same when reducing size in this way. However, if reducing a graph or chart to a more appropriate size makes it hard to interpret, consider replacing it with a table.

With qualitative data, which usually comes in the form of quotes, the choices are between presenting the quote in-line within a paragraph, "*Like this*", or in a separate paragraph and indented;

> *"Much like this."*

Presenting the quote in-line is less disruptive to the flow of the paragraphs around it, but only if the quote is short, taking up no more than a line and a half on the page. If the quote is larger than that, then you should use an indented presentation. Whether in-line or indented, highlighting the data using italics or some other distinctive formatting is also recommended to help distinguish the quote from the text around it.

You should aim to keep any quote as short as possible, focusing only on that part of what was said or written that is relevant to the point you are making with the quote. As such, you should feel free to cut the quote short at the start or end (or both) or remove a part in the middle, if the section removed has no relevance. You should indicate any missing section with three dots "... *and it would look like this*". If the effect of removing a section makes the remaining quote hard to understand, you can include an explanatory word or two inside square brackets to clarify.

> In Alicia's research she is interested about where the players have learnt their playing style. There is one quote which offers a good example of one such influence.

> "I switched to my current coach six years ago after my family moved to this city, and it's from him I learnt to pay attention to what your opponent is trying to achieve."

As she is only interested in what they learnt and who from, Alicia can reduce this quote as follows to focus on the key points.

> "... it's from him [the coach] I learnt to pay attention to what your opponent is trying to achieve."

▶ ADVANCED

Why don't we say prove and disprove?

It is a common practice among researchers to avoid saying that their findings 'prove' or 'disprove' a hypothesis or theoretical model, preferring instead to talk about 'supporting' or 'failing to support' it. On the surface, this may seem like an arbitrary choice between two synonyms. However, there is an important principle at play here. To fully explore the reasons for choosing 'support' rather than 'prove' we would need to return to some of the same territory in the philosophy of science that we looked at in the method section when discussing logical positivism (See: Positionality, p. 81). Any such exploration would also become concerned with epistemology, the branch of philosophy which explores the nature and limits of human knowledge. While such a full exploration of this issue is beyond the scope of this chapter, we can shed some light on at least one key difference between the terms 'supported' and 'proven', namely the extent to which both terms invite further discussion on that matter.

If we describe a finding as 'proving' something, it implies that the finding has settled the matter once and for all. After all, once something is 'proven' or 'disproven' then your search for an answer is over and there is no need to gather any more evidence. This, in turn, implies that our knowledge and understanding of that issue is now complete. However, most scientists believe that their knowledge of any area of research will never be complete and is always evolving. From this perspective, each piece of new evidence adds to our knowledge and helps us to understand a little more about that area, but we will never reach a point where we know everything there is to know about that area. While it is true that not every scientist shares this view of how knowledge operates in their subject, it does represent the dominant paradigm in most sciences. For this reason, it is recommended that you use terms which describe your findings as either fitting in (supporting) or not fitting in (failing to support) with the current understanding of that area of research. Such terms reflect the viewpoint that any finding is only one piece of a much larger process of collecting evidence. The terms also recognise that no matter how much evidence we collect, we never stop looking for more evidence, since there is always room to improve our understanding of that area.

If you are unconvinced by the reasons I am offering here for avoiding terms like 'proved' and 'disproved', then the good news is that even the principle that "no question can ever be considered closed" is itself still open for debate. If you feel that there is more to this issue than has been discussed here, you should first inform your opinions by learning more about the philosophy of epistemology and how it applies to science and then join the debate. You too can then contribute to our understanding of whether or not things can ever be 'proven' in science.

Additional testing

When conducting a quantitative analysis, there are a number of additional tests you can include as part of the analysis which act as checks on the reliability of the measures or suitability of the data used. While it is generally agreed that you should always carry out these tests to ensure that your measures and data are as reliable and suitable as they can be, opinion is divided as to whether you need to mention them in your report. Considering the limited space available to discuss all your analyses, unless these additional tests reveal a major issue, it can feel as if they are not worth mentioning. However, a closer inspection will reveal that none of these tests offer a result that is black and white, pass or fail. Qualities such as reliability or suitability are measured on a sliding scale and while some scores are better than others, there is no such thing as a perfect result. Even so, a good result on one of these tests, such as a result suggesting your data is suitable for analysis, can still reveal a lot that is of interest to your audience about the rigour of your analysis and the amount of confidence they can have in its findings. It may feel as if reporting any weaknesses in your data or your measures is counterproductive, if the point of mentioning these additional tests is to impress your audience with the rigour of your methods. There will be a temptation to 'paper over the cracks', but it is important not to confuse rigorous methods with flawless ones. Real research is messy and imperfect; rigour comes from trying to manage those imperfections as best you can, which includes publicly acknowledging them so your audience can factor those imperfections into their reading of your report. As such, making space to include these additional tests and their outcomes in your report, no matter what the tests have found, is well worth the effort involved.

One type of additional test you could include are those tests which check the suitability of your data prior to analysis, such as tests for skewness or outliers. Certain types of quantitative analysis operate on the assumption that your data has specific qualities, such as normality or homogeneity. If you plan to use such an analysis, then there are various tests that check for these qualities in the data which you should carry out first. You would then report that these tests were conducted as one of the first steps in the analysis, before you discuss the main analysis and its findings. As always, you should aim only to report those details that are essential, which in this case means it is enough to say the test was carried out and to state the main finding of the test, which can usually be summarised in a single score. A more complete run-down of these tests does not need to be included in the results section, but could be included in an appendix (See: Appendices: The basics, p. 159).

Another type of additional test worth including are the tests of reliability such as the Cronbach's alpha reliability test. These tests were mentioned several times in the chapter on the method section, including in the discussion regarding developing your own materials and the use of a pilot study (See: Materials, p. 68, Pilot studies, p. 77 and Using existing materials vs developing your own, p. 79). In addition to the results of reliability tests carried out before you collected main study data, which are reported in your method section, you should also carry out a reliability analysis using the main study data itself and report the results of that in the results section. This is another type of test that you would report as a step in your analysis which comes before the main analysis and its findings. Similar to the other additional tests, you only report those details that are essential, namely the fact that a reliability test was carried out and the main finding of the test. Sometimes there will be one reliability score for the whole measure, but if the measure contains sections there can often be a reliability score for each section.

Either way, you can report the reliability score or scores in the results section, while a more complete run-down of the test can be included in an appendix (See: Appendices: The basics, p. 159).

> *In John's research, he plans to discuss the findings of the ANOVA, but first he needs to report on two additional tests. The additional tests are in **bold**]*

[In John's sub-section on his ANOVA analysis] **The Shapiro-Wilk Test for normality was non-significant (p = 0.827), indicating that the data was normally distributed. The Levine's test for homogeneity was also non-significant (p = 0.663) indicating homogeneity of variance between the groups**. *The results of the ANOVA show a significant difference between the strategy groups in terms of their average game score (F(2,27) = 1.62, p = 0.03).*

When the findings from the additional tests show that your data and measures are all within the boundaries of reliability and suitability, it is simple enough to report that fact and then move on to reporting the findings of the main analysis. A more interesting situation develops when these tests identify any issues with your data or measures. How you manage those issues can depend on a few factors.

In the case of tests of normality, it can depend on how much the data deviates from normality and if your planned statistical analysis is robust. Small deviations from normality in your data usually mean you can continue with your main analyses as planned, but you should tell your audience about the deviation and urge them to treat the findings with caution. What you mean by 'treat the findings with caution' is that you recognise that your data is imperfect but you feel that it is still possible to learn something from analysing it. Alternatively, some statistical methods of analysis are also known to be 'robust', which means they are less affected by small deviations from normality in the data. If your chosen method of analysis is one of those robust methods, then you can mention that as your response instead of urging caution with the results. What you are saying, in this case, is that there may be a minor deviation from normality in the data, but the findings of the statistical analysis won't be affected by it.

For more serious deviations from normality, simply urging caution or relying on the robustness of your method of analysis may not be enough. One potential solution would be to remove any data points that are outliers; an 'outlier' being a data point which disrupts the normality of the data by being so different from all the other data. If that doesn't work, then it may be necessary to switch the type of analysis you are using to one of the non-parametric analyses which don't require normally distributed data. If you do end up removing outliers or switching to a non-parametric analysis because of issues with the data's normality, then you should mention it when discussing that analysis in the results section. Since these actions will affect the findings of the analysis, it is important for your audience to know your reasons for taking them.

In the case of tests of reliability, findings which show that the materials have only a moderate level of reliability can be addressed, much like small deviations from normality in the data, by suggesting your audience treat the findings with caution. On the other hand, weak or very weak reliability scores can sometimes be addressed by removing parts of that measure which the reliability test has identified as the source of the poor reliability scores. For example, the result of the Cronbach's alpha test can tell you how much the reliability of a questionnaire would improve if certain questions were 'dropped', meaning that the data from those questions would not be used in the analysis. In this way, you can remove questions which are dragging down the overall reliability of your questionnaire. You then use only the data from the remaining, more reliable questions, in your main analysis. If you cannot bring the overall reliability of a measure up to an acceptable level in this way, then you may need to face the fact that the data from that measure cannot be used, and so the analysis which uses that data cannot take place. This would be a last resort, but it should be considered if the reliability score is low enough. Better to cancel the analysis than to produce potentially invalid findings by using unreliable measures.

The final point to consider is how you decide what qualifies as a 'minor' deviation from normality or an 'acceptable' level of reliability and how you then justify that decision to your audience in your report. Usually, such justifications are based on a comparison between your reliability or normality scores and the same scores in another published sources. One such comparative source can be other research using a similar method to your research. Another such source would be a published standard of reliability or normality, which specifies values for week and strong scores to be used by all researchers. As such, when interpreting the findings of these tests there should be a published source you can site as a basis for that interpretation.

▶ CHAPTER 5: EXERCISES

Exercise 1: MCT

1) Which of the following is NOT part of the purpose of the results?
   A. Taking the answers to the research questions and relating them to the wider context.
   B. Presenting the key findings for each method of analysis.

C. Identifying which method of analysis and data was used in each analysis.

D. Identifying the answers to the research questions that are suggested by the findings.

2) Why is it recommended to discuss each method of analysis in a separate sub-section?

A. To make it clear which findings were produced by which methods of analysis.

B. It helps your audience to see when the discussion on one method of analysis has ended and the discussion of new method is beginning.

C. It helps to clarify which method of analysis is being used to analyse each type of data.

D. All of the above.

3) Discussing the _____ for a method of analysis means exploring the answers to the research questions that the findings have revealed, whereas discussions on the _____ are where you either clarify what the finding means or to add more detail to what that finding is saying.

A. findings of the analysis, relevance of the findings

B. elaborations on the findings, findings of the analysis

C. relevance of the findings, elaborations on the findings

D. relevance of the findings, findings of the analysis

4) The point of explaining how a method of analysis was set up is...

A. to demonstrate how that analysis is the appropriate analysis for the research question.

B. to explain how the analysis works to those in the audience that are not familiar with it.

C. to explain which approach to the analysis was used, if more than one approach is possible.

D. to clarify which data was analysed by that method of analysis.

5) The main results are those few results produced by the analysis which are relevant to the research questions, whereas the key finding _____.

A. is relevant to the wider context.

B. explains what the main results mean.

C. is relevant to the research area.

D. None of the above.

6) When you are providing additional data you should always aim to present the smallest amount of data necessary because _____.

A. the purpose of the additional data is to clarify things and so you want to keep it simple.

B. too much additional data can mean that the key findings will be overlooked.

C. your audience only needs to see the data that is relevant to the point you are making.

D. All of the above.

7) You should avoid saying that your results 'prove' something when discussing _____ analyses, whereas saying a result is 'significant' is not suitable when discussing _____ analyses.

A. any, qualitative

B. qualitative, any

C. quantitative, any

D. any, quantitative

8) When it comes to including a more complete picture of one of your analyses in an appendix, which of the following is NOT recommended.

A. Including a mention of that appendix in the sub-section where that method of analysis is being discussed.

B. Including as much additional detail about the analysis as you can in the appendix because there is no way of knowing which bits your audience will be interested in.

C. Including a more complete picture of an analysis in an appendix when the results of an analyses didn't find anything of interest.

D. All of the above.

9) If the result of a test of normality on your data shows a large deviation from normality, you should respond by either _____ or _____.

A. urging your audience to treat the findings with caution, referring to the robustness of your analysis.

B. urging your audience to treat the findings with caution, switching to a non-parametric method of analysis.

C. eliminating any outliers in your data, switching to a non-parametric method of analysis.

D. eliminating any outliers in your data, referring to the robustness of your analysis.

10) Which of the following details does NOT need to be included when discussing a method of analysis?

A. A listing of all of the types of data included in that analysis.

B. An exploration of the findings of that analysis in more depth.

C. An explanation of what the findings of that analysis reveal about the research questions.

D. An explanation of what an analysis of that type is supposed to do.

Exercise 2: How serious are these mistakes?

A common problem faced by many first-time report writers is judging the relative importance of all the different rules and requirements involved in report writing. Is it a big deal if you don't completely understand a method of analysis you are using? How serious an issue is it if you explain your method of analysis more than you should? With this in mind you will find, in alphabetical order, 10 common mistakes made by first-time report writers when writing their results. You need to put each of them in one of three categories of importance: serious errors, moderate errors and minor errors.

- Including unedited tables and figures from a statistical output file in your report.
- Making a mistake in how you report the main results.
- Not fully understanding a method of analysis you are using.
- Not mentioning the type of data used or which method of analysis was used.
- Not reporting the key findings or relating them to the research questions.
- Not explaining how the method of analysis was set up or not elaborating on the findings.
- Reporting too many findings or including too many graphs or tables.
- Reporting a result as being almost significant.
- Trying to explain too much about method of analysis that you are using.
- Using the wrong terms to report the findings of your analysis.

▶ CHAPTER 5: ANSWERS

Exercise 1: MCT

Q1: Ans = A (See: The basics, p. 90 ↔ Relevance of the findings, p. 97)
Q2: Ans = D (See: Structuring your analyses using sub-sections, p. 91)
Q3: Ans = C (See: Findings of the analysis, p. 93 ↔ Elaborations on the findings, p. 95 ↔ Relevance of the findings, p. 97)
Q4 Ans = C (See: Method of analysis, p. 93 ↔ Explain your findings, not your statistics, p. 101 ↔ Type of data, p. 92)
Q5: Ans = B (See: Findings of the analysis, p. 93)
Q6: Ans = D (See: Elaborations on the findings, p. 95 ↔ Summary data, tables and graphs, p. 104)
Q7 Ans = A (See: Mind your language, p. 102 ↔ Why don't we say prove and disprove? p. 105)
Q8: Ans = B (See: Trying to report too many findings, p. 98 ↔ Dumping stats clutter into the results, p. 100 ↔ Additional testing, p. 106)

Q9: Ans = C (See: Additional testing, p. 106)

Q10: Ans = D (See: Type of data, p. 92 ↔ Elaborations on the findings, p. 95 ↔ Relevance of the findings, p. 97 ↔ Explain your findings, not your statistics, p. 101)

Exercise 2: How serious are these mistakes?

Serious errors

(Not fully understanding a method of analysis you are using. ↔ Not mentioning the type of data used or which method of analysis was used. ↔ Not reporting the key findings or relating them to the research questions.)

All of these are serious errors, either because they completely undermine the central purposes of the results, which is to provide a clear understanding of the findings and how they were produced, or because they risk introducing what may be a fatal flaw in your analysis. While it is true that an incomplete understanding of your analysis is not guaranteed to result in an invalid analysis or findings, it greatly increases the chance of that happening. More importantly, it is the scale of the potential damage which is the real threat with this mistake. If they are recognised as being invalid, your flawed findings will undermine the credibility of both the results and discussion sections of your report. But, even if they are not spotted as being invalid, in that case you have only "succeeded" in presenting false answers as the truth, and that is no victory for anyone that considers themselves a researcher. As far as the other errors in this category are concerned, leaving out details such as the type of data, method of analysis, key findings or relevance of the findings, these are more obvious errors but just as serious. Without these details it is much harder, if not impossible, for your audience to understand your findings or how they were produced. Each of these details represents an indispensable part of the puzzle, and so all of them need to be present for the findings to make sense to anyone other than yourself.

(See: The basics, p. 90 ↔ Type of data, p. 92 ↔ Method of analysis, p. 93 ↔ Findings of the analysis, p. 93 ↔ Relevance of the findings, p. 97 ↔ Know your analysis, p. 103.)

Moderate errors

(Making a mistake in how you report the main results. ↔ Not explaining how the method of analysis was set up or not elaborating on the findings. ↔

Reporting a result as being almost significant. ↔ Using the wrong terms to report the findings of your analysis.)

All of these are moderate errors owing to the fact that, while they do make your work much less effective, they do not fatally undermine it the way the serious errors do. At first glance, making a mistake in the reporting of your main results sounds like a serious error; however, the mistake here is only in the reporting of the analysis, not in the analysis itself. The researcher who makes this mistake has usually carried out their analysis correctly and understands their results, but makes some basic error in how they communicate the results in the results section. This kind of mistake will still confuse your audience because the incorrectly reported results will not align with the findings. However, as long as the results and discussion are based on valid findings, the damage of this error is limited to the results section and so is moderate rather than serious. Similarly, leaving out an explanation of the set-up of the analysis or the elaboration of the results are moderate errors, rather than serious ones, because these are important details but not essential. Their absence will make it harder, but not impossible, to interpret the results. Finally, using incorrect or invalid terms, such as reporting a result as almost significant, may appear trivial but it can represent a serious lack of understanding of the analysis. At worst, using these wrong terms can lead the researcher to draw invalid conclusions from valid findings, and at best they still demonstrate poor understanding of the analysis which can undermine credibility in their findings and conclusions.

(See: Findings of the analysis, p. 93 ↔ Method of analysis, p. 93 ↔ Elaborations on the findings, p. 95 ↔ Significance is an all-or-nothing quality, p. 99 ↔ Mind your language, p. 102 ↔ Why don't we say prove and disprove? p. 105.)

Minor errors

(Including unedited tables and figures from a statistical output file in your report. ↔ Reporting too many findings or including too many graphs or tables. ↔ Trying to explain too much about method of analysis that you are using.)

All of these are minor errors in the sense that, although they have a negative impact on the effectiveness of your results, the extent of their impact is much more limited than the moderate errors. All three errors share a similar problem, in that they are likely to introduce a lot of unnecessary additional information into the results. This can have a number of negative effects, such as not leaving enough space to discuss more important information properly or burying key findings so that the audience overlooks them. While none of this will cause serious damage to your results, it falls short of what should be the aim for any memorable results section, too tell your audience only those things they need to know in the least amount of space possible. Overall then, these are mistakes you should generally try to avoid making, but you should not worry too much about it if you do end up making one.

(See: Trying to report too many findings, p. 98 ↔ Dumping stats clutter into the results, p. 100 ↔ Explain your findings, not your statistics, p. 101 ↔ Summary data, tables and graphs, p. 104)

6 The discussion

The discussion is the section where you explore and apply the findings of your research, while also critically evaluating the research itself. You do this by first reviewing the answers to your research questions, reflecting on their relevance to the research area and wider context, as well as exploring the links between your findings and the findings of past research. You also evaluate your research design, reflecting on both its strengths and weaknesses. Finally, you look ahead, considering potential practical applications for your findings as well as future research ideas to carry on where your research leaves off. By the end of the discussion section, your audience should be aware of the wider theoretical and practical implications of your findings, the lessons learnt regarding methodology and what is next for research in this area.

▶ BEFORE YOU BEGIN THIS CHAPTER...

Before you are ready to begin writing your discussion, there are a number of steps in the research process you will need to complete first.

- Complete your data collection and analysis.
- Consider the implications of your findings for both the research area and the wider context.
- Identify the implications in your findings for any previous research.
- Reflect on both the strengths and weaknesses of the methodology of your research.
- Consider the potential for practical applications of your research findings.
- Evaluate the potential for future research in the same research area.

DOI: 10.4324/9781003107965-6

- Once you have completed all of these steps, then you are ready to begin writing this section of the report.

▶ THE BASICS

The discussion section can be divided into six sub-sections: wider implications, past research, methodological issues, future research, practical applications and conclusions. You should structure these sections as separate paragraphs, but it is optional whether you identify each of them using sub-headings. It is useful to divide up the discussion section in this way as it helps both you and your audience to keep track of all of the different topics you will need to cover in this section.

Wider implications

The first thing you need to do is to review your key findings and the answers to the research questions again and consider what implications these answers might have for the research area and wider context in which your research is located. Since you have already stated your findings and the answers to the research questions in the results section (See: Findings of the analysis, p. 93 and Relevance of the findings, p. 97), your audience only needs a very brief reminder of those findings and answers here in the discussion. As such, there is no need to state what kind of analysis was used or to provide another summary of the results in the discussion; it is enough simply to restate the key findings. As well as summarising the findings, you need to mention what answers to the research questions those findings indicate, since that reminds your audience what the findings mean. Again, to save time and avoid too much repetition of the results section, it is usually enough to state what the answer to the research question was without needing to restate the question itself. Doing all this in-brief allows you to move on quickly to discussing the implications of those findings and answers.

Once you have re-stated the findings and the answers to the research questions, you should relate those answers to your research area and the wider context. The aim here is to explain to your audience what insights those answers provide to the research area or wider context. At its most basic level, sharing an 'insight' means helping people to gain a new understanding or new perspective on something (See: Insight, p. 213). As such, if you want to figure out whether the answer to a research question offers any insight into the research area, you should ask yourself whether the answer reveals anything about the deeper structures or processes which explain how the research area works. You will have suggested what some of those deeper structures and processes are in your theoretical model in the introduction (See: Outline the theoretical model, p. 15). Do the answers to the research questions confirm or contradict any parts of your model? Alternatively, it may be that the answers add something new to the model, a new way of looking at the research area. Similarly, if you want to know whether an answer to a research question offers an insight into the wider context, you should ask yourself whether the answer inspires any new ideas or strategies to understand or tackle the issues that exist in that wider context (See: Introduce the research context, p. 14).

Kate is exploring the links between the use of make-up by women and evaluations of their appearance by others. She asked both male and female participants to rate the attractiveness of a series of sample female faces which varied as to which types of make-up they used. The types of make-up were divided into two categories: 'enhancers' which increased the attractiveness of key facial features (such as lipstick enhancing lip colour) and 'perfectors' which remove blemishes or imperfections (such as foundation creating the appearance of flawless skin). Her research question asks if 'perfecting' make-up will have a bigger impact on attractiveness than 'enhancing' make-up.

[In Kate's Wider implications] The results of the analysis found that 'enhancing' make-up (such as lipstick or eye-shadow) had no impact on the attractiveness ratings offered by men or women in response to the sample faces. On the other hand, three out of the four types of 'perfecting' make-up (foundation, concealer, fake tan) did produce a significant improvement in attractiveness ratings from both men and women. Therefore, 'perfecting' make-up does have a bigger impact on attractiveness than 'enhancing' make-up. What this suggests, is that make-up's most important benefits come from the appearance it hides rather than the appearance it creates. This supports the theoretical model which suggested that hiding flaws is a more successful strategy than promoting advantages when attracting a mate. It also means that the promotion of products which claim to conceal or correct flaws may have a stronger relationship with unhealthy body-image than other beauty products or promotions.

One thing to aim for, when you are explaining the relevance of the findings to the research area or wider context, is to use simple non-technical language wherever possible. It may seem to you like you are stating the obvious, but a basic rule to remember is that *you* understand your research much better than your audience ever will, and so what may seem obvious to you is not always obvious to them.

Past research

Following your discussion of the wider implications, the next step is to relate your findings to the findings of the key pieces of previous research mentioned in your introduction and literature review (See: Outline the theoretical model, p. 15 and Identifying the foundations and unresolved questions, p. 41). The aim here is to compare your results to the results of that previous research and to comment on the similarities and differences. You are also considering whether your findings have added to, or changed, the understanding of the research area created by that previous research. If your findings add to, but don't radically change, the understanding of the research area created by the previous research, then you can say that your findings are consistent with that previous research. However, if your findings do radically change the understanding of the research area, then you can say your results are inconsistent with that previous research. Furthermore, if your findings were the exact opposite of the results found in a piece of previous research, you might go so far as to say that your findings contradict or challenge the findings of that research. As well as making the comparison, you may also wish to offer a comment on what the consistency or lack of consistency might mean.

> [In Kate's Past research] *The findings of the current research indicate that covering imperfections or flaws had a bigger influence on attractiveness than highlighting positive attributes. These findings appear to be consistent with Gartz (1992) who reported that "overlooks my flaws" was a more common response than "finds me attractive" among people asked about the qualities they look for in a long-term partner. This supports the idea that most people see their flaws as a critical element affecting their attractiveness. However, my findings were not consistent with Steinhauer (1997), who found that in conversations when out on a date, people expend more effort emphasizing their positive qualities than downplaying their negative ones. This suggests that people might take a different approach when managing their appearance verbally then when they are managing it physically.*

You don't need to compare your results to every piece of previous research you have mentioned in the introduction or literature review. You can focus on the key research that appeared later on in each section of your literature review, the research which was the biggest inspiration for your research questions (See: The funnel, p. 48 and Identifying the foundations and unresolved questions, p. 41).

Methodological issues

Having related your findings to past research, the next step is to review any potential issues with your methodology. The aim here is to critically evaluate your methodology, considering both strengths and weaknesses and identifying any aspects of your research design that should be carried over, or improved on, if the research were to be repeated in the future.

The element of the methodology which is most often mentioned in this sub-section is the materials. This is because the materials are the most complex element of the methodology both practically and theoretically. This extra complexity means more chances for problems, but also more potential for fine-tuning and improvement. Evaluation of the materials tends to focus on whether they worked as expected, as well as discussing any problems or potential improvements that emerged during the research. If you were able to carry out a pilot study (See: Pilot studies, p. 77) or any reliability analyses (See: Additional testing, p. 106) on those materials, then this is a good place to comment on the overall results from those activities. You should avoid repeating too much information from previous sections about those activities, focusing instead on what they revealed overall regarding the reliability or validity of the materials or any ways they could be improved.

In comparison to the materials, conducting the procedure or selecting the participants are more straightforward activities, which means less chance of error but also less room for improvement. Consequently, the procedure or participants are usually only worth discussing in this sub-section when there were notable problems with them during the research. In most cases, serious problems with the participants or procedure may have already been mentioned in the method section. However, it would only be here in the methodological issues sub-section of the discussion that you can reflect on the impact of those issues as well as make suggestions for improvements in future research.

In addition to identifying areas of potential weakness in your methodology, you should also seek to identify any strengths. An example of a strength would be any precautions you took to ensure that the data collection was reliable and valid such as designing part of your methodology to control a confounding variable. Again, this may be something you have already mentioned in the method section (See: Controlling confounding variables, p. 78) but it doesn't hurt to remind your audience of the benefits of this design feature in the discussion.

[In Kate's Methodological issues] *An important element of the methodology for this research was the use of the FaceSim software to generate the sample faces. By using computer generated faces, I was able control all other elements of the image, ensuring that the type of make-up used was the only element that changed from picture to picture. This avoided the impact of potential confounding variables such as lighting and facial expression, noted in other research such as Dornacu (1993). However, in the debriefings, some participants said they were unsure if they were meant to rate the face based on their own opinion or give it the rating they thought most people would give. This raises the possibility of participants interpreting the instructions differently, and so should be clarified in the instructions for future research of this type.*

Any methodological issues you mention can be inspired by your own reflections on the research, but another potential source of inspiration can be anecdotal feedback from your participants. 'Anecdotal feedback' is the name given to any small-talk you may have had with the participants; casual conversations that are not part of the formal data collection. If your participants say anything about their experience that highlights a weakness in your method, anything that was confusing or did not work properly, then those are examples of anecdotal feedback. Other times, it may not be something that was said, but rather things you noticed, such as a step in the procedure where the participants seemed unsure what to do and needed help to continue. Wherever the inspiration is from, if there is any aspect of your method that might have affected the findings of your research in a positive or negative way, then it deserves a mention here.

Practical applications

Once you have finished reflecting on the pros and cons of the research design, the next step is to explore the difference your findings might make out there in the real world through a discussion of the practical applications of those findings. The aim of this sub-section is to demonstrate that your research findings could be used to help in real-world situations which are part of the wider context in which your research is located (See: Introduce the research context, p. 14). That help can come from your findings providing new information or a new way of looking at things, so as to give people a better understanding of that situation. Other times, the help might can come in the form of your findings leading to suggestions for an intervention. An 'intervention' is a series of actions taken either by those people already in the situation, or someone who is supporting them, which are aimed at improving the situation. Whatever form your practical application takes, you need to make sure that both the benefits of the application and its link to your findings are clear.

> [In Kate's Practical applications] *Given that the current research found that 'perfecting' make-up had the biggest impact on attractiveness ratings, it is likely to have a strong appeal to anyone with low self-esteem relating to their appearance. As such, parents and teachers could be advised to be on the lookout for high levels of use of 'perfecting' make-up among children around the ages 12 or 13, known to be common starting point for body dysmorphia and eating disorders (Balakin, 1995).*

One question that first-time report writers often ask is whether they are limited to the findings of their own research when suggesting practical applications. As a rule, it is better to stick to your own findings when discussing such applications. Otherwise, you will be discussing the applications of other researcher's findings, and so most likely repeating what those researchers have already said in their own reports. One exception to this rule is that, on some occasions, you might speculate about applications that could come from the findings of future research which follow up on yours. When doing so, you should keep your claims very simple, since you are applying findings which haven't happened yet (or may never happen) and so it is best not to overstate what those findings will be or what can be done with them.

Another question that first-time report writers struggle with is what you should say about applications if the results of your analysis were non-significant, such as when you looked for difference between groups but don't find one. Can you do anything practical with a finding like that? While a non-significant result can feel less exciting, it can still be of practical use. Being able to show that nothing is going on is sometimes a very meaningful insight. For example, if you found that reducing class sizes had no effect on the performance of the students in that class, then that is a finding with important practical implications. Yet another situation that first-time report writers find challenging is when the findings of their research simply confirm existing practice and they wonder if it is permitted to suggest no changes to the way things are currently being done. The simple answer is yes; after all, a practical application is as much about providing new information as suggesting new practice. If your research provides fresh evidence of the effectiveness of current practice, that is new information and well worth knowing.

Future research

Having discussed the applications of your research in the wider world, the next step is to look to the future and consider where research in this area goes next. The aim of this sub-section is to provide ideas for research questions that other researchers can use as the inspiration for their research.

When proposing future research, you need to go beyond merely recycling your research minus any mistakes you made. That being said, you also need to be careful not to go too far in the other direction and propose future research which seems completely unconnected to your research. Future research works best when it can be seen to grow out of your research rather than simply appearing out of thin air. As such, you need to strike the right balance, with future research proposals which include some elements of your research but combine them with something new in an attempt to answer new research questions.

It is this idea of changing the research questions that really helps to separate your research from the future research. The best way to achieve that change is to propose adding something new to the theoretical model for your research (See: What is a theoretical model (and why do I need one), p. 29). That usually means bringing in a new element or suggesting a new relationship between elements. A good example of bringing in a new element is to introduce a new variable and a good example of suggesting a new relationship would be to argue that this new variable has an effect on one of the other variables in the model. In addition to telling your audience what the future research should look at, you should explain why that research is worth doing. The best way to do this is to propose at least one benefit to the research area or wider context that might come from answering the new research questions connected to this future research. However, keep in mind that you're not required to provide a full blueprint for this future research, just the idea, and so the briefest outline is enough.

[In Kate's Future research] *Future research in this area could explore if this difference between 'perfecting' and 'enhancing' make-up operates in the same way at all levels of self-esteem. Touchstone (2001) found that people with lower self-esteem were more likely to rate make-up and clothes as important elements affecting their confidence in social situations. As such, future research could examine if the difference between "perfector" and "enhancer" make-up is larger in a low self-esteem group compared to a high one. Establishing the role of self-esteem could help to determine if the pressure to appear flawless is coming from values within the person or as a social pressure they feel coming from others.*

Conclusion

As the final sub-section of the discussion, the job of the conclusion is to take a step back and reflect on the discussion as a whole, highlighting those discussion points which are of the greatest importance. The aim of this sub-section is to craft the 'take-home' message of your research report. Of all the points you have made in your discussion, which ones do you most want your audience to remember and why?

It is important to note that a conclusion is not a summary, and so you should avoid repeating all the main points from your discussion here. Instead you should look at this as an opportunity to review all the points you made across all the other sub-sections of the discussion and select a few points which you think are more important than the others. How you judge the importance of each point is completely up to you; there are no fixed rules for doing this. Your reasons can be entirely your own, the only catch being that, for each point you highlight in the conclusion, you need to explain to your audience why you are highlighting it.

If you find you are struggling to come up with any conclusions, there are some prompts below to help you kick-start your thinking on this task. These prompts have been divided up by the sub-sections of the discussion since you never can tell where the most important point in your discussion may be found.

- **Wider implications:** Did any of your findings make a big difference to the way you see the research area or the wider context to which it belongs? If so, explain what that difference is and why it feels like an important difference to you.
- **Past research:** Did your findings raise an important question about any of the previous research? Did you challenge any previous findings or come down on one side of any debates in the literature? If so, explain why challenging that past research matters or what it would mean to settle that debate.
- **Methodological issues:** On the negative side, were any of the problems with the methodology serious enough that they undermine the findings of the research? If so, explain why they are so serious and what the implications are for the credibility of your findings. On the positive side, does an improvement in your methodology represent an important step forward in the way this area should be studied? If so, explain why it is that important.
- **Practical applications:** Are the findings of your research important enough to make a big difference when applied to the real world? If so, explain what difference that application would make and why would it matter.
- **Future research:** Would any of the future research proposals represent an important step forward in this research area? If so, explain why it is so important and what makes it stand out from other potential research advances.

[In Kate's Conclusions] *In conclusion, by highlighting the importance of 'perfecting' make-up in appearance modification, the findings of this research could offer a valuable new tool to parents and other guardians looking to identify self-esteem issues among the youth. While this would be only one of the tools needed for such a task, high levels of use of 'perfecting' make-up would offer an easily recognised signal of esteem issues which could then be followed up with more detailed investigation and support.*

Keep in mind that conclusions work best when they are focused and credible. Focus comes from not trying to offer too many conclusions, and the credibility comes from being modest in your claims about the importance of any point you have made. A conclusion that highlights just one point, which is only slightly more important than the other points you made in your discussion, can still be a good conclusion. As long as it is something your audience believes and remembers, then your conclusions sub-section has done its job well.

▶ COMMON MISTAKES

Not every discussion will contain all of the sub-sections

You should not assume that every discussion section is going to contain all six sub-sections. While the wider implications, past research and conclusions sub-sections are essential, and so almost always included, points relating to the other sub-sections are more optional and so their inclusion depends on the importance of the point and the space available. With finite space to work with, a good researcher should always consider if the space used to make a point about methodological issues, practical applications or future research could be better used making another point belonging to another section. This means that any of those three sub-sections could end up being left out if the points within that sub-section are less important than the points that could be made elsewhere.

The weak literature review strikes again!

Weaknesses in your literature review are going to show up very clearly in the discussion section, especially in the Past research sub-section where you relate the findings of your research to the findings of previous research. The biggest problems occur when first-time report writers invent research questions first and then conduct their literature review later, a strategy which regularly leaves them high-and-dry and struggling to find any research relevant to those questions (See: Research questions emerge from the literature review, not the other way around, p. 46). This usually results in a weak literature review, containing lots of research which appears to be in the same research area as your research, but under closer inspection turns out to be not directly related to your research or your research questions. If your audience hasn't already seen through the illusion behind that kind of literature review in the literature review section, it is going to collapse right in front of their eyes in the discussion section.

For the comparisons in the Past research sub-section to work, your research and the previous research need to be directly related, which usually means having elements in common, such as the same variables coming up in both. This connection will be strongest with the pieces of previous research used to generate the research questions for your research (See: Identifying the foundations and unresolved questions, p. 41). However, if none of the previous research in the literature review is the source of the research questions for your research, then there may not be any elements in common, making it hard or even impossible to compare your findings to theirs. This doesn't just look bad, it also shows up a flaw in your research design. No clear origin for your research questions means no clear basis for your theoretical model, and once your theoretical model starts to look shaky so does your whole research. This is one of the reasons why it is so important to establish a good theoretical basis for your research by using previous research, mentioned in your literature review, to help generate your research questions.

Unnecessary repetition of details from the literature review

When you are relating the findings of your research to previous research you will end up re-visiting some of the points you made about that previous research in your literature review. While some repetition is therefore inevitable, that doesn't mean you should drag your audience through a full replay of the literature review in the discussion. One possible reason that many first-time report writers re-visit too much of the literature review is because they know they are supposed to relate their research to the previous research, but are unsure which previous research to talk about. Their "solution" is to include as many pieces of research from the literature review as they can, hoping that the research they need to cover is in there somewhere.

As a rule, you only need to make mention of a piece of previous research, in the Past research sub-section, if the findings of your research are directly relevant to it. Usually this means that both your research and the previous research have some element in common, such as the same variable being measured in both pieces of research. Other times it means that a finding from your research relates to a claim made in the previous research. Either way, it should be possible to say that the findings of your research are either consistent or inconsistent with the findings or claims from that previous research. However, any piece of previous research where it is not possible to make that kind of connection does not need to be mentioned in the discussion.

Another example of unnecessary repetition is the inclusion of details from the methodology of previous research when that research is mentioned in the discussion. While the methodology of previous research may have received the occasional mention in the literature review, in the discussion all your audience needs to know about each piece of previous research are their key findings. After all, the key findings are usually the only thing you need if you want to compare findings between your research and the previous research. One exception to this rule is when your results are inconsistent with the findings of a piece of previous research and you think methodological differences may be responsible. In such a case, you might highlight the methodology of a piece of previous research in your discussion so that you can use that methodology to explain the difference in results.

Discuss your own findings, not the findings of others

Research doesn't always turn out as you expect, and while any researcher might be a little less enthusiastic to discuss research whose findings go against expectations, first-time report writers seem to struggle with this more than most. This is odd, because, as you will see in the rest of this chapter, no matter what the outcome of the research there should always be plenty of interesting things to talk about. Unexpected results, such as not finding what you hoped for, or mistakes you have made can all be a rich source for ideas and insights. As such, there is no reason to do what some report writers do when faced with disappointing findings, which is to ignore them and spend a large section of their discussion talking about the findings of other research instead.

In these cases, the findings of their own research get only the bare minimum of attention. The Past research section is almost all about the findings of previous research with the findings of their own research hardly being mentioned. Even more blatant, it is the findings of the previous research that are being applied in Wider implications, Practical applications or the focus of the Conclusions subsection. Like a parent who keeps wondering out loud why their child can't be more like someone else's child, it can be embarrassing to watch a researcher treat their own research as second best. The lesson here, therefore, is that the previous research of others should never outshine your research in the discussion. The findings of previous research should only ever be mentioned when comparing to or expanding on the findings of your research.

Sampling is a more complicated issue than it appears to be

One of the most common methodological issues cited by first-time report writers is to criticise the sample used in their research, claiming either that the sample was too small or it wasn't representative. It is not surprising that these supposed flaws are so commonly mentioned, since most first-time research is carried out in a rush, recruiting anyone who is available at the time. Thus, for many first-time report writers, half-hearted participant recruitment is the guilty secret of their research, making it the first potential flaw that pops into their mind.

The problem with this criticism is that sampling is not a simple issue and so explaining why a sample is inadequate often involves a much more complicated argument than a first-time report writer may realise. For example, having a small number of participants is not always a flaw, and having more participants does not always make research more reliable. Often, a detailed understanding of your method of analysis is needed in order to know when the size of the sample affected the reliability of that analysis. Unless you understand your analysis well enough to be able to make this kind of judgement, it is best to avoid commenting on the size of your sample as either a strength or weakness.

As for the supposed issue that the sample was not 'representative', the most common reason for this claim is that all the participants were recruited from the same place, such as from among fellow students on the course. Your sample is supposed to be representing the wider population, such that the results you get with the sample can also be said to apply to the population (See: Participants, p. 66). Thus, criticising the fact that all your participants have been recruited from one place works on the assumption that this must make them less representative of the population. Again, this is a very simplistic argument, and representativeness is not such a simple issue. Any sample will differ from the general population in some ways, but it is worth considering what these differences will be and, most importantly, whether the differences will influence the findings of your analysis. Unless you can explain how the differences between your sample and the population affected the data you collected, and so influenced the findings of your analysis, you should avoid suggesting that your sample is not representative.

Don't over-reach when suggesting practical applications

When offering a suggestion for a practical application, it is best to be cautious about the scale of your suggestions. Almost all undergraduate research and much postgraduate research will involve small-scale research which explores relatively minor issues. When applying the findings from such research, it is best to make comparably small suggestions regarding how much your findings reveal about the situation they relate to, or how much of a change should be made based on those findings. Claims of very deep insights or suggesting revolutionary changes from such low-level research can sound a little ridiculous and spoil the opportunity to offer genuine insight or interventions that can come from such findings. A practical application doesn't need to be dramatic to be impressive. By keeping it small-scale and making suggestions which are more in proportion with your findings, you will demonstrate a much better awareness of the real value of those findings.

Future research is not just your research again plus fixes

When proposing future research, you should avoid the trap so many first-time report writers fall into where they simply suggest carrying out their research again but with all the methodological issues fixed. While technically that would be a different piece of research, as a proposal for future research it is uninspired and unnecessary. There is no need to suggest that it would be better to carry out your research again without the mistakes; that goes without saying, and it misses the point of making future research proposals in the first place. Future research is about identifying new directions for the research area, and fixing mistakes does not qualify as a new direction. Future research should involve new variables or a radical change to the methodology, but most important of all, there needs to be a change to the research questions. Without a change to the research questions, no matter how much you dress it up, it is just your research being proposed all over again and there is nothing futuristic about that.

Clichéd endings

When writing the final sentence in the conclusion section, even experienced writers find it hard to resist the temptation to end on a flourish, some kind of memorable statement that will stick in the mind of the audience. The problem is that memorable final words are very hard to create and so a lot of report writers end up trotting out one of a small number of standard endings which are so over-used as to have become clichés. Examples include some variation on, "More research is needed in this area", "By adding new elements, future research may be able to understand this research area better" and "The current research area is very important and understanding it better could make a big difference to society in the future". While all of these claims are true they are also all generic and clichéd through over-use. There is always more research to be done, it will always involve new elements or discoveries and it will always be of some use to society. If you feel you must wrap up your conclusion in a final sentence, try to avoid these tired clichés and find something original to say. Then again, you shouldn't feel like you have to. After all, there is nothing wrong with a conclusion section which just ends.

▶ REFINEMENTS

Citing sources to support your points

When discussing topics such as methodological issues and future research, many writers do not attempt to support their points with cited sources. Some even believe that citations aren't needed for points relating to methodological issues, practical applications and future research. This belief is not entirely untrue, as the points in these sub-sections often originate with the findings and experiences found within your research. As such, on first glance it might appear that evidence from your research is the only basis necessary for the points in these sub-sections.

That being said, while it is true that citations may not be an absolute requirement when discussing future research or practical applications, we shouldn't overlook the possibility that something which is not essential can still add considerable value. Any point you make which is supported by citing a source that supports it is usually a stronger point as a result of that citation. Thus, citing a source to support a methodological issue demonstrates that the other researchers agree that this issue is an important enough in that research area to have affected the results of your research. Similarly, a citation which supports your proposal for future research demonstrates that other researchers agree that the variables you have proposed to be included in that future research are relevant to the research area and worthy of research.

It is not always possible to find a cited source to support every point you may wish make on these topics. After all, certain methodological issues may be unique to your research, or a practical application may be entirely original. It is for this reason that a citation is not an absolute requirement here, but having one can be a strength. As such, even though it means extra work to find those sources which support the methodological, practical and future research points in your discussion, your report will be the better for them.

Exploring the impact of methodology on the results

If you plan to identify any issues with your methodology, then you need to go further than just pointing them out; it is essential to explain what impact that issue had on the findings of the research. Thus, all reflections on the methodology, good or bad, should be driven by one question, "How did this affect the results?"

One way to approach this is to reflect on whether the issue under consideration affected the behaviour of the participants, the accuracy or validity of the measures, the conditions under which the research was being carried out or things of that nature. When discussing such an issue you should talk specifics, such as explaining how the issue may have caused a certain score to be higher or lower than it otherwise would have been. Linking a methodological issue to a specific effect on the results in this way has value for both your audience and yourself. For your audience, it helps them to see how this issue you have identified has made a difference to the results and therefore why it is worth mentioning. For yourself, it requires you to think about how the issue interacted with the specific details of your research, which prevents you from mindlessly including the same issues in every report.

In addition to being able to identify the impact that a methodological issue had on your results, your claims regarding the importance of this issue are strengthened if you can cite a source to support those claims (See: Citing sources to support your points, p. 130). Support may come from other research which had a similar issue, or which used a methodology to avoid that issue. Alternatively, if your claim is that something affected the outcome of your research, it would help if you could find research which confirms that this 'thing' does have an impact on the topic your research is exploring. Finally, if the methodological issue you are discussing was a flaw in your methodology, it helps to suggest what should be done by future research to avoid having this flaw reoccur.

> [In Kate's Methodological issues] *One potential methodological issue with the current research was that the participants' sexuality was not measured. O'Hannagain (1995) found that people used a narrower range of attractiveness ratings when evaluating others who were incompatible with their sexuality (for example, heterosexual men evaluating other men). If a large percentage of the participants in this research did not see the sample females as compatible sexual partners, this narrower range of scores could make it less likely to find a difference between faces that did or didn't use 'perfecting' make-up. In future, sexuality should be measured alongside gender to control for its effects.*

Introducing previous research in the discussion section

It is a common practice that all of the research mentioned in the discussion section will have been mentioned first in the literature review section. While this is a good practice, there is no rule which prevents you from introducing a piece of previous research for the first time in the discussion section. However, if you do so, you will need to tackle the unspoken question, which will occur to many of your audience, as to why this is the first time that research is being mentioned. After all, it is not unreasonable to expect that if this previous research is relevant to your research, it should have been included in the literature review.

One reason that research might be introduced for the first time in the discussion is if it is a minority viewpoint which is being used to explain an unexpected finding of your research. Typically, your research questions and hypotheses will be based on the outcome that the majority of the previous research leads you to expect. While there may be a minority of previous research that disagrees with the majority, there won't always be time and space to mention all those minority viewpoints in your literature review. Consequently, it may only be when your result fails to match the majority expectation, that you introduce a piece of previous research in your discussion which holds a minority viewpoint that explains the unexpected finding. In a similar vein, previous research which can offer an explanation regarding a methodological or theoretical issue may also get introduced for the first time in the discussion (See: Citing sources to support your points, p. 130). This is because the issues being explained were unplanned, whereas the job of the literature review is to make a case for the planned outcomes, not the unplanned ones. One other place where previous research might be introduced for the first time in the discussion is in proposals for future research. If the previous research in question has little connection to your research, but could be used to justify a proposal for future research, then it makes sense that the Future research sub-section of the discussion is the place where it is first introduced.

In conclusion, the literature review remains the best place to introduce the majority of the previous research you intend to mention in your report as long as you remember that there are some exceptions to this rule.

▶ ADVANCED

Deeper connections to past research

When comparing the findings of your research to the previous research, the initial focus tends to be on the level of consistency between your findings and theirs. However, merely noting the presence or absence of consistency represents only a surface level of comparison and beneath it can lie a number of additional potential levels of reflection.

For example, if your research findings are consistent with those of the previous research, you may then wish to consider how your research has added to the understanding of the research area. For example, if your research design included new variables or new methodology, then you can talk about how these additions expand on what was already known about the research area. You may also wish to explain the relative importance of these additions. Their importance can be evaluated by considering how much they are adding to what is known, or how big an impact they will have on our understanding of the way the research area operates.

On the other hand, if your research findings are inconsistent with the previous research, then you may wish to look at your methodology as a potential cause for this inconsistency. Changes in your measures, procedure or sample, in comparison to the previous research, may explain why your findings differ from theirs. If you do identify such a difference between your method and theirs, you will need to explain what impact that difference had on the data so as to justify why it might have affected your findings. Another way to explain why your findings differ from the findings of previous research would be to identify a theoretical issue which explains this difference. One example of theoretical issue which could explain such a difference is a confounding variable, a variable that neither your research nor the previous research measured or controlled for, but which affected the outcome (See: Controlling confounding variables, p. 78). Undetected variations in this variable could explain why your research and the previous research produced different findings.

You may encounter a situation where the findings of your research are consistent with the findings of one group of previous research (which we will call the consistent group) but inconsistent with the findings of another group (the inconsistent group). If this occurs, it is important to consider how the reasons you offer to explain the difference in findings will apply to both groups of previous research. For example, imagine a methodological difference between your research and the previous research which you say explains the inconsistency between your findings and the findings of the inconsistent group. For this explanation to be true, it would also need to be the case that this methodological difference was not present when comparing methodologies between your research and the consistent group. Being able to demonstrate that a methodological difference is present where the results are inconsistent and absent where the results are consistent would be very strong evidence that the methodological difference is indeed responsible. The same is the case for theoretical explanations, namely that they would need to be present for the inconsistent group and absent for the consistent group.

> [In Kate's Past Research sub-section] *The responses from the participants in the current research showed they were aware of the type of make-up being worn on the different sample faces, suggesting they were aware of which types of make-up were associated with the more attractive faces. These results are inconsistent with Tolhido (1998) who found that make-up users were unable to judge which type of make-up would have the most positive impact on their own appearance. One possible explanation for this contradiction is that people rate the impact of make-up on their own face differently than its impact on the faces of others (Diderichs, 2014). This might explain the difference in findings between the current research, which looked at the effectiveness of make-up on the faces of others, and Tolhido (1998) where participants were considering the effectiveness of make-up on themselves.*

Reflexivity

The majority of the guidance in this chapter is based on a traditional positivist approach to research, where the researcher aims to be an objective outsider, disconnected from the events they are studying (See: Positionality, p. 81). One alternative to this approach would be to take a more interpretivist approach to the discussion section where, in addition to the other elements already discussed in this chapter, you would also recognise and explore your connections to the context you are researching. This can be achieved by introducing an additional layer of reflection into the discussion.

There are different levels of reflection that you can aim for. The most basic level would be a descriptive approach where, at some point in the discussion section, you include a personal evaluation of how things went in the research. At this level, your own point of view tends to be the only one included and your perspective is often limited to a static, post hoc reflection, looking back after the research has been completed. Often, the individual elements of this kind of reflection are discussed separately without any attempt at synthesis. A common mistake found in many first-time report writers' efforts at reflection is a tendency to present their reflections as seemingly 'omniscient' pronouncements about what "really happened" or what it "really means", said with the apparent benefit of hindsight. This can occur if you believe that reflection and hindsight mean that you should know better now than you did before, when in fact that is by no means guaranteed. Moreover, while insight can be a product of reflection, it is not inevitable, nor is it the only outcome of value. Strange as it might sound, acknowledging greater uncertainty on some aspect of the research as a result of reflection can be just as valuable, especially if it better captures your true understanding (or lack thereof) of your own research.

As your experience with reflection grows, your use of these basic elements may evolve. The reflections you offer may begin to incorporate the participants' points-of-view in addition to your own. At first, comparisons between these points of view may be little more than observing similarities and differences. However, in time, you can explore how each point-of-view offers us a new perspective on the others. You may also find a growing awareness of the way in which your perspective and understanding of the research have changed over time and look to incorporate a recognition of that change in your discussion.

In the long term, your reflections may continue to evolve, producing ever more complex patterns. The act of reflection can itself become a factor, where changes in your perspective and understanding can be attributed to the process of reflecting. There may also be evidence of the reflection leading to changes within you, in terms of how you see yourself, your research or the process of research itself. At this level, you may begin to attempt to synthesise the various elements of reflection, striving for a deeper insight, but in a self-aware manner that acknowledges the limitations and personal nature of the insight, resisting the 'omniscient' pronouncements mentioned before.

While reflexivity is more common in qualitative research, there is nothing about it that makes it incompatible with quantitative research. In truth, any research could benefit from reflexivity in the discussion. There is no specific sub-section of the discussion where these reflections belong. In practice, it is up to you how much reflection you include to where you include it. While it may seem like reflexivity is something you need to fully embrace or not at all, in reality, you can dip in and out of it as you see fit. Rather than treating it as an either-or choice between positivism and interpretivism, think of it more like adding a sprinkle (or a dash) of reflection and self-awareness to add a little depth and complexity to the 'flavour' of your research. That being said, I will add one final word of caution on this topic. Given how reflexivity departs from the traditional positivist approach to research, it is advisable to discuss reflexivity with your supervisor or publisher before including a large amount of it in your report.

Further analysis

One option you have for enhancing the points you make in your discussion is to use further analyses to support those points. These further analyses should not be confused with the additional data or additional testing mentioned in the chapter on the results section (See: Summary data, tables and graphs, p. 104 and Additional testing, p. 106). These additional tests or data are intended to enhance the main analyses and assist in answering the research questions. In contrast to that, a further analysis is completely separate from all of the main analyses and, more critically, the further analysis is not attempting to answer any of the research questions. Instead, the purpose of a piece of further analysis is to enhance the credibility of a point made in the discussion by providing some evidence to support it. For example, it may be possible to use further analyses to test for the impact of a methodological issue or confounding variable. Alternatively, a further analysis could demonstrate the relevance of a variable which is part of a proposal for future research. Lastly, further analyses could explore your findings in more detail, possibly attempting to answer a new question raised by a discussion of those findings in the Wider implications sub-section.

Further analyses should be seen as unplanned in the sense that they are reactive to the outcomes of the main analyses of your research. This means that the further analyses are not part of the original research design and so there were no plans to collect the data needed for a further analysis as part of the main the data collection. For that reason, the data used in further analyses will always have an improvised quality to it. This may be data which is being repurposed, originally collected for a different reason, possibly even part of a different planned analysis, but which is serving a second purpose as part of a further analysis. For example, a further analysis might involve analysing the response to just one question from the questionnaire, where the main analysis had used the total based on responses to all the questions. If it is not possible to repurpose existing data, the data for a further analysis may need to be collected some other way. For example, if the researcher becomes aware of the need for data for a further analysis after the main data collection is over, it may be possible to return the same participants with follow-up questions.

It is not necessary to report the details of further analyses in the same way as you did the main analyses. The most obvious difference is that further analyses are only mentioned in the discussion, and they are not included in the results section. You would typically mention the results of a further analysis in the same paragraph as the point it is attempting to support. When reporting a further analysis, it is enough to identify what variables were included, what type of analysis was used and what the key finding was. All of this could be compacted into one sentence or possibly two. You should keep your interpretation and discussion of further analyses short so as to not distract too much attention from the main analyses. Don't make the mistake of trying to compensate for a disappointing result in your main analyses by focusing more on results of further analyses. These results are intended to be a side show, not the main event. In a similar vein, you should also be quite cautious regarding the claims you make based on further analyses. Owing to its improvised nature, a further analysis often doesn't have all the elements it needs to be truly rigorous. Possibly you are analysing one question when you really want a new questionnaire that focuses on that specific issue. Maybe there are other variables you would need to measure in order to analyse this new issue more completely. These shortcomings don't invalidate the further analysis, but they should produce a sense of caution when drawing conclusions from such an analysis. As such, the conclusions from any further analysis will need confirmation from a more detailed future research into the same area and your comments should reflect this.

[In Kate's Future research] *In order to confirm that it was the make-up affecting people's ratings of the sample faces, in addition to rating each sample face the participants were asked to identify which make-up was being worn. Using these responses which identify the make-up being used, a further analysis was conducted, using a repeated measures ANOVA, to check the accuracy of people's ability to spot make-up use for all the different types of make-up. The results found significant differences, with mascara being the type of make-up most-likely to go unnoticed and lip-stick the least likely. Future research may wish to further investigate if the notability of a type of make-up affects who uses it and the reasons it is used.*

CHAPTER 6: EXERCISES

Exercise 1: MCT

1) Which of the following is NOT part of the purpose of the discussion?
   A. To relate the findings of your research to the previous research and the wider context.
   B. To explore the strengths and weakness of the methodology of your research.
   C. To propose new areas of research and practical applications.
   D. To repeat all the key points from all the other sections of the report.

2) When discussing the wider implications of your findings, it is recommended that you mention the _____ and the _____, but it is usually not necessary to mention the _____ or the _____.
   A. key findings, types of analysis used, research questions, answers to the research questions
   B. research questions, answers to the research questions, key findings, types of analysis used
   C. key findings, research questions, types of analysis used, answers to the research questions
   D. key findings, answers to the research questions, types of analysis used, research questions

3) The main purpose of reviewing the previous research in the discussion is to...
   A. remind the audience of all other important findings in the same research area as your research.
   B. provide an opportunity to introduce any previous research that there wasn't room enough to include in the literature review.
   C. allow comparison between your findings and previous findings to see where they agree or disagree.
   D. provide you with a selection of other findings to use in your practical applications if your research didn't find anything useful.

4) When writing about the methodological issues of your research it is usually a good idea to avoid...
   A. speculating how an issue may have affected the results.
   B. basing your points on anecdotal comments made by the participants.
   C. considering the issues around sample size and representativeness.
   D. suggesting solutions to the issues you have identified.

5) When making suggestions for practical applications, _____ are to be avoided because they _____.

A. speculations about the findings of future research, might not turn out as expected.
B. applications of non-significant findings, cannot be applied if they didn't find what they were looking for.
C. dramatic claims, can appear unrealistic coming from small-scale research.
D. confirmations of existing practices, have no value unless a new practice is being suggested.

6) The purpose of future research is to....
A. suggest fixes to the methodology of your research based on those methodological issues that you have identified.
B. identify new areas of research that are different from your research but in the same research area.
C. propose methods of replicating your research so as to confirm its findings.
D. All of the above.

7) Which of the following is worth including in the conclusion section of your discussion?
A. The suggestion that more research is needed to understand this area properly.
B. Stating that your research area is important and so understanding it better could make a big difference to society in the future.
C. A summary of the key points made in the methodological issues and future research sections.
D. An example of one way in which your research has added something of value to our understanding of the research area.

8) Why does it cause such a big problem in the discussion section if your research questions were not based on any specific pieces of previous research?
A. It means your literature review is much more likely to entirely consist of research which has little or nothing in common with your research.
B. If your research and the previous research have no elements in common, it won't be possible to compare your and their findings.
C. Without a link to previous research there is no basis for your theoretical model which means it lacks credibility.
D. All of the above.

9) Why might you introduce a piece of analysis in your discussion that wasn't mentioned in your results section?
A. As an alternative analysis used to answer a research question if the main analysis was inconclusive.
B. To support a suggestion for a methodological issue or future research.
C. To introduce an element of reflexivity into your discussion.
D. You wouldn't, all analyses must be introduced for the first time in the results.

10) In the discussion section it is NOT acceptable to...
   A. change the research questions for your research to make them a better fit for the findings.
   B. introduce previous research not mentioned in the literature review to support a proposal for future research.
   C. suggest methodological issues or practical applications based entirely on your research with no external sources cited.
   D. leave out entire sub-sections such as methodological issues, practical applications or future research.

Exercise 2: How serious are these mistakes?

A common problem faced by many first-time report writers is judging the relative importance of all the different rules and requirements involved in report writing. How important is it to relate your findings to previous research? How serious a problem is it to not discuss the wider implications of your findings? With this in mind you will find, in alphabetical order, 12 common mistakes made by first-time report writers when writing their discussion. You need to put each of them in one of three categories of importance: serious errors, moderate errors and minor errors.

- Discussing the types of analysis used or repeating all the results figures.
- Discussing previous research that is unrelated to the findings of your research.
- Making dramatic claims in your proposals for practical applications.
- Not basing your research questions on previous research.
- Not citing any sources in the methodological issues or future research.
- Not discussing any methodological issues, practical applications or future research.
- Not discussing the wider implications of the key findings.
- Not offering any conclusion.
- Not relating the findings of your research to the previous research.
- Proposing future research which is just your research again with fixes.
- Using findings from previous research as the basis for wider implications or practical applications.
- Using sampling as one of your methodological issues.

CHAPTER 6: ANSWERS

Exercise 1: MCT

Q1: Ans = D (See: The basics, p. 118 ↔ Wider implications, p. 118 ↔ Past research, p. 119 ↔ Unnecessary repetition of details from the literature review, p. 127)

Q2: Ans = D (See: Wider implications, p. 118)

Q3: Ans = C (See: Past research, p. 119 ↔ Discuss your own findings, not the findings of others, p. 128)

Q4: Ans = C (See: Methodological issues, p. 120 ↔ Sampling is a more complicated issue than it appears to be, p. 128 ↔ Exploring the impact of methodology on the results, p. 131)

Q5: Ans = C (See: Practical applications, p. 122 ↔ Don't over-reach when suggesting practical applications, p. 129)

Q6: Ans = B (See: Future research, p. 123 ↔ Future research is not just your research again plus fixes, p. 129)

Q7: Ans = D (See: Conclusion, p. 124 ↔ Clichéd endings, p. 130)

Q8: Ans = D (See: The weak literature review strikes again!, p. 126)

Q9: Ans = B (See: Further analysis, 136 ↔ Reflexivity, p. 134)

Q10: Ans = A (See: Introducing previous research in the discussion section, p. 132 ↔ Citing sources to support your points, p. 130 ↔ Not every discussion will contain all of the sub-sections, p. 126)

Exercise 2: How serious are these mistakes?

Serious errors

(Not basing your research questions on previous research ↔ Not discussing the wider implications of the key findings ↔ Not relating the findings of your research to the previous research ↔ Using findings from previous research as the basis for wider implications or practical applications.)

All of these are serious errors either because they completely undermine the central purpose of the discussion, which is to explore and apply the findings of your research, or because they reveal what may be a fatal flaw in your research design. While it is true that a discussion won't always have all of the sub-sections mentioned in this chapter, the wider implications and past research sections are so central to the purpose of the discussion, it is hard to see how it can achieve that purpose without them. Research which isn't being linked to either the wider world or the previous research in the same area has little or no value, which is the reason that exploring the connections to those things in these two sub-sections is indispensable. It is much the same issue with the dissertation which spends most of its time applying the findings of previous research when it should be applying the findings of your research. Regarding the research questions which are not connected to any previous research, again it is a lack of connections that makes it hard for the discussion to achieve its purpose. The fact that this error is revealing a flaw in the research design which happened long before the discussion was written doesn't make it any less serious. If anything, it makes it worse because it usually means that it is much too late to fix it.

(See: The weak literature review strikes again! p. 126 ↔ Wider implications, p. 118 ↔ Past research, p. 119 ↔ Discuss your own findings, not the findings of others, p. 128)

Moderate errors

(Discussing previous research that is unrelated to the findings of your research ↔ Discussing the types of analysis used or repeating all the results figures ↔ Not offering any conclusion ↔ Proposing future research which is just your research again with fixes.)

All of these are moderate errors owing to the fact that, while they do make your work much less effective, they do not fatally undermine it the way the serious errors do. The first two errors, where you include previous research unconnected to the findings or details of the analysis already explained, are problems because this content is unnecessary in the discussion. If it seems harsh to label unnecessary information as an error, we need to keep in mind that there is always limited space in any section of the report and so each piece of unnecessary information means less space to discuss the things that are necessary. By contrast, leaving out the conclusion, something that is usually necessary to achieve the main purpose of the discussion, is also seen as a moderate error. The absence of this sub-section is less serious than the absence of the wider implications or past research subsections because, although the lack of a conclusion means the discussion will be much less effective, it can still achieve its purpose without a conclusion. Finally, the use of fixes as suggestions for future research demonstrates a lack of awareness that future research should represent progress in the research area. Suggesting the same research again with fixes is unlikely to provide future researchers with much inspiration for new research questions.

(See: Design: Unnecessary repetition of details from the literature review, p. 73 ↔ Wider implications, p. 118 ↔ Conclusion, p. 124 ↔ Future research is not just your research again plus fixes, p. 129)

Minor errors

(Making dramatic claims in your proposals for practical applications ↔ Not citing any sources in the methodological issues or future research ↔ Not discussing any methodological issues, practical applications or future research ↔ Using sampling as one of your methodological issues.)

All of these are minor errors in the sense that, although they have a negative impact on the effectiveness of your discussion, the extent of their impact is much more limited than the moderate errors. It should be noted that none of these is guaranteed to be a mistake, there can be legitimate reasons for doing any of them; however, they are more likely to be done in error than appropriately. Good examples of this principle are making dramatic claims or using sampling as an error, where it is rare for the report writer to understand the technical requirements needed to do those things properly. In the case of leaving out the sub-sections named here or not citing supporting sources, these could be seen less as errors and more as missed opportunities. A discussion without any of those sub-sections or supporting sources will usually not be making its case as effectively as it could, and so they should be included where possible. Overall then, these are mistakes you should generally try to avoid making, but you should not worry too much about it if you do end up making one.

(See: Don't over-reach when suggesting practical applications, p. 129 ↔ Citing sources to support your points, p. 130 ↔ Not every discussion will contain all of the sub-sections, p. 126 ↔ Sampling is a more complicated issue than it appears to be, p. 128)

Abstracts, references and appendices

► AN OVERVIEW

Unlike the other chapters of this book, each of which focuses on a single section of the report, this chapter covers three sections: the abstract, the references and the appendices. The reason for combining them into a single chapter is that they are relatively minor sections compared to the others, by which I mean they are less complex, both in structure and content. Because they are less complex, they are easier to write and there are fewer chances to make mistakes; however, it also means they are less important and so are unlikely to impress the audience no matter how well they are done. When was the last time you were 'blown away' by the references list in an article you were reading? That being said, less important does not mean unimportant. Like the service you get in a restaurant, it's not why you are there; but if it is done badly, it can spoil the whole experience and overshadow what should be the real focus of the event, the meal itself. As such, your aim in all of these sections is to be as efficient as possible, communicating quickly and clearly so as to keep your audience's focus where it should be, on the other sections of the report. The ultimate goal for these sections is to do their job so well that you hardly even notice they are there.

► ABSTRACT

The abstract is the section where you summarise the entire report in a single paragraph. The purpose of having an abstract is to allow your audience to preview what your research is about without needing to read the entire report. You do this by first summarising the wider context and research area. This is followed

DOI: 10.4324/9781003107965-7

by paraphrasing the research questions and then including a brief description of the research methodology. After that, you highlight one or two of the key findings and then include one or two examples of discussion topics. By the end of the abstract, your audience should feel that they have an overview of the entire research, thus allowing them to decide if they want to know more by reading the rest of the report.

Before you begin this part of the chapter...

As the abstract requires information from every other section of the report, not only is it necessary to have completed all the stages of your research, but also you will need to have finished writing the rest of the report too. This means that when you have completed your final draft of every other section of the report, only then will you be ready to begin writing this section.

The basics

The abstract appears at the very start of the report and contains a summary of a selection of the key details from each of the other sections of the report, except for the references and appendices. Although the abstract is technically the first section in the report, given that it draws upon almost every other section, the abstract tends to be the last part of the report to be written. The following table indicates which key details are most often included in the abstract as well as where in the report they can be found.

Key detail	Taken from...
Which research area/issue was the research investigating?	Introduction (wider context or research area)
What research questions were being asked?	Introduction (research questions)
Who took part?	Method (participants)
What were they asked to do?	Method (materials and/or procedure)
What were the key findings of the analysis?	Results
What insights emerged from this research?	Discussion (conclusion)

The abstract is written in the past tense as a single paragraph. As a rule-of-thumb, the length of your abstract should fall between 200 and 600 words. This means that you won't be able to include every key detail for each of the sections mentioned above and instead will have to choose those details you think are most interesting and important. How you decide the importance of each detail is entirely up to you. The shortness of the abstract also means that for each key detail you should aim to summarise it so that it can be explained in a sentence or two. Indeed, working within such a confined space can be one of the biggest challenges in writing the abstract, deciding which details to include and how to find the space to include them. Don't be surprised if this section takes you far longer to write than its length would suggest.

Common mistakes

The longest summary

One of the most important things to remember about the abstract is the need to keep it short. A long abstract is almost a contradiction in terms. The most common reason that first-time report writers make their abstract too long is the mistaken belief that they are required to summarise *all* of the key details in each section, such as including all the steps in the method or all the key findings. It's almost as though they are trying to turn the abstract into a crib-sheet, a summary which tells you everything you need to know so that you don't need to read the full thing.

Instead, the abstract should be thought of as being like the trailer for a film, sharing just a few highlights so as to convince the audience that it is worth their time to see the full movie, but without giving the whole story away. As such, it is completely acceptable to include only one or two of the key details from any section in your abstract. For example, you may choose to mention only one or two of the more interesting key findings from the results, the ones most likely to grab the attention of your audience. All you need to do with the abstract is spark their interest. If you manage that, then you will then have the rest of the report to tell the story of your research properly rather than trying to cram it all into the tiny space of the abstract.

Refinements

Citing references in the abstract

In your abstract you are typically working hard to find the space to say everything you wish to say about your research, which usually doesn't leave much time or space in this section to start diving into any previous research. Consequently, on most occasions it is unlikely you will need to cite any other sources in the abstract.

One exception would be, if your research topic is heavily based on any theory, concept or methodology which exists in multiple competing definitions or versions. There is likely to be debate among researchers as to which version is the most valid, and as such, it may be helpful to include a citation in your abstract so as to identify the source of the version you are using. Doing this will signal your position regarding the debate surrounding that theory or concept, something your audience is likely to want to know from the outset when reviewing your research. Another possible exception would be if you were introducing a new theoretical or methodological element which represents a major departure from the previous research in the area. Citing the source of this new element is a good way of highlighting it in the abstract, communicating to your audience that this particular element is going to be important in your research and is worthy of their attention from the start.

One thing to keep in mind is that, even in those examples mentioned above where the inclusion of a citation can be useful, it is never critical. As such, if you are finding it hard to make enough space to include details about your research which you think are critical, dropping the citations should be your first choice to make that space. Think of them as luxuries not essentials, nice to have but you can always manage without them.

Advanced

Departing from the standard abstract 'formula'

The list of key facts which are identified in 'the basics' for this section represent those things you are likely to find in most abstracts. However, the contents of a good abstract are not set in stone and you should treat this list as a set of recommendations not rules. You are perfectly entitled to add things not mentioned on that list or to leave out things that are. The only requirement for including something in the abstract should be that it will attract the attention of your audience. Showing a little creativity in what you include or how you present it is one way to achieve that. If the abstract is like a trailer for a movie, much like an advert for your research report, then the secret to making an advert effective is to make it stand out from the crowd.

If you want to see some examples of this in action, you may wish to re-read the abstracts of all the articles you read when conducting your literature review. In each case, see if you can identify what it was that caught your eye about those abstracts, what drew you in and convinced you to read the full text of the article. Key words linking that article to your chosen research area will have played a part, but unless you read every single article with a matching keyword, there will be other tricks and techniques they used to 'reel you in' and convince you that *this* was an article worth reading. It may have been an effective turn of phrase or a clarity in their language which was the key. They may have highlighted just the right findings or conclusions to catch your attention. Although it may be done in a different way in each abstract, paying more attention to how other researchers have done it will fire up your imagination when it comes to turning your own abstract into an 'attention magnet'.

There is no standard formula I can recommend to achieve this since departing from the standard formula is often the best way to achieve it. One thought exercise which can help is to imagine you are out at a party and someone asks you about your research. It's a social situation, so you want to keep it quick, simple and interesting. What would you tell them? It's likely to be some mix of the bare essentials they would need to understand your research and a choice selection of those tidbits they would find most interesting. Feel free to play around with the mix until you get it right and remember that when it comes to the abstract, nothing is indispensable.

Brevity is the soul of wit

Sometimes, a good abstract is as much about what is left out as what is included. Leaving out the less critical details can help to make the important things stand out a little bit more. Your audience certainly won't complain if you skip the formalities and get right to the point. When you have dozens of abstracts to read, the appeal of an abstract which gets right to the point and tells you all you need to know quickly and clearly should not be underestimated. With this in mind, it is worth noting that however short your abstract is, it could almost certainly be shorter.

Some of this can be achieved by learning to be more economic with your language, paring it down to just the words needed to make the point and no more. Practice and a thesaurus are very useful here. Other times the cuts are harder to make, requiring you to weigh up two or more points and decide which is the point that stays while the others go. Rather than including every point you can up to the limits of the allowed space, for each point you add to the abstract you should consider how much additional value does that point contribute above what was provided already? It may add to the clarity or the appeal of your abstract, but by how much? At the stage where each addition only offers a marginal increase in value, you should consider drawing the line there and adding no more.

It is worth noting that many academic journals will only allow you 200 words for an abstract and so practising to be more concise in your abstracts is a valuable skill.

Sometimes these draconian size restrictions can be the all-important motivator, forcing you to push your limits and discover new ways of phrasing things or presenting information in a more concise manner without sacrificing the essentials. If you ever find yourself agonising about details lost to such cuts, it is worth considering that most readers will have made up their mind as to whether they will read your report long before they finish your abstract. Like the first few pages of a novel or the first ten minutes of a movie, you either hook your audience quickly or not at all. This may be why the journals set the limits they do. Chances are, if you haven't hooked your audience by the time you get 200 words into your abstract then it is unlikely that adding more words will make any difference.

▶ REFERENCES

The references section is where you provide all the information needed to identify and locate every source that is relevant to your research. The structure and content of this section is determined by the 'referencing system' that is required by your course or publisher. Given that the choice of referencing system is usually made on behalf the researcher by someone else, the researcher's role is to learn the rules of that system and implement those rules precisely. The rules of the referencing system are what determine whereabouts in the report each full reference is included, what information is provided, how that information is presented and can even determine if a source should be included. It's not intended that the references section would ever be read from start to finish. It's a section your audience would consult to find out the full details of a specific source. After consulting the references section in this way, your audience should have all the information they need to locate that source and read it for themselves.

Before you begin this part of chapter...

Unlike most of the other sections of the report, your references section may not be something you write from start to finish in one continuous process. You could end up adding to it as you go. As such, if we consider for a moment the writing of a single reference, there are a number of steps in the research process you will need to complete first.

- Find out which referencing system you are expected to use.
- Determine which type of source you are going to be referencing.
- Consult the formatting guide for the chosen referencing system on what information is required for that type of source and how that information should be presented.

- Gather all the information about that source that is required.
- Once you have completed all of these steps then you are ready to add a reference to this section of the report.

The basics

The references section is a list (or series of lists) where each entry on the list represents a source that is relevant to your research. The purpose of the list is to provide enough information about those sources so as to make it possible for the audience to identify, evaluate and potentially locate any source they wish to. In order to identify a source, it is necessary to provide the name of the source as well as the names of its authors. For example, in the case of a book it would be the name of the book and its authors or editors, whereas for a journal article it would be the name of the article and its authors. To allow the audience to locate and evaluate the source, it is also necessary to reveal when and where it was published. For example, in the case of a journal article this will mean providing the name, date and issue of the journal in which it was published, whereas for a website it will mean providing the URL needed to locate that website on the internet.

As we saw when discussing sources in the literature review, the credibility of a point partially rests on the credibility of the sources used to support that point (See: Use high quality sources, p. 50). For this reason, one of the purposes behind providing a full reference is to allow your audience to evaluate the credibility of each source. A full reference is necessary to make that kind of evaluation as it will reveal the conditions under which the source was published and therefore the level of scrutiny and verification it will have received. For example, a journal article is considered more credible than a website because unlike the website, the journal article will have been peer reviewed.

The other purpose behind providing a full reference is to allow your audience to locate the original source and read it for themselves. This can form part of the evaluation process, determining if your report has represented the findings of the previous research completely and correctly, although this level of verification is uncommon as it is so time-consuming. A more likely reason for your audience to wish to read the source for themselves would be to explore some aspect of that source in more detail. Using the reference information in one source as the means to find related sources in the same research area is a common feature of the literature review process, and providing full references for each related source is what makes that possible.

Referencing systems

While a references section will always be seeking to provide the information needed to locate and evaluate the sources relevant to your research, where and how that information is provided is decided by the referencing system in use. There are a number of different referencing systems: APA, Harvard, MHRA, Chicago and Oxford to name but a few. The differences between these systems can vary from minor differences over formatting and punctuation, to major differences over where the full reference is provided or what sources need to be included in the references section. While the sheer number of different referencing systems can be intimidating at first, it may help to know that they can be organised into just three different types of system.

Parenthetical systems – When a source is cited in the text, the surnames of the authors and the date of publication appear in brackets (also known as parentheses) in the text. The full references for all the citations throughout the report are provided in a separate section which comes in between the discussion and appendices. In this section, there is a single list for all sources used throughout the report, and the list is arranged alphabetically based on the surname of the lead author of the source. Each source appears only once in this list no matter how many times it is cited in the report.

Footnote systems – When a source is cited in the text, it is identified by a number indicating the order in which that source appeared among all the other sources cited on the page. The full references for all the citations on that page are provided in the footnotes area of the page. The list is arranged chronologically, based on the order in which the citations appear on the page. A source which gets cited more than once can appear more than once in the reference section.

Endnote systems – When a source is cited in the text, it is identified by a number indicating the order in which that source appeared among all the other sources cited in that section. The full references for all the citations throughout the report are provided in a separate section which comes in between the discussion and the appendices. In this section, there is a separate list for each of the sections of the report, with each of these lists arranged chronologically based on the order in which the citations appear in that section. A source which gets cited more than once can appear more than once in this references section.

References list vs. bibliography

When you are using a parenthetical referencing system (such as APA, Harvard or MLA among others), there are two ways in which the list of full references can be listed either as a references list or as a bibliography. Both lists follow the same rules of parenthetical referencing mentioned above, but they differ in terms of which sources need to be included.

In a 'references list', also known as 'works cited', you include a full reference for only those sources that are cited in-text somewhere in the report. Any source which doesn't get cited in the report should not be included in your references list. There may be some sources you read which influence your general thinking about the research or report, but did not contain any specific fact or claim you wished to cite in the text of the report. Since those sources have not been cited, they should not get mentioned in a references list, but they may be mentioned in a bibliography.

In a 'bibliography', also known as 'works consulted', you include a full reference for all of the sources you have read which have influenced the research or the writing of the report. This means that cited sources are included in a bibliography, but so are any other sources you have read which are relevant to the research or the report, even if those sources are never cited in the report. There are no formal rules about what qualifies a source as being 'relevant', that is entirely up the researcher to decide.

Sometimes the referencing system will specify whether you should provide a references list or a bibliography or both. Other times, it will be decided by the same people who decided which referencing system you are expected to follow. Whichever type of list you are providing, you should label the list clearly so your audience knows which kind it is. If you are asked to use both types of list, they should be provided as two separate lists, labelled accordingly. On some occasions, when both a references list and a bibliography are presented together, the bibliography will focus only on those sources which are relevant but were not cited. This helps to avoid the bibliography duplicating contents of the references list. Again, this is something that is decided by the same people who chose the referencing system, so you should ask them what they want you to do here.

Formatting your references

Both citations and full references are always presented in a very specific format, and achieving the required formatting means following a set of rules as to how the citation or full reference should appear on the page. These rules detail everything about the appearance of the citation or reference, from the information about the source which needs to be included, down to where you place every full stop and comma. First-time report writers nearly always find these formatting rules to be a headache. There are a lot of rules to remember and they can be very detailed. The rules are necessary to ensure that each citation and reference is clear. By standardising the way that citations and references appear on the page using very specific rules, we can make sure that no matter who is writing the report section, they will provide the same information in the same way. You can pick up a references section written by anyone and use it to locate all of the sources listed there.

Each of the different referencing systems has its own set of formatting rules. The full set of formatting rules for each system is quite long, because there are many different types of sources and there needs to be rule to cover every type. Don't feel intimidated, you don't need to learn the formatting rules for every type of source straight away. Most undergraduate researchers only use a few different types of sources in their research. Typically, once you learn the formatting rules for a book, a journal article, an online source and a secondary cited source, you will find this covers the vast majority of the sources that you use. Even if you do end up using a less usual type of source at some point, all you need to do then is to look up that type of source in the full set of formatting rules for the referencing system. These formatting rules are almost always available via the web, and with practice, checking the rule for an unfamiliar type of source becomes no harder than looking up the spelling of an unfamiliar word.

Common mistakes

Double-check your names and dates

While it might seem to go without saying that all of the sources cited in the text should be included in the full list of references, it is not uncommon to find 'orphan' citations, namely citations without a matching full reference in a references section. Sometimes the full reference is not missing, but rather there is an accidental difference between the citation and the full reference such as one of them having a misspelled author name or incorrect publication date.

The most likely reason for these 'orphan' citations is inadequate proof reading. While you should be adding a full reference at the same time as you add any citation, with citations being added and removed from one draft to the next, it is only natural that you might lose track. As such, you should always plan to make one final check of all citations and matching full references as part of your proof reading of the final full draft of your report. The final full draft is the one you produce after all other changes and corrections have been made. With no further changes to be made, all cited sources should have a matching full reference. A good way to carry out this check is to either print out the full list of references or open them in a separate document on a different screen. This allows you to do a page-by-page comparison of all citations and matching full references to ensure none are missing, misspelled or incorrectly dated.

Which referencing system?

With so many different referencing systems, it shouldn't be surprising that a common mistake among first-time report writers is to use the wrong one. The wrong referencing system is any referencing system other than the one you were expected to use. One reason that the first-time report writers get confused on this issue is if they have learnt referencing using one system on a different course or an earlier level of study, but then move to a new course or level of study which uses a different system. This means you should not assume that the referencing system you used on a previous report is the same one you should be using on your current report. The same goes if you are moving from one publisher to another. You also need to be careful if you are simultaneously studying a combination of different subjects, as each subject may require a different referencing system when writing about that subject. The best way to avoid this mistake is to always double-check for each report you are writing, which referencing system your course or publisher expects you to use for that report.

Alphabetical or chronological?

One common area of confusion is the order in which the full references should appear in your references section. In parenthetical referencing systems (such as Harvard), the references list and/or bibliography is presented alphabetically, based on the surname of the lead author. It is easy to get this confused with the footnote or endnote systems (such as Oxford), where the full references appear in chronological order based on the order in which they were cited in the text. A sign that this kind of confusion may be occurring is if the same source appears more than once in your references list or bibliography. Multiple appearances by the same source is fine in a chronological system like a footnote or endnote, but it should never happen in alphabetical system like the references list. If it does, then chances are that you are applying a chronological order where it does not belong.

Confusing a references list and a bibliography

The other common area of confusion is between a references list, which includes full references for cited sources only, and a bibliography, which includes a full reference for all relevant sources, cited or not. Given that a bibliography and references list are so similar, it is easy to see how you might confuse them or accidentally apply the rules of one to the other. It can help you to keep them straight if you remember that the entries on a **REFER**ences list must REFER to citations somewhere in the report. As long as you can keep that in mind, it is easy to remember which one you are dealing with and so which sources should be included.

Refinements

Reference as you cite

Tracking down all the details of a source, in order to create a full reference, can be time-consuming and a little tedious, and so it is a common practice to put off this job until after the rest of the report is written. While some of the reason for doing that is nothing more than avoiding a boring job, there are some advantages to this approach. For example, re-drafting your work can result in a citation being dropped. Therefore, waiting until the final draft is decided before searching for those full references can, in theory, save you the time you would have spent finding full references for citations that ended up not being needed.

However, there is also some merit in referencing as you cite, by which I mean tracking down the full reference information at the point when you first add the citation to the text. This approach forces you to double-check that you can locate all the details for each source before you commit to using that source as a citation in your report. That might end up being a very prudent precaution, as there have been many researchers who have discovered, to their dismay, that they cannot locate the full reference information for a source they have been citing throughout their report. It can be a real headache to only discover this as the submission deadline approaches. Report writers can be left with the equally unpleasant options of scrambling to remove all citations which mention the missing source, as well as removing any points that depend on those citations, or desperately searching for replacement sources to cite in the place of the missing one. If you are ever unlucky enough to have to do this once, you will never want to be in that position again.

Ultimately, the decision to reference as you cite or to leave it to the end can depend on other elements of your writing and planning style. If your writing style involves a large number of extensive re-writes, adding in and then taking out large amounts of text, then waiting until the end to search for the full information of the surviving citations may be best for you. On the other hand, if you have a habit of leaving things to the last minute, 'diving across the finish line' as the deadline expires, then referencing as you cite could be just the thing to keep you safe from that last-minute-missing-source panic and all the havoc it creates.

Advanced

Be honest about your secondary sources

If you read some information where it was first written, for example, reading the journal article where a theory was first proposed, then you are said to have consulted the primary source for that information. Alternatively, if you read about the primary source somewhere else, for example, you read a book where the author talks about a theory located in a journal article they have read, then you are said to have consulted a secondary source for that information. In general, consulting primary sources is a sign of criticality and good scholarship (See: Criticality, p. 214), qualities you would want to demonstrate as often as you can. While it is not always practical, or even possible, to consult the primary source every time, the more information and understanding you can gather from primary sources the better.

When it comes to citing and referencing your sources, in principle, you should always indicate in each citation and full reference whether you consulted that source directly as a primary source or learnt about it via secondary source. However, in practice, there are times when sources that the researcher has learnt about via a secondary source, get cited and referenced as if the researcher had consulted the primary source. Sometimes the reason for this is just convenience. Finding and reading the primary source, when the secondary source has already told you everything you wanted to know about that primary source, can feel like a waste of time. By comparison, it is much easier to simply copy the full reference of a primary source from the references section of the secondary source where you read about it. This is more of a shortcut than an attempt at misleading anyone. Other times, the tendency to refer to all sources as primary sources can be driven, in part, by a reluctance to admit how many sources in your literature review are sources you have not read yourself. And of course, the most seductive element behind presenting all your sources as primary sources is that, most of the time, no one except you will ever know.

However, there are two good reasons to be as open as you can be about your use of secondary sources. First, if your audience begins to suspect there are a large number of unacknowledged secondary sources in your report, it lowers their confidence in your work a whole. Second, the need to publicly acknowledge your use of secondary sources can be a very effective spur for you to make the effort to actually locate and read more primary sources. Putting the real number of primary and secondary sources you have consulted on display, where you and your entire audience can see what you are finding out for yourself, can be a powerful motivation to 'up your game' in this area. We need to be realistic and acknowledge that finding primary sources requires effort, and the motivation to make that effort needs to come from somewhere. Embracing the principles of good scholarship is a start, but at the same time, subjecting yourself to public scrutiny while upholding those principles can give you that important extra boost you need to get it done.

▶ APPENDICES

The appendices section is where you include any information which can make an important contribution to your audience's understanding of your research, but which was not suitable for inclusion in any of the other sections of the report. You do this by creating a separate appendix for each type of information you want to include, giving each appendix an identifying name and label. This allows you to create a link to that appendix in another section of the report, inviting your audience to consult the contents of that appendix before they finish reading that other section. The additional information they receive by consulting the appendix should make a worthwhile contribution to their understanding of the related section.

Before you begin this part of the chapter...

Unlike most of the other sections of the report, your appendices section is not likely to be something you write from start to finish in one continuous process. Instead, you are more likely to write it an appendix at a time. As such, if we consider for a moment the writing of a single appendix, there are a number of steps in the research process you will need to complete first.

- Gather the information to be included in the appendix.
- If necessary, convert that information into a digital format.
- Consider how much of the information is needed to allow your audience to understand the aspect of the research the appendix is concerned with.
- Decide how to present the information in the clearest and most concise way.
- Once you have completed all of these steps you are ready to begin writing an appendix in this section of the report.

The basics

Sometimes you will want to mention a piece of information in your report, but there isn't a suitable place to put it. Maybe it would take up too much space or it goes into more detail than is needed by the majority of your audience. While you should always reflect on whether this information is something your report can do without, if the conclusion you reach is that it should still be included somewhere, then the best place for it may be in the appendices at the end of the report.

The appendices is always the final section of the report and is divided up into a series of sub-sections. Each of these sub-sections is called an appendix and is intended to hold extra information which might help your audience to get a better understanding of some element of your research. Each appendix will typically be related to one section of the report, possibly even a specific sub-section within that section. In that other part of the report there should be a 'link' to the appendix, a suggestion to the audience to check out the contents of that appendix if they wish to learn more about the issue that other section of the report is discussing.

For example, an appendix might contain a sample copy of one of the materials you employed in your data collection, such as a blank copy of your questionnaire. Having something like this in an appendix means you can include a link to this appendix in the materials sub-section of the method section, inviting your audience to review the questionnaire that you are describing to them. Another example would be an appendix which contains a more complete version of the results from one of your analyses. You could include a link to this appendix when discussing this method of analysis in your results section. This would allow your audience to explore other aspects of your results in addition to the ones you relate to your key findings, potentially providing them with an extra insight into your results.

Layout for the appendices

Each appendix should have a name and a label at the top of the first page of that appendix. The name contains the word "Appendix" followed by a letter of the alphabet which indicates the order of the appendices. The first appendix is "Appendix A", the second one is "Appendix B" and so on. The label for an appendix should provide a short description of what the appendix contains. For example, an appendix which contains a sample of the images that were presented to participants as part of the data collection might have the label "Sample images" or "Data collection images".

Sometimes it is helpful to include headings within the appendix, offering a more detailed breakdown of what the appendix contains. For example, if the appendix of images contained three different kinds of images presented in three separate groups, it might help to include a heading above each group to indicate which type of images they are, for example, "Images of everyday objects", "Images of dangerous objects" and "Images of valuable objects". Such headings are optional since they will not always be needed. Sometimes the label for the appendix, along with the information your audience has already received in the other parts of the report, may be enough to make sense of the contents of an appendix without additional headings.

Common mistakes

Appendices are not used to prove your honesty

For some reason, first-time report writers tend to include things in the appendices whose only purpose appears to be to provide evidence that they really did what they have claimed to have done in the rest of the report. An example of this kind of 'evidence for the defence' includes copies of all the raw data collected, consent forms signed by the participants or emails confirming ethical approval. It is not always clear why they feel the need for this kind of proof. Possibly the severe penalties for academic misconduct, such as data fabrication, are scary enough to make them feel that safe is better than sorry. Whatever the reason, these 'proofs' are almost always unnecessary and only serve to leave your appendices looking like a guilty conscience. Double-checking the requirements of your course will usually tell you what kinds of evidence, if any, are needed in your report. Any kinds of evidence they don't explicitly ask for, you can assume they don't need.

Be selective about what you put in an appendix

The appendices can become a dumping ground if you don't exercise some good judgement when it comes to deciding what you include there. Some first-time report writers employ a just-in-case philosophy, throwing everything up-to-and-including the kitchen sink into an appendix out of fear that they might leave out something important. This usually results in a bloated appendices section where the occasional piece of genuinely interesting information is lost in a sea of dross.

To avoid this, there are three key principles you should follow when it comes to constructing your appendices. The first principle is that every appendix needs to have a purpose. You should have clear reason in mind why it is necessary to have an appendix with those materials in your report. This purpose should include what the appendix adds over-and-above what is already available in the rest of the report and why that addition is important. For any appendix, if you can't explain to yourself why it is needed, then the contents of that appendix are almost certainly not needed. The second principle is that every appendix should be integrated with the rest of the report. This means that for every appendix, in one of the other sections of the report there should be a link which says "See Appendix X on page Y for an example of Z". If you ever find yourself including an appendix, but you haven't made a link to it anywhere in the report, then that is a sign that the contents of that appendix are not needed. The third principle is that you should only include the minimum amount of material in each appendix needed to achieve the purpose of that appendix. For example, if you are providing people with a sample of something in an appendix, then you only need to include some, not all, of the thing you are sampling.

Be careful about confidentiality issues with your appendices

Whether it is including raw data, emails from gatekeepers or using completed questionnaires as examples of materials, you should consider if sharing these in an appendix might reveal things about those involved in your research. The most basic rule for including any materials connected to someone who was involved in your research, whether they were a participant, gatekeeper, confederate or something else, is that the materials included should never reveal their identity. But, even if you were to anonymise the materials, you should also consider if sharing the materials themselves would still be breaching confidentiality. The people connected with those materials may feel that some detail contained within the anonymised materials would still reveal their identity in some other way. Alternatively, they may simply feel uncomfortable with having something shared with the world that they assumed would only be seen by the researcher. As such, where possible you should avoid sharing these kinds of materials in an appendix, using something else in their place where possible (for example, using a blank questionnaire as an example, not a completed one). If you have to use materials connected to someone involved with the research, you should seek their permission first and only use the materials if they grant that permission. Remember that ethical protections extend to all those involved in your research, not just the participants, and they cover the entire research process including the report, not just during data collection.

Refinements

Tidy up those statistical appendices

In the chapter on the results section, a point was made about the cluttered outputs from most statistical software and how unsuitable they are for including in the results section (See: Dumping stats clutter into the results, p. 100). What was suggested in that chapter was to create your own simplified output tables and graphs for inclusion in the results section and leave the more complex outputs from the statistical software for the appendices.

That does not mean you can simply cut-and-paste the outputs from the statistical software directly into an appendix without changing them; there are still a number of things you will need to do to present those results clearly, even in an appendix. The most important thing to do is to tidy up the formatting. Make sure that the tables and figures fit into the pages of the report cleanly, without extending too far into the margins of the page or ending up divided between two pages. Most statistical software does not label the tables or figures correctly (See: Labelling tables and figures, p. 209) and so you will need to do that manually. Remember to continue the rule about numbering each table and figure consecutively throughout the report. As such, the number of the first table in the first appendix should follow on from the number of the last table in the rest of the report, with the same rule applying for the figures as well. Try to present the results in as compact a format as you can. This can include using a smaller font size than you did in the other sections of the report, single-line spacing and reducing the size of figures and other images as much as you can while keeping them legible. You can consider this an extension of the principles of good presentation used for presenting summary data in the results (See: Summary data, tables and graphs, p. 10).

One final point to consider is to decide what details are necessary to include from the output in the appendix. While it was always the intention that the appendix would be a more complete report of all the results from that analysis, you do not need to include the entire output down to the last full stop. There are likely to be a number of elements in the output which are by-products of the software that created it and not the statistics being done. Examples may include the names of the data files used in the analysis or a record of the settings for the analysis in the software. These elements can usually be left out of the appendix. Even among the statistical results, there may be elements of the analysis which even the most diligent audience member is unlikely to want or need to see. This is because statistical software can sometimes 'throw everything at the wall' when it comes to analysis, carrying out any and all tests associated with that type of analysis in the event that they may be needed. While there is no formal method to decide what is or isn't necessary to include in the appendix, a simple rule-of-thumb might be if the element of the analysis is one you don't understand or have never needed to consult yourself, then you can probably leave it out of the appendices.

▶ CHAPTER 7: EXERCISES

Exercise 1: MCT

1) Why should the abstract, references and appendices be considered minor sections of the report?
   A. They are the final three sections to appear in the report.
   B. Their combined length is shorter than the length of any one of the other sections.
   C. They are less complex than the other sections.
   D. None of the above.

2) The purpose of the abstract is to summarise....
   A. all the key details or the report.
   B. the aims and key findings of the report only.
   C. the most important and interesting details of the report.
   D. the previous research that inspired your research.

3) In an abstract it is typical to see details such as _____ and _____ but it is usually not necessary to include _____.
   A. a few details about the participants, a result from one of the analyses, a suggestion for a practical application
   B. a research question, a brief summary of the ethical precautions taken, a conclusion from the discussion
   C. a brief summary of the key sources that inspired your research, an example of a questionnaire item, a suggestion for future research
   D. a brief summary of the procedure, a key finding of one of the analyses, an example of a questionnaire item

4) You should only be citing other sources in the abstract if...
   A. you have the space.
   B. it identifies which definition you are using for a debated concept.
   C. it highlights an important innovation in your methodology.
   D. All of the above.

5) The purpose of the references section is...
   A. to lend credibility to the points made in the report by demonstrating the quality of the sources those points are based on.
   B. to allow your audience to locate specific sources you have mentioned in the report that interest them.
   C. to provide your audience with the chance to check for themselves if you are correctly presenting the findings of the sources you have cited.
   D. All of the above.

6) When it comes to location, in parenthetical and _____ systems, the references section is located between the discussion and appendices. When it comes to arranging the order of the references, in footnote and endnote systems the order is _____.
   A. footnote, chronological
   B. endnote, alphabetical
   C. footnote, alphabetical
   D. endnote, chronological

7) The difference between a references list and a bibliography is that the references list _____ while the bibliography _____.
   A. only includes sources that were cited in the text, also includes sources that were not cited
   B. is arranged alphabetically, is arranged chronologically
   C. only includes each source once no matter how many times it is cited, includes a source multiple times if it is cited multiple times
   D. All of the above.

8) The purpose of the appendices section is...
   A. to include everything connected to your research in case the audience needs to see it.
   B. to include only those things mentioned in the report but not included in any other section.
   C. to include a copy of the sources on which your research is based so that the audience can access them if they wish to.
   D. to provide proof that the claims made in the research regarding the methodology and results are accurate.

9) Which of the following belongs in an appendix?
   A. A completed questionnaire which has been filled in by one of the participants.
   B. Your raw data.
   C. A complete set of the materials used in your research.
   D. Additional details from your analyses that weren't included in the results section.

10) Which of the following is NOT a valid rule about presenting materials in an appendix?
   A. Appendices containing materials need to be signed by the researcher to authenticate them.
   B. Each appendix should have an identifier and a title.
   C. You continue the numbering system for tables and figures used in the rest of the report in the appendices.
   D. Each appendix should be referred to somewhere in the rest of the report.

Exercise 2: How serious are these mistakes?

A common problem faced by many first-time report writers is judging the relative importance of all the different rules and requirements involved in report writing. How important is it to keep your abstract short? How serious a problem is it to list sources chronologically in a bibliography? With this in mind you will find, in alphabetical order, 10 common mistakes made by first-time report writers when writing their abstract, references or appendices. You need to put each of them in one of two categories of importance: moderate errors and minor errors.

- Arranging the references in a references list or bibliography in chronological order.
- Claiming a source as a primary source in your references when you have only read about it in a secondary source.
- Citing a source for which there is no matching full reference.
- Constructing an abstract which tries to include all the key details from every section.
- Including something in an appendix without seeking permission from the person who provided it.
- Including an appendix without a purpose or there is no link to it anywhere else in the report.
- Including a reference in a references list, footnote or endnote that was not cited in-text.
- Providing more details than are needed in an appendix.
- Providing information in an appendix as proof that a claim made in the report is accurate.
- Using a referencing system other than the one that is expected.

▸ CHAPTER 7: ANSWERS

Exercise 1: MCT

Q1: Ans = C (See: An overview, p. 145)
Q2: Ans = C (See: Abstract: The basics, p. 146 ↔ The longest summary, p. 147 ↔ Brevity is the soul of wit, p. 149)
Q3: Ans = D (See: Abstract: The basics, p. 146 ↔ Departing from the standard abstract 'formula', p. 148)
Q4: Ans = D (See: Citing references in the abstract, p. 147)
Q5: Ans = D (See: References: The basics, p. 159)
Q6: Ans = B (See: Referencing systems, p. 152 ↔ Alphabetical or chronological? p. 155)

Q7 Ans = A (See: References list vs bibliography, p. 152 ↔ Referencing systems, p. 152 ↔ Confusing a references list and a bibliography, p. 155)

Q8: Ans = B (See: Appendices: The basics, p. 159 ↔ Appendices are not used to prove your honesty, p. 160 ↔ Be selective about what you put in an appendix, p. 160)

Q9: Ans = D (See: Appendices are not used to prove your honesty, p. 160 ↔ Be selective about what you put in an appendix, p. 160 ↔ Be careful about confidentiality issues with your appendices, p. 161)

Q10: Ans = A (See: Layout for the appendices, p. 159 ↔ Be selective about what you put in an appendix, p. 160)

Exercise 2: How serious are these mistakes?

Unlike the previous sections, there are only two categories of mistake for these three sections: moderate and minor errors. The reason why there are no serious errors for these sections is because serious errors are the ones that completely undermine the central purpose of that section or reveal a fatal flaw into your report. Given that the abstract, references and appendices are a relatively uncompleted sections, it is very hard for any mistake to completely undermine them. Similarly, their status as minor sections means that even if you were to execute them poorly, that is unlikely to result in a fatal flaw to your report. As such, even the larger mistakes you can make tend to be only moderate errors overall.

Moderate errors

(Including an appendix without a purpose or there is no link to it anywhere else in the report ↔ Citing a source for which there is no matching full reference ↔ Using a referencing system other than the one that is expected. Claiming a source as a primary source in your references when you have only read about it in a secondary source ↔ Including something in an appendix without seeking permission from the person who provided it.)

All of these are moderate errors, owing to the fact that while they do make your work much less effective, they don't fatally undermine it the way a serious error would. Nonetheless they are still to be avoided. Including pointless or un-linked appendices is likely to make the necessary linked appendices more time-consuming to locate. Your audience may find this off-putting, making them less likely to make use of the appendices and thus reducing the effectiveness of the appendices section as a whole. The next two errors, with unreferenced citations and the use of the incorrect referencing system, both interfere with the main purpose of the references section, which is to provide the information needed to identify and locate every source that is relevant to your research. With no information available about a source, or if the information is unclear or hard to find because it is not where it is expected to be, your audience's ability to evaluate the quality of your sources or find them for themselves will be seriously disrupted. The final two issues are not technical issues, as much as they are moral issues. Incorrectly claiming to have read something as a primary source or including materials without permission may not harm the effectiveness of your report, but they will harm your reputation if discovered and remain unethical, discovered or not.

(See: Double-check your names and dates, p. 154 ↔ Which referencing system? p. 155 ↔ Reference as you cite, p. 156 ↔ Be honest about your secondary sources, p. 157 ↔ Be selective about what you put in an appendix, p. 160 ↔ Be careful about confidentiality issues with your appendices, p. 161)

Minor errors

(Arranging the references in a references list or bibliography in chronological order. Including a reference in a references list, footnote or endnote that was not cited in-text. Constructing an abstract which tries to include all the key details from every section. Proving information in an appendix as proof that a claim made in the report is accurate. Providing more details than are needed in an appendix.)

All of these are minor errors in the sense that, although they have a negative impact on the effectiveness of your abstract, references or appendices, the extent of their impact is much more limited than the moderate errors. For example, while arranging references in the wrong order or including references without a matching citation will make it harder for your audience to get what they need from the references section, the level of disruption will only be minor. The final three issues are all concerned with including information that is not needed in an abstract or appendix, either to prove honesty or simply misjudging how much information is needed to achieve the purpose of that section. While it may be well intentioned, the excess information dilutes the impact of the rest of the abstract or appendices, and so both sections would be better off without it. Overall then, these are mistakes you should generally try to avoid making, but you should not worry too much about it if you do end up making one.

(See: The longest summary, p. 147 ↔ Alphabetical or chronological? p. 155 ↔ Reference as you cite, p. 156 ↔ Appendices are not used to prove your honesty, p. 160 ↔ Be selective about what you put in an appendix, p. 160)

Desk-based research

▶ AN OVERVIEW

The guidance on report writing found in this book is intended to be relevant to the writing of reports in a wide variety of subjects. That being said, the approach to report writing outlined in all the other chapters does assume that you will be gathering and analysing some kind of data and using the results of that analysis to answer your research questions. In other words, this book assumes that you will be carrying out some form of empirical research. While report writing is more common among subjects that use the empirical research method, it is not limited to just to those subjects. For that reason, this chapter explores how you should approach writing a research report if you are using a non-empirical research method, often referred to as 'desk-based research'.

There are many different desk-based research methods out there but we will be focusing on two of the most common methods: a systematic literature review and theoretical research. For each one, we will review the ways in which writing a report for that desk-based research method compares to writing a report for empirical research, noting both similarities and differences. In this way, the advice outlined in this chapter will help you adapt the general guidance on report writing found in the other chapters to the specific requirements of your preferred type of desk-based research.

▶ BEFORE YOU BEGIN THIS CHAPTER...

As this chapter is intended to complement the other chapters in this book, sometimes agreeing with the approach in those other chapters and other times

DOI: 10.4324/9781003107965-8

modifying that approach, it raises the question as to whether you should read this chapter or other chapters first. It could work either way but reading this chapter first is recommended as it will put you in the right frame of mind when you read the other chapters afterwards. This approach means you will know at first glance which elements of those other chapters are relevant to your chosen desk-based method and which are not. You may even find that there are entire chapters which have very little relevance to the type of desk-based report you are writing (for example, there is no method section in a Theoretical research report). Reading this chapter first could save you a lot of time, allowing you to focus on just those bits that are relevant. One other thing to note is that the abstract, references and appendices sections are virtually the same for both empirical and desk-based research reports, and so you won't find them discussed in this chapter. Instead, you can consider the guidance provided in the chapter which focuses on those three sections to apply no matter what kind of research report you are writing.

Finally, a common mistake among first-time report writers when it comes to desk-based research is to underestimate it. The fact that you do not need to recruit participants, collect data or learn a formal method of analysis can make writing a desk-based research report sound much easier than an empirical report. However, writing a desk-based research report can be every bit as challenging as any empirical report. Systematic literature reviews require you to look a research collectively, looking for deeper patterns in the assumptions and methods of that research as a whole. Theoretical research requires you to deconstruct the assumptions and language used. If you have not had any practice at doing this before, learning to look at research in this way for the first time can be just as difficult as learning any of the methods used to analyse data. Also, carrying out desk-based research is no time-saver. Time saved by not needing to chase after participants or carefully note interview responses is spent instead trawling through library databases and carefully noting search terms and hit rates or reading and re-reading theoretical positions so as to identify inconsistencies and contradictions. In the end, you may find that the desk-based report plays more to your strengths than an empirical report does, but you should take a careful look at the challenges involved in both types of report before you decide if that is true. Whichever type of report you end up choosing, you should never expect it to be easy.

▶ SYSTEMATIC LITERATURE REVIEW

The basics

A systematic literature review is a piece of research where you review a selection of the literature related to your chosen research area in order to learn more about the theoretical assumptions and methodology used in that literature. The aim is to see if the theoretical or methodological approach taken by the other researchers had an impact on what they found or how they interpreted those findings. In essence, you are researching the literature, seeking to answer questions about the assumptions, theories, concepts and methods which were used in that literature. The aim is to get a deeper understanding of the findings of the literature, an understanding that gives you a new insight into why they found, what they found and what those findings mean. Among the benefits of this new understanding is the potential to inspire a new approach to applying the findings of that literature in practical settings or new methodologies to be used in future research.

Overall structure

In a systematic literature review report, the order of the sections is as follows: Introduction, Method, Literature Review and Analysis, Discussion, References and Appendices. In the introduction, you first discuss the wider context and research area in which the review is located, before laying out your theoretical model and research questions. The method section outlines the scope for the literature review and the ethical precautions. In the literature review and analysis you discuss the literature, analysing the assumptions, methods and findings of that literature, before relating the results of that analysis back to your research questions. In the discussion, you relate the findings of you review back the wider context again before focusing on methodological issues, practical applications and future research directions arising from those findings. After all that, the references and appendices contain full reference information and any additional materials cited elsewhere in the text.

Introduction

The introduction is where you explain the purpose behind your research. You start by talking about the wider context behind your research and why it matters, before focusing in on the research area within that context which you will be exploring in greater detail. You outline the theoretical model that you plan to use when conducting that exploration and then finish off by stating the questions that your research seeks to answer. By the end of your introduction your audience should have a clear idea of what your research is about, which research questions you are trying to answer and why those answers matter. The introduction section for a systematic literature review report is very similar to that of an empirical report. As such, while you can get general guidance on this section here, you may also wish to consult the chapter on the introduction section to get some additional guidance on how to present the content in each of the sub-sections described below (See: Chapter 2, Introduction, p. 13).

The first sub-section in the introduction is the 'wider context', in which you discuss the real-world situation or issue that your research is connected to, with the aim of demonstrating to your audience why your research matters. Following that, the second sub-section is the 'research area', in which you identify the area within that wider context that you will be focusing on, explaining your choice of that area and why it is important to the wider context. As both of these sub-sections are written in the same way for a systematic literature review report as they are for an empirical report, you may find the guidance on them in the introduction chapter useful here too (See: Introduce the research context, p. 14 ↔ Identify the research area, p. 14).

The next sub-section is the 'theoretical model', in which you identify patterns or issues in the theoretical or methodological approaches used by the literature in your chosen research area, which you are proposing have affected the findings in this area. For example, you might propose that certain assumptions, definitions or methodological approaches in the literature have influenced what was found. Furthermore, if there are debates among the scholars in this research area over definitions of key concepts, you might propose that whatever side a researcher takes in that debate will affect what they find or how they interpret that finding. One thing to keep in mind about each of these proposals is to keep them short. Here, in the introduction section, you just briefly outline how these approaches may be affecting the findings of the literature. It will be in the literature review and analysis section, later on in the report, where you fill in all the details.

Rosella is conducting a systematic review of the literature on the practicality of electric cars and other vehicles. In particular, her research area focuses on the literature concerned with the battery life of these vehicles and the factors that influence it.

[In Rosella's Theoretical Model] *There are a number of methodological differences between the various pieces of research testing the efficiency of electric vehicles which may have affected their findings. One such difference is the way in which they evaluated the capacity of the vehicle's battery. In some research, theoretical models are used, while others chose practical measures, such as the amount of work completed by the battery before it was exhausted. It is also worth noting that among the researchers that used practical measures, the two most commonly used measures were distance travelled and time spent active. Furthermore, the choice between a lab-based or field-based research design, when conducting these practical measures, is another important methodological decision which may be influencing findings in this research area.*

Finally, at the end of the introduction, is the 'research questions' sub-section. Here you highlight specific proposals made in the theoretical model sub-section and pose a question about that proposal that the research seeks to answer via the analysis of the literature. As this is another sub-section written in much the same way for an empirical report as for a systematic literature review report, you will find the guidance in the introduction chapter useful here too (See: Research questions, p. 18). One thing to note is that the typical research questions found in a systematic literature review are similar to qualitative research questions in empirical research, in that they seek to understand the reasons why things happen or what difference something makes. As such, a structured literature review might include research questions asking why the literature takes a certain approach or is based on certain assumptions. The questions might also ask what difference it makes to the research findings if a researcher adopts one approach or one definition over another. For further advice on phrasing research questions for a systematic literature review, you should consult the guidance on phrasing qualitative research questions (See: Your research questions will decide your methodology, p. 25).

[In Rosella's Research Questions]

What factors influence the choice between practical measures and theoretical models of battery capacity?

How does the choice between the practical measures of distance travelled and time spent active affect conclusions in the literature about battery capacity?

How does the choice between lab-based and field-based research effect findings in the literature on battery capacity?

Method

The method section is where you tell your audience how your research was carried out. You do this by telling them what your research was designed to do, how the data were collected and what steps you took to ensure it was all done ethically. By the end of the method section you should have provided just enough detail such that your audience can understand exactly what was done in your research and, if they wish to, recreate it themselves.

While the method section in a systematic literature review report serves a very similar purpose to the method in an empirical report, it is likely to be much shorter and have fewer sub-sections. As such, it is unlikely that you will find the chapter on the method for empirical reports much help when writing a method for a structured review. As such, for this section you should focus on the guidance found in this chapter alone.

The first sub-section of the method for a systematic review is the 'searches' sub-section, which is concerned with the search parameters. This contains information regarding which collections or databases of literature were included in the literature search and what the search criteria were, such as year of publication, source type or search terms. Any reasons for the choices made in selecting these parameters should be included here as well.

> [In Rosella's Searches sub-section] *The journal databases used were Compendex, Knovel and IEEE Explore, as these are the three most widely used engineering databases. The search was limited to empirical research articles in peer reviewed journals between the years 2010 and 2020. This time period covers the most recent generation of Li-ion batteries. The search terms used were 'electric', 'battery-powered', 'vehicle', 'car', 'efficiency', 'evaluation', 'practical', 'effectiveness' and 'benchmark'.*

The other sub-section in the method is the 'ethics' sub-section, where you discuss the ethical precautions taken in your research. Most systematic literature reviews only draw on the findings of published sources, and since these will have already been subjected to ethical scrutiny there are no additional precautions needed when using these sources. Nonetheless, your method sub-section still needs to explain to your audience that this was the case. In addition, it is possible for a systemic literature review to include a mix of sources, some of which may not be published. This will require you to take appropriate precautions to protect the ethical rights of the individuals connected to those unpublished sources and report what those precautions were in this sub-section. Furthermore, there are versions of the systematic literature review which involve combining and analysing data from multiple pieces of literature (See: Quantitative meta-analysis, p. 180). Since this involves analysing and publishing actual participant data, it deserves the same ethical precautions as any piece of empirical research would and again these precautions need to be reported here. In summary, whether the ethical precautions were taken by you or by others, it is important to indicate what was done and by whom in the ethics sub-section of a systematic literature review.

Literature review and analysis

The literature review and analysis section is the heart of a structured literature review report. In this section you will both present and analyse the literature you have located in your review. You will also use the conclusions from that analysis to offer answers to your research questions. This is very different from an empirical report where the literature review section is used to pose new research questions, rather than answer them, and where the analysis is reported in a separate results section. Given these differences, you will find that most of the guidance in the literature review chapter or the results chapters is not relevant when writing this section in a systematic review. Instead, you should focus on the guidance on this section found here in this chapter. There are one or two specific sections from the literature review chapter that can be helpful here, and these are identified below.

The literature review and analysis section is structured into sub-sections, with each sub-section focused on the research issue behind one of your research questions. The analysis of the literature relating to that issue will be used to answer that question. Therefore, within each sub-section of the literature review and analysis section, you would need to do all the following things: identify the research question, critically review the relevant literature in relation to the question, present a conclusion which results from that review and relate that conclusion back to the research question. Identifying the research question is done very briefly at the start in a sentence or two at most. Framing the sub-section in this way will help the audience to recognise the relevant information about each piece of literature you mention after that point. It should also help make the whole sub-section appear to be one overall point, focused on that research question, rather than simply a collection of separate pieces of literature. When it comes to critically reviewing the literature, unless you are combining quantitative data in a meta-analysis (See: Quantitative meta-analysis, p. 180), there is no formal method of analysis which must be followed. However, there are some general guidelines which are useful to keep in mind. When you are deciding which literature to include in each sub-section, you should start with the most relevant piece of literature and then ensure that each additional piece mentioned after the first one is adding something new and of value to the understanding provided by the previous pieces (See: Criticality, p. 214).

[The start of one of the sub-sections of Rosella's Literature review and analysis] *While there has been a large amount of research exploring the impact of ambient temperature on battery life, there is a noticeable difference in the findings from lab-based research compared to field-based research on this issue. This is relevant to the research question on the impact that the choice between lab-based and field-based research has on the findings in this area. The findings of Adams and Baron's (2009) widely cited lab-based research, which showed that battery life is reduced by 50% for every 15 degrees F that the battery temperature rises above 77F, has been supported by the majority of research that has followed. However, as Cecil (2014) has shown, the effects of ambient temperature on batteries in field-based research can depend on insulation, with different types of insulation reducing the temperature variation by as much as 80%. Further-more, Dangar and Elim's (2019) field-based research found that vehicle colour can affect how much the vehicle as a whole, including the battery, is heated by sunlight, with black cars heated up to 27F more than white ones under the same conditions.*

This approach, where each new piece of literature adds something new to what the previous ones have said, ensures that each piece of literature is relevant to the previous ones and avoids repetition where you have multiple pieces of literature all making the same point. It should also mean that, when all the literature in the sub-section is considered together, it will help you reach a conclusion which offers a new understanding of that research issue which you can relate back to the research question. If you find you need some additional guidance on achiev-ing that new understanding, you should consider some of the methods recom-mended for achieving insight (See: Insight, p. 213) or those suggested for use in resolving debates in the literature (See: Debates in the literature, p. 53). Finally, when it comes to relating your conclusion back to the research questions, this is a very similar activity whether being done in a systematic literature review report or an empirical report. As such, you may find much of the guidance about re-lating empirical findings back to research questions in the chapter on the results section helpful here too (See: Wider implications, p. 118).

Discussion

The discussion section is where you explore and apply the findings of your re-search, while also critically evaluating the research itself. You review the answers to your research questions, reflecting on their relevance to the research area and wider context. You also evaluate your research design before looking ahead to consider potential practical applications for your findings as well as future re-search ideas. By the end of the discussion section, your audience should be aware of the wider theoretical and practical implications of your research findings, the lessons learnt regarding methodology and what is next for research in this area.

The discussion section in a systematic literature review report is very similar to that of an empirical report, with almost all the same sub-sections found in both types of report. The only exception is the past research sub-section which appears in an empirical report but is not needed in a systematic literature review report. Given all this similarity between the discussion sections in the two types of report, while you will find some general guidance on the discussion section here, you may also wish to consult the chapter on the discussion section to get additional guidance on how to present the content described below (See: Dis-cussion, p. 176).

The discussion section in a systematic literature review report starts by considering the wider implications of the answers to the research questions, relating them to both the wider context and research area (See: Wider implications, p. 118). Implications which relate to the wider context might come in the form of insights regarding the real-world situation to which the research is connected. The review may have revealed something about that real-world situation, a new way of looking at it perhaps. Implications of this type often lend themselves to suggestions for actions which can be taken to improve that real-world situation, and so points you begin in this section can be expanded on later in the practical applications sub-section. Implications which relate to the research area typically come in the form of insights into the approach being taken by researchers in this area or about their findings. Implications of this type usually lend themselves to suggestions for new avenues for research and so points you begin in this section can be expanded on later in the future research sub-section.

[In Rosella's Wider implications sub-section] *One of the conclusions which emerged from this review was the role that funding can play in the choice between practical measures and theoretical models of battery capacity. Research which is funded by businesses which manufacture electric vehicles tend to favour theoretical models. The results reported by research using theoretical models are consistently higher than those using practical measures, and this represents a benefit for the manufacturers who can report these higher results in the adverts for their vehicles. While all the research reviewed openly acknowledged their funding sources, the adverts are not required to state that the results they are citing are based on theoretical models. All of this raises important questions about the relationship between business and research in this area.*

The next sub-section focuses on the methodological issues arising from your research (See Methodological issues, p. 120). It is important to note that the methodological issues discussed here are those connected to your systematic literature review itself and not any wider methodological issues that your review may have found in the literature. The type of issue that might be considered here are the choices you made in setting up the search parameters, such as choosing which sources to search or which search criteria to use. Similarly, any issues you encountered in executing the search or interpreting the findings can be mentioned here. It is important that the discussion of any methodological issue should mention the impact that issue had on the findings, as the only methodological issues worth mentioning are the ones that affected the outcome of your research.

Following methodological issues comes the practical applications sub-section, where the aim is to make suggestions as to how the research findings can be translated into practical solutions and improvements (See: Practical applications, p. 122). While this section is very similar in both empirical and systematic literature review reports, one difference is that the findings from a systematic literature review can allow you to make much stronger suggestions in terms of the scale or the scope of the changes you are suggesting. It is more reasonable to make a suggestion for widespread or significant change based on a review which has found a large amount of research that has all reached the same conclusion than it would be to make the same recommendation based on a single piece of empirical research.

After that comes future research, which involves making proposals for future research to address questions and issues that have been raised by the review (See: Future research, p. 123). Again, there is very similar sub-section in both empirical and systematic literature review reports. That being said, one form of future research proposal which tends only to be made as a result of a systematic review are the more general suggestions for a whole area of future research, as opposed to proposals for one specific piece of future research. General suggestions might be concerned with changes in the methodology or theoretical assumptions made by a large amount, or indeed all, of the research in this research area. Again, it tends only to make sense to be making such a widespread suggestion if it is based on a wider review of the literature rather than on one piece of research.

> [In Rosella's Future research sub-section] *Given the role that temperature can play in battery capacity, and differences in battery temperature resulting from battery position and vehicle colour, future field-based research on battery capacity should measure battery temperature directly, as opposed to recording ambient temperature. Temperature gauges which are integrated with the battery or placed within the insulation housing can achieve this. This should apply to all field-based research, not just those that are researching the impact of temperature, owing to the fact that temperature can affect the outcome of any research on battery capacity.*

Finally, you have the conclusion sub-section, where you take a step back and reflect on the discussion as a whole, highlighting those discussion points which are of the greatest importance. The aim of this sub-section, which remains the same whether it is found in an empirical or systematic literature review report, is to craft the 'take-home' message of your research report (See: Conclusion, p. 124). Keep in mind that conclusions work best when they are focused and credible. Focus comes from not trying to offer too many conclusions and the credibility comes from being modest in your claims about the importance of any conclusion you are offering.

Common mistakes

A review is not just a summary

Many first-time report writers make the mistake of thinking that a systemic literature review is nothing more than an immense summary, a long list of all the research they can find related to the research area. Often there will be no specific research questions, beyond asking "What are the findings or conclusions of the literature in this research area?". The two main problems with this 'summary' approach are that it lacks focus and purpose. Without more specific research questions, it is hard to justify why the chosen literature was included, as opposed to other literature in the same research area, and it is equally hard to explain what the point of the review is. A systematic literature review needs to be focused on specific research questions and it needs to be trying to answer those questions for a good reason. That 'good reason' is usually based on the fact that the chosen questions are about issues which have an impact on the findings of the research in that area. Answering the research questions will help to determine what impact is. This is why the theoretical model and the research questions play such critical roles in any systematic review. Producing a theoretical model focuses the review on specific issues and requires the report writer to explain what impact those issues are having on the research in this research area. Following on from that, creating research questions requires the report writer to clarify for themselves and for their audience what they want to know about each of these issues. This also explains why the theoretical model and research questions are both included in the introduction section because the focus and purpose of any research are qualities you want to establish early on in the report.

Refinements

Detailing your search

In addition to the basic details mentioned earlier regarding your search parameters (See: Systematic literature review: Method, p. 173), there are some additional details you can provide to give a more complete picture of this key element of your research design. After all, exactly where and how you went about searching for the literature is likely to have had a big impact on what you found.

One type of additional detail you could provide would be to report the total number of hits, reviews and selections for each search. 'Hits' represents the number of sources that matched your search criteria, 'reviews' are the sources you read completely and 'selections' are the ones you actually mention in the report. Providing these details can help to demonstrate the diligence of your search as well as helping to put the claims you make in the report in perspective by showing the true scope of the search that produced them. Another type of additional detail would be to expand on the rationale you provide for the parameters of your search, offering a basis for your choice of specific databases or the reasons for limiting the scope of your search to certain years, source types or search terms. The rationale for these choices, much like the rationale for any academic argument, can be based on evidence in the form of supporting sources or logical argument. An example of the type of source you could cite would be another systematic review which used a similar approach. Alternatively, a logical argument for the search parameters could be based on aspects of the research area, the wider context or practical concerns and limitations. It is important not to become defensive or self-conscious when acknowledging the limitations of your search or the subjectivity of your rationale for those limitations. Instead, you should adopt the style and mentality used in a positionality sub-section in an empirical report (See: Positionality, p. 81). The aim is not to justify your choices, but rather to help your audience to understand your viewpoint so they can take that viewpoint into consideration when reviewing your findings.

Advanced

Quantitative meta-analysis

When conducting a systematic review of a research area where quantitative methods of analysis are widely used, there is the option to conduct a meta-analysis. In a meta-analysis, you carry out your own statistical analysis which combines either the data or the results from multiple pieces of previous research. When combining the data, you are typically merging multiple similar datasets from different pieces of research and carrying out the same analysis that each piece of research did separately, but on the combined dataset. In addition, if the datasets differ in some way that could be represented as a new variable, for example, if they were collected from different groups, it may be also possible to use this new variable to carry out a new analysis.

If the datasets are not available or not compatible, then the alternative is to do a meta-analysis of the research results instead. When combining the results from multiple pieces of previous research, each piece of research becomes the equivalent of a participant and the results from that research become a set of data points. An example of this kind of meta-analysis would be to compare effect sizes across multiple pieces of research. Effect sizes are often used for this kind of analysis as they represent a standardised measure that can be used to compare results where a variety of different analyses and data types were used.

There are a number of advantages with a meta-analysis; for example, it can help to resolve debates or contradictory findings within the research area. It may also make it possible to answer some questions which could not have been answered by the individual pieces of research, such as a comparison across groups or situations, where the individual pieces of research only focused on one group or situation each. A meta-analysis is also thought to have greater 'power', which in statistical terms means a greater chance of finding an effect if there is one to be found. Finally, a meta-analysis can help to compensate for distortions in individual datasets, such as those caused by skewness or outliers (See: Additional testing, p. 106).

However, there are also a number of challenges and potential errors which can be introduced when attempting a meta-analysis. It is too simplistic to assume that a larger data-set from a meta-analysis will always be more valid and reliable merely by being larger (See: Sampling is a more complicated issue than it appears to be, p. 128). Indeed, there is the potential that adding more data increases the chances of producing a false-positive, appearing to find an effect when there is none. There is also the risk that combining the outcomes from several pieces of research into one overall outcome loses important findings within each piece of research. Finally, if sets of data or findings are combined without consideration for the quality of each set, this can harm the accuracy of the meta-analysis findings.

One thing that should be clear from all of this is that the level of statistical expertise necessary to carry out a meta-analysis is quite high. As such, it should only be considered by a report writer who either has a high level of statistical experience themselves or who can call on a high level of support from someone with that experience.

▶ THEORETICAL RESEARCH

The basics

In a piece of theoretical research, you carry out a theoretical investigation into a concept, theory or issue which is widely mentioned by the literature in a given research area. This is done by critically evaluating things such as fundamental assumptions, definitions, the validity of the evidence and the manipulation of language which are all elements in a particular point of view on that concept, known as a 'perspective'. The validity of the assumptions, definitions and other elements is evaluated through rational argument. This involves presenting a series of claims, backed up by justifications and using an approach which is clearly explained and internally consistent. In essence, you are using rational argument to deconstruct the theoretical frameworks which support that perspective on the concept, so you can assess their validity and make suggestions as to how those frameworks might be revised. The idea is that, by proposing revisions to the framework, you will change people's perspective on the concept, and that will affect any research past or future that is linked to that concept.

Overall structure

The structure of a theoretical research report is very different from the structure of an empirical report. There are only three types of section in a theoretical research report; the introduction, the sub-questions and the conclusion. In the introduction, the research context is explained and the main research question is identified. The main research question is broken down into sub-questions and each of these sub-questions is explored in a separate sub-question section. Within each of these sub-question sections you will take a position on that sub-question and critically evaluate that position so as to produce an insight on the main research question. It is important to note that while there will only ever be one introduction section at the start and one conclusion section at the end, there can be several sub-question sections in the middle, each one looking at a different sub-question. Finally, in the conclusion, the insights from the sub-questions are combined and synthesised so as to provide an answer to the main research question.

Given the considerable difference between the structures of an empirical report and a theoretical research report, the majority of the guidance in the other chapters in this book will not apply here, and some chapters (Method and Results) will have no relevance at all. Instead, guidance on the structure and content of a theoretical research report can be found almost entirely within this chapter. Where there are parts of the other chapters that are relevant to a theoretical research report, they will be highlighted here.

Introduction

The introduction section is where you explain the purpose behind your research; what you are trying to do and why you are trying to do it. To achieve this, you need to identify the wider context to which your research is related, before focusing in on the research area within that context that your research will explore in greater detail. You finish off by stating the question that your research seeks to answer. In that way, by the end of your introduction your audience should have a clear idea of what your research is about, the research questions that you are trying to answer and why those answers matter.

You start this section by identifying the wider context or issue to which the research relates, so as to help your audience to understand why your research matters. While this wider context can be a 'real-world' issue, in the case of theoretical research it can be an entirely theoretical issue, such as the discussions in the literature surrounding a concept or theory. Connecting to a wider context is something that needs to be done in empirical research as well, and so the guidance on the wider context sub-section in the introduction chapter may be of some help here (See: Introduce the research context, p. 14).

> *Himari is conducting a piece of theoretical research exploring the justifications behind denying prisoners the right to vote in elections. She is exploring this issue through a combination of perspectives from both social and political philosophy.*

> [In Himari's Introduction] *In the last few years, a number of prominent legal challenges have placed the question of prisoners being denied the right to vote firmly in the public eye. The significance of this question in both moral and legal terms should not be underestimated. The number of people incarcerated in most developed countries varies between 0.001 and 0.002% of the population, although it can range as high as 0.006% in the US. As they are all of voting age, the impact on the electorate could be significant, with the margin of difference which decides the outcome of some elections being 0.002% of the electorate or less.*

Once the wider context has been established, you then direct attention onto one part of the wider context, the research area, which will be the main focus of your research. The selection of a research area is done for practical reasons as much as anything else, as it would not be possible for a single piece of research to properly explore the entirety of the wider context. Nevertheless, it is still necessary to explain to the audience why this particular research area was selected and why it is relevant to the wider contact. Again, much the same thing needs to be done in an empirical report, and so the guidance on the research area in the introduction chapter would be of use here (See: Identify the research area, p. 14).

As well as identifying the research area, you should give the audience some idea of the approach you plan to take when exploring this area. This is done by highlighting some of the key theoretical concepts or approaches you plan to use. You should not go into much detail about them at this early stage, all that is needed is a very general outline of the intended approach. This is similar to the theoretical framework provided in an empirical report, and so yet again you may find the guidance on that issue helpful here too (See: Outline the theoretical model, p. 15).

> [In Himari's Introduction] *This research will explore the justification for imprisonment using Adam's (1854) arguments on the relationship between incarceration and justice, in order to argue that justice can only serve the few and not the many. I will*

also consider the limiting of suffrage, contrasting Babcock's (1952) 'true electorate' with Carlisle's (1981) 'voting citizen'. The overall aim here is to establish if a discontinuous approach can cope with doctrinal diversity and better address the question of limited voting rights.

The final element in the introduction is to state the research question. The research question is a question that you are trying to answer by carrying out your research. A theoretical research report would typically have one overall research question, which would then be broken down into sub-questions. The reason for breaking the main research question down in this way is that a research question usually contains certain assumptions, conceptual definitions or theoretical positions which need to be critically evaluated before the question can be answered. Breaking the question down allows you to tackle these tasks individually. It is worth noting that some researchers refer to the research question in a theoretical research report as the 'topic' which is broken down into 'sub-topics'. The only difference here appears to be the label used, as topics and research questions seem to function in the same way.

[In Himari's Introduction] *Consequently, this research asks is it just to deny prisoners the right to vote? In order to answer this, we will consider three sub-questions. The first sub-question asks how imprisonment can be reconciled with a belief in freedom as an inalienable right? The second sub-question explores the concept of justice in asking whom does justice serve? The third sub-question considers who is entitled to participate in an election?*

Sub-questions

Each sub-question will have its own section devoted to it, and within each of these sections you will find the following elements: taking a position, critical review and resolution.

The first step involves you taking a position on the sub-question that is the focus of the section. When taking a position on the sub-question, you are proposing your own answer to that question. There are many types of position you can take, but some examples of the most common types include: a challenge to an existing position on that sub-question, an agreement with an existing position or an original position that has not previously been proposed. While your position should be derived from the literature relating to sub-question, it can still be considered 'your' position. This is because ownership is determined by the unique way you present and defend that position in your critical review of the literature.

The next step involves the critical review of the literature relating to the sub-question. The literature contained within this review can include other theoretical research on the same or related questions as well as empirical research carried out in the same research area as the sub-question. A critical review is an exploration of any issue which attempts to incorporate a variety of perspectives on that issue (See: Criticality, p. 214). Typically, the most widely known, or 'dominant', perspective is the first to be considered, but following that, additional perspectives are then considered and compared to the dominant one.

The purpose of this review will vary depending on whether the position you have taken on the sub-question is compatible or incompatible with the dominant perspective. On the one hand, if your position is compatible, you use your review of the literature to demonstrate why the dominant perspective is valid and how it is linked to the position you are taking. The review would also need to consider any challenges to the dominant perspective or alternative interpretations which would undermine your position. In these cases, arguments should be presented as to why these alternatives were invalid or irrelevant to the sub-question and the position you have taken. On the other hand, if your position is incompatible with the dominant perspective, then the whole process runs in reverse. This time, the aim is to present arguments as to why the dominant perspective is invalid or irrelevant as well as why the challenges or alternative interpretations are valid and how one or more of those alternatives are linked to the position that you are taking.

Whether you are supporting or challenging the dominant perspective, in a critical review it is always necessary to consider additional perspectives. There are a number of ways in which these additional perspectives can be used. They can be used to question the fundamental assumptions of the dominant perspective, challenge the definitions of key concepts or the validity of the evidence used in that perspective. New perspectives can also be used to explore the manipulation of language in the dominant perspective, including the way that words are used to frame the issue and how they can reveal the author's agenda. Adding new perspectives may mean bringing together, or 'synthesising', two bodies of literature that have not been combined before and assessing whether the new perspective created when you bring them together is internally consistent and coherent. It may also mean bringing together concepts that are usually explored separately and considering how they relate to each other. It is not necessary that each new perspective must disagree with the ones that came before; however, they should bring something new to the discussion, adding to the audience's understanding of the issue.

The final step in this section is the resolution, where you explain what insight your position on that sub-question has given you regarding the main research question. It is important to explain this link because the main purpose behind answering the sub-questions is to shed light onto the main research question. Doing this also helps to link all the sub-question sections together by showing how each one is part of the larger puzzle that is the main research question. The actual linking together of all the sub-questions will need to wait until the conclusion section. In the resolution step of a sub-question section, all you need to do is to establish the insight that one sub-question provides on its own. The challenge of providing insight is common to many types of academic writing and so you may find the guidance on insight included in the chapter on academic writing useful here too (See: Insight, p. 213).

[In the resolution step from one of Himari's sub-question sections] *In summary, I would argue that imprisonment is not incompatible with a belief in freedom as an inalienable right, when viewed from the perspective of Agander's (2001) position that all rights have inherent limits. Thus, there would be nothing inconsistent in the recognition of a right in one context, while also accepting the restriction of that right in another context. By this logic it would be valid to endorse the right to vote for all citizens while also restricting that right in prisoners.*

Conclusion

In the conclusion section of a theoretical research paper, you revisit the main research question stated in the introduction and present your answer to that question. Ideally, this answer should be influenced by the positions you have taken on the various sub-questions, as this would demonstrate why it was necessary to answer the sub-questions in order to find an answer to the main question. It is important that the conclusion offers a synthesis not a summary. If you were to repeat the position you took on each of the sub-questions as a series of separate points in the conclusion, that would be a summary and should be avoided. Instead, the aim is to combine all these positions into one larger point that only becomes obvious when the positions are considered together, which is a synthesis. One way to approach it would be for your answer to the main research question to call on ideas that were mentioned in the various positions you took, so that your audience can see the connection, but without you needing to explicitly state which idea is coming from which position.

As well as presenting an answer to the main research question, the conclusion will usually contain some evaluation of the limitations of your research and some suggestions for future research. Regarding the limitations, the aim here is not to find fault with the execution of your research, but rather to acknowledge the necessary choices you made which shaped what the research did and did not discuss. These limitations have a lot in common with the methodological issues relating to search parameters in the discussion section of a systematic literature review and so you may find the guidance on that section relevant here too (See: Systematic literature review: Discussion, p. 176). One of the reasons for acknowledging such limitations is to use them as the basis for proposing a different approach to exploring your chosen research area or the wider context behind it. However, it is important to note that this suggested future research is not intended to correct or replace the findings of your research, but rather add to them.

Common mistakes

Theoretical research is not a matter of opinion

A common misconception among first-time report writers is the belief that theoretical research is all a matter of opinion and that you can take a position on a sub-question entirely based on your own personal opinions. The problem with this belief is that personal opinions are usually based on personal experience, with little or no awareness of any literature or application of any rational argument. Because of this, personal opinions lack credibility, not because they are wrong, but rather because they offer no reason why the audience should believe them to be right. This mistake can happen in many forms of academic writing, and so the guidance on personal opinions in the academic writing chapter may be of some help here as well (See: Personal opinion vs informed opinion, p. 211). Instead of personal opinion, report writers should base their positions on an *informed* opinion; that is,, an opinion that they have arrived at through a critical review of the literature, supporting their position by connecting it to the writings of others and rational argument. Presenting an informed opinion in this way helps the audience to see how the report writer's position relates to the views of others in the literature. It also helps the audience to see how the report writer formed that opinion in the first place, and why they agree or disagree with the views of others. All of this allows the audience to form their own informed opinions on the positions they are reading about in the report.

Refinements

Deciding which perspectives to include

Even experienced report writers can suffer from uncertainty as to which perspectives they should be including in their discussion of any sub-question. There will always be more perspectives you could discuss than there is space available in the report, and so the challenge is to whittle them down to the most important perspectives. However, this simply raises the question as to how you decide which are the most important ones. The approach to selecting perspectives mentioned in the basics was based on the prominence of a perspective in the literature, and its ability to add something new to the audience's understanding of the issue being discussed. While this approach will, to a certain degree, reduce the list of potential perspectives to choose from, it is likely that there will still be too many perspectives to include them all.

As such, you need to develop the ability to judge the relative importance of the various perspectives, establishing how important each perspective is compared to the others. One technique you can use to develop this skill is that, before you begin writing a sub-section, you first make a list of all the points you want to include. Then, imagine that you were asked to drop one of the perspectives from the list. Pick the one you would choose to exclude. This is a good way to start because you will find it much easier to make the cut when it is only a single perspective you need to leave out. The trick is to repeat that process multiple times, each time picking a new perspective to exclude from among those that remain after excluding the previous one. While the choice gets harder the further you go in this process, you may be surprised how this enables you to whittle down the list to only a handful of perspectives. In doing this, you establish the relative importance of all the perspectives on your list, from the least important, which was first to get excluded, to the most important ones that survived the longest. Once you have established the relative importance of each perspective in this way, you can begin to write the section, adding the perspectives from your list in order of importance, continuing to add perspectives until you run out of space. In that way, you can be confident that any perspectives which had to be left out will not to be missed, as they are less important than the ones you included. Similarly, if you need to go back later and cut a section down because the whole report is too long, the last point in the section can be the first to go as you know it is the least important one.

Advanced

Does a theoretical research report need a method section?

In the basic guidance on a theoretical research report in this chapter, there is no method section mentioned, but the question of whether a method section is needed in this type of report is a matter for debate. Some would argue that a piece of theoretical research does not have a method in the same way that a piece of empirical research does. There are no measures, participants, procedure or their equivalents in theoretical research. Those who reject the idea of including a method section in a theoretical research report would argue that the methods employed in theoretical research are demonstrated through their execution, in other words, through the writing of the report. From this perspective, a separate method section which describes the method is redundant, as reading the report allows the audience to see first-hand the means by which the validity of the assumptions, definitions and other elements of the main research question are evaluated through rational argument.

However, there are some who would distinguish between 'methods' and 'methodology'; the former being the tools and steps employed in the research while the latter is the overall approach being adopted. From this perspective, while it is still true to say that the methods are being demonstrated through the writing of the report, theoretical research also has a methodology which could be articulated in a method section. For example, the report writer could discuss the rationale for their chosen methods of interpretation, such as choosing between interpretive versus descriptive phenomenology or deconstruction versus radical hermeneutics. Similarly, they might discuss the rationale for choices they made regarding the scope of the sources of literature they reviewed, in much the same way that the report writer of a structured literature review might do (See: Systematic literature review: Detailing your search, p. 179). The aim here is not to justify any of these choices, but rather to help the audience to understand the rationale behind the choices. In this way, this form of method section would have some similarities with a positionality sub-section in a qualitative empirical report, and so some of the guidance on that may be helpful here too (See: Positionality, p. 81).

Thus, we can see that the question of whether a method section is needed or not remains within the discretion of the report writer, but should you decide that one is needed, hopefully the guidance offered here can help you to write that section more effectively.

▶ CHAPTER 8: EXERCISES

Please Note: As you are only likely to be using one of the two types of desk-based research at any one time, the exercises have been divided to two separate groups, with one group focused on systematic literature reviews and the other on theoretical research. This allows you to focus your exercises on the type of research you are planning to use right now. As you may end up using the other type of research at a later date, it is better not to look at the answers for any exercises you are not completing this time around.

Systematic literature review

Exercise 1: MCT – Systematic literature review

1) In a systematic literature review the purpose of reviewing the literature is to _____, whereas in a piece of empirical research, the purpose of the literature review is to _____.
   A. pose new research questions, answer the research questions.
   B. answer the research questions, pose new research questions.
   C. answer the research questions, summarise the existing research.
   D. summarise the existing research, pose new research questions.

2) In a systematic literature review, the theoretical model...
   A. is not included because it is only used in empirical research.
   B. identifies shared methods or concepts that influence the outcome of the research in this research area.
   C. identifies deeper concepts and relationships which help explain how things work in the real-world situation which is the focus of the research area.
   D. None of the above.

3) Which of the following information is NOT needed in the method section of a systematic literature review.
   A. A discussion of the ethical precautions that were taken.
   B. The number of sources located in each search and how many were read.
   C. A description of the methods used to access each archive and database.
   D. All of the above.

4) Alphonse is reviewing the literature relating to injury and recovery among professional rock-climbers. His research question seeks to understand the link between the type of safety ropes and injuries. His plan is to locate all the research which includes information about safety ropes and injuries and identify which type of ropes each piece of research found to be the safest. He believes that this will reveal the type of rope which is found to be the safest by the majority of the research. Why would this be a weak analysis?
   A. This might show which type of rope is safest but not the reasons why it is safer than the others.
   B. The analysis does not answer his research question because if you want to understand the links between ropes and injury you need to find out what makes a rope 'safe'.
   C. To properly compare the various pieces of research, you need to combine their data or results, not just count which type of rope each piece of research found to be safest.
   D. All of the above.

5) Among the results from Alphonse's review, he has identified the most effective method of arranging the ropes to avoid injury. He has also found that focusing only on physical injuries can lead the researcher to underestimate the recovery time after a serious accident. In Alphonse's discussion, both of these findings would first be mentioned _____, with the rope arrangement finding further explored in _____ and the focus on physical injury finding explored further in _____.

A. Wider implications, practical applications, methodological issues.
B. Wider implications, past research, methodological issues.
C. Wider implications, practical applications, future research.
D. Past research, practical applications, future research.

Exercise 2: How serious are these mistakes?

A common problem faced by many first-time report writers is judging the relative importance of all the different rules and requirements involved in report writing. How important is it to include an ethics section? How serious a problem is it if you don't relate the results of your analysis back to a research question? With this in mind you will find, in alphabetical order, six common mistakes made by first-time report writers when writing a systematic literature review report. You need to put each of them into one of three categories of importance: serious errors, moderate errors and minor errors.

- Believing that the main aim of a systemic literature review is to pose new unresolved research questions.
- Expecting a systemic review report to be easier or quicker than an empirical report.
- Leaving out the ethics sub-section.
- Not having any search parameters or not mentioning them in your report.
- Not relating the results of your analysis back to your research questions.
- Using an empirical report structure, with separate literature review and analysis.

Theoretical research

Exercise 3: MCT – Theoretical research

1) Titus wants to research misanthropy, a concept which describes the fact that some people prefer being alone. Which of the following would be an example of theoretical research in this area?

A. Comparing stress levels in those people who define misanthropy as a choice they have made to those who define it as a trait they were born with.

B. Comparing findings of the research which explore the relationship between misanthropy and mental health in teenagers to the research looking at that relationship in the elderly.

C. Comparing depictions of misanthropy in popular culture to those in clinical literature.

D. None of the above.

2) Why does a theoretical research report not normally have a method section?

A. The method in a theoretical report is usually demonstrated in the writing of the report and so a method section is not needed.

B. Theoretical research does not involve collecting data and so there is no methodology to report.

C. The methodology in a theoretical report has already been explained in the introduction section instead.

D. None of the above.

3) To take a 'position' on a sub-question in theoretical research means that you are....

A. taking the answer to that sub-question and relating it back to the central research question.

B. criticising the most widely known answer to that question, known as the dominant perspective.

C. expressing your personal opinion on what you think is the answer to that question.

D. presenting your answer to that question based on the literature you have read.

4) The research question is broken down into sub-questions because...

A. it is usually too complex to try and answer it directly.

B. that allows the report writer to break up the research question into smaller parts that can be explored in separate sections.

C. answering the sub-questions will lead to an answer for the research question.

D. All of the above.

5) Which of the following is NOT needed in the conclusion section of a theoretical research report?

A. Repeating the main research question.

B. A summary of the positions you took on the various sub-questions.

C. A review of the limitations to the choices you made during the research.

D. Suggestions regarding future directions for the research in this area.

Exercise 4: How serious are these mistakes?

A common problem faced by many first-time report writers is judging the relative importance of all the different rules and requirements involved in report writing. How important is it to relate the insight from each sub-question back to the main research question? How serious a problem is it to take a position entirely based on personal opinion? With this in mind you will find, in alphabetical order, six common mistakes made by first-time report writers when writing a theoretical research report. You need to put each of them into one of three categories of importance: serious errors, moderate errors and minor errors.

- Expecting a theoretical research report to be easier or quicker than an empirical report.
- Including a method section in a theoretical research report.
- Not identifying any wider context for the research in the introduction section.
- Not relating the insight from each sub-question back to the main research question.
- Summarising your position on each of the sub-questions in the conclusion section.
- Taking a position based entirely on personal opinion.

CHAPTER 8: ANSWERS

Systematic literature review

Exercise 1: MCT – Systematic literature review

Q1: Ans = B (See: Literature review and analysis, p. 174 ↔ A review is not just a summary, p. 178)
Q2: Ans = B (See: Introduction, p. 171)
Q3: Ans = C (See: Introduction, p. 171 ↔ Detailing your search, p. 179)
Q4: Ans = D (See: Literature review and analysis, p. 174 ↔ Quantitative meta-analysis, p. 180)
Q5: Ans = C (See: Discussion, p. 176)

Exercise 2: How serious are these mistakes?

SERIOUS ERRORS

(Believing that the main aim of a systemic literature review is to pose new unresolved research questions. ↔ Not relating the results of your analysis back to your research questions.)

Both of these are serious errors because they completely undermine the central purpose of a systematic literature review, which is to answer research questions about the assumptions, theories, concepts and methods which are behind the research being reviewed. To begin with you cannot achieve this aim if you are more focused on posing new unresolved research questions, which is the main aim of a literature review in an empirical report, rather than answering them, which is the aim of a systematic literature review. Furthermore, presenting an analysis of the literature by itself does not achieve this aim if you don't use the results of that analysis to answer research questions. As such, it is vital that your report identifies the research questions and makes it clear what answers to those questions are provided by the systematic review. (See: Introduction, p. 181 ↔ Literature review and analysis, p. 174 ↔ Discussion, p. 176 ↔ A review is not just a summary, 178.)

MODERATE ERRORS

(Expecting a systemic review report to be easier or quicker than an empirical report. ↔ Not having any search parameters or not mentioning them in your report.)

Both of these are moderate errors owing to the fact that, while they do make your work much less effective, they don't fatally undermine it the way the serious errors do. The search parameters are an important element of the credibility of that review. Not having any parameters is the more serious version of this error, as a haphazard review with no defined parameters is vulnerable to unintentional bias and misrepresenting the research area. If you have parameters but never mention them in your report, this is still a problem as it leaves your audience uncertain what your parameters were, or doubting that you even had any, either of which will undermine their confidence in the report. Underestimating the challenge presented by a systematic literature review is also a problem as it can lead you to be underprepared for the time and effort needed, meaning you don't have enough of either to do the report justice. (See: Before you begin this chapter…, p. 169 ↔ Method, p. 173.)

MINOR ERRORS

(Using an empirical report structure, with separate literature review and analysis. ↔ Leaving out the ethics sub-section.)

Both of these are minor errors in the sense that, although they have a negative impact on the effectiveness of your systematic literature review, the extent of their impact is much more limited than the moderate errors. For example, it should still be possible for your audience to see how the findings of your review of the literature resulted from the review itself, even if the review and findings are in different sections. However, your audience will need to work harder to make those links compared to a layout where the analysis was part of the review. As for the ethics section, although most systematic reviews are entirely based on published sources, which means the ethical precautions needed are minimal, saying as much an ethics section will help your audience to reach the same conclusion. Overall then, these are mistakes you should generally try to avoid making, but you should not worry too much about it if you do end up making one. (See: Literature review and analysis, p. 174 ↔ Method, p. 173.)

Theoretical research

Exercise 3: MCT – Theoretical research

Q1: Ans = C (See: The basics, p. 181)
Q2: Ans = A (See: Does a theoretical research report need a method section? p. 188)
Q3: Ans = D (See: Sub-questions, p. 184 ↔ Theoretical research is not a matter of opinion, p. 187)
Q4: Ans = D (See: Introduction, p. 182 ↔ Sub-questions, p. 184)
Q5: Ans = B (See: Conclusion, p. 186)

Exercise 4: How serious are these mistakes?

SERIOUS ERRORS

(Not relating the insight from each sub-question back to the main research question. ↔ Taking a position based entirely on personal opinion.)

Both of these are serious errors because they completely undermine the central purpose of a piece of theoretical research, which is to deconstruct the theoretical frameworks relating to a concept, proposing revisions to the frameworks and thereby change people's perspective on the concept. Merely taking positions on the sub-questions does not achieve this aim, unless the insights from those positions are related back to the main research question. If your audience cannot see how the answer to the main research question was inspired by your positions on the sub-questions, it will leave them wondering how that answer was achieved and what the point of the sub-questions was. Similarly, it is not possible to achieve this aim by taking a position entirely based on personal opinion as this approach is not using rational argument and so cannot offer a credible revised framework which would change someone's perspective on the concept. (See: The basics, p. 181 ↔ Sub-questions, p. 184 ↔ Conclusion, p. 186 ↔ Theoretical research is not a matter of opinion, p. 187.)

MODERATE ERRORS

(Expecting a theoretical research report to be easier or quicker than an empirical report. ↔ Not identifying any wider context for the research in the introduction section.)

Both of these are moderate errors owing to the fact that, while they do make your work much less effective, they don't fatally undermine it the way the serious errors do. Regarding the first error, underestimating the challenge represented by a theoretical research report can lead you to be underprepared for the time and effort needed, meaning you don't have enough of either to do the report justice. Regarding the second error, if you do not explain to your audience how your research is connected to a wider context, it may cause your audience to doubt the importance of the research findings. Making the connection to a wider context demonstrates that this research matters and so the findings will also matter. While it is true that neither of these negative outcomes is guaranteed to happen as a result of these errors, there is an unacceptably high likelihood that they could happen, and so the errors should definitely be avoided. (See: Before you begin this chapter..., p. 169 ↔ Introduction, p. 182.)

MINOR ERRORS

(Summarising your position on each of the sub-questions in the conclusion section. ↔ Including a method section in a theoretical research report.)

Both of these are minor errors in the sense that, although they have a negative impact on the effectiveness of your theoretical research, the extent of their impact is much more limited than the moderate errors. For example, while it is wasting space to repeat your position on each sub-question in the conclusion, having already stated those positions earlier in the report, the amount of space wasted is not large and so the amount of harm done is small. The second issue, including a method section in a theoretical report, is not guaranteed to be an error. In some theoretical reports a method section could actually be of use and is worth including. In those cases where the method section was not needed it is a waste of space, although not likely to be a large one. Overall then, these are mistakes you should generally try to avoid making, but you should not worry too much about it if you do end up making one. (See: Conclusion, p. 186 ↔ Does a theoretical research report need a method section? p. 188.)

9

Academic writing

Unlike the majority of other chapters in this book, each of which focuses on a different section of the report, this chapter will explore a style of writing known as 'academic writing' which you are expected to use throughout the report. The aim of academic writing is to provide insightful answers, and it achieves this aim by presenting evidence and then drawing conclusions from that evidence. All of this is done within a pre-arranged structure which helps to ensure clarity and consistency. Other important elements of the academic writing style include techniques such as drafting and signposting, as well as aiming to be concise and being precise in your use of language. When done correctly, the academic writing style should ensure that your report is read and understood by the widest possible audience, while also making sure that they find the points you make both credible and persuasive.

▶ THE BASICS

When we first learn to write, the act of writing is presented as having a single purpose, 'communication'. At that early stage, our learning focuses on mastering the rules of grammar and spelling so that we can communicate clearly and without error. It is only later that we begin to learn about other styles of writing with other purposes, as well as the structures and techniques used to achieve those purposes. Examples include poetry, where we employ metre and symbolism for the purpose of producing an emotional response or drama where we divide the story into acts and limit the amount of information provided to our audience for the purpose of building tension.

DOI: 10.4324/9781003107965-9

As we progress through our education we encounter a style of writing known as the 'academic writing' style. We are encouraged to use this style more and more in the assignments and exercises we write. Just like the other writing styles we have discussed, the academic style has a purpose and it employs various techniques and structures to achieve that purpose. Using a research report as our example of a piece of academic writing, we will now discuss what the purpose of a report is, and how it achieves that purpose through the use of academic arguments and structure.

Purpose

The central purpose behind all academic writing is a search for the truth. While that might sound very lofty and abstract, it will sound more familiar if you think of it as a search for an answer to a question, where the correct answer is the 'truth'. In academic writing activities there is always a question in need of an answer, whether it is the essay question at the heart of your essay or the research questions at the heart of your report. When you write your report you are attempting to answer the research questions. However, answering research questions is a complex job, and the secret to completing any complex job is to have a plan, a 'blueprint' which helps you to break the job down into less-complex tasks and ensures that you don't forget any of those tasks. In the case of a research report your plan is ready and waiting for you, in the form of the report structure.

Structure

There are many different types of academic pieces, with essays and reports being the two types you are likely to know best. Each type has a structure, a pattern that anyone writing that type of piece is supposed to follow. The research report has one of the most complex structures of all the different types of academic pieces. Learning all the ins and outs of that structure for the first time can feel both intimidating and stifling, as if the endless rules of report writing were designed to make the job harder. In reality, while all the details of the report structure are undeniably challenging to learn, once you get to know it, you may start to see how all that structure can actually help you in a number of ways when it comes to achieving effective writing.

The structure takes the overall job of the report, which is to answer the research questions, and breaks it down into separate tasks, with each section of the report assigned a specific task. When we reviewed each of the sections of the report in the other chapters of this book, the task that has been assigned to any section or sub-section was referred to as its 'aim'. Achieving its aim should be the focus of any section, and every piece of information in that section should be helping to achieve it. You can use this focus as a filter, helping you to decide what information does or does not belong in each section and sub-section. Therefore, when you are thinking of adding any piece of information to any section of the report, you should always be asking yourself how this information helps to achieve the aim of that section? Any information which does not help to achieve the aim of the section probably does not belong there.

The other benefit of the structure, apart from helping to break the job down, is that it acts like a blueprint, providing the report writer with an identifiable space for each and every bit of information they need to include in the report. Report writing becomes about placing each piece of information about that research in the section or sub-section to which it belongs. In the same way you might pat your pockets before you leave the house to make sure you haven't forgotten anything important, checking each of the sections and sub-sections of the report structure can give you a warning about forgotten or misplaced information. Finding any section left empty or incomplete tells you that you have forgotten to include some information or put it in the wrong section.

Argument

While the structure of the report does most of the work in telling you what to include and where to put it, there is one key ingredient that is expected in almost every section, and that is academic argument. In everyday language an 'argument' usually refers to a dispute or disagreement between two or more people. In academic writing, however, presenting an 'argument' refers to presenting your audience with some evidence and then offering a conclusion based on that evidence. As such, in academic writing there do not need to be two sides or a disagreement for it to be referred to as an 'argument'.

The essential components of an academic argument are evidence and a conclusion based on that evidence. Thus, each time you present your audience with some evidence and draw a conclusion based on that evidence you are presenting an argument. Sometimes the conclusion comes first and the evidence for that conclusion follows-on afterwards, such as when you tell your audience about a choice or decision you have made and then offer reasons for that choice.

You will find that you are including academic arguments throughout your report. In the introduction you talk about many of the choices you have made, such as the wider context you have chosen or the research area within that context you have decided to focus on, in both cases presenting reasons for those choices (See: Introduce the research context, p. 14 and Identify the research area, p. 14). In each of the sub-sections of your literature review you present evidence in the form of the findings from related sources and offer a conclusion at the end of the sub-section which identifies the key finding or unresolved question from those sources (See: Structuring your review, p. 38). Similarly, in each of the sub-sections of your results you present evidence in the form of the analysis and key finding, before sharing a conclusion in the form of the answer to the research question that key finding has demonstrated (See: Relevance of the findings, p. 97). Finally, in your discussion you are offering conclusions on many things, such as the relevance of your findings to other research (See: Past research, p. 119) or the effectiveness of your methodology (See: Methodological issues, p. 120).

As such, throughout your report, whenever you are including evidence you should be asking yourself where you will be providing a conclusion on that evidence? Similarly, if you are talking about a choice or decision, you should be asking yourself where you have provided reasons for that choice? There are some places in the report where it may look like this rule does not apply, such as in the abstract, method, references and appendices sections. In those sections you will often be presenting evidence but not offering any conclusions. This is because the conclusions about that evidence are offered elsewhere in the report. For example, while there is evidence about your sources in the references section, the conclusions about those sources and what they reveal are offered in the literature review section. Similarly, much of the evidence about the methodology is mentioned in the method section, but most of the conclusions about the suitability of that methodology are in the discussion section. So, as you can see, the evidence in these sections is still part of an evidence-conclusion pair which forms an academic argument, although it is harder to spot owing to the fact that the evidence and conclusion are in different sections. Thankfully, everywhere else in the report your evidence and conclusions will appear together within the same section. This should make it easier for you to notice when you leave out either one and so fail to form an argument.

▶ COMMON MISTAKES

Failing to form an argument

Although an academic argument requires a combination of evidence and a conclusion, first-time report writers sometimes make the mistake of presenting one or the other but not both. On the one hand, they may know what the evidence is saying but are unsure what conclusions to draw from it. In these situations, they may cling to the false hope that as long as they 'pile on' more and more evidence, the sheer amount of it will somehow be its own conclusion. Instead, stating a lot of facts but not offering any conclusions will come across as being too descriptive or will be said to lack insight or critical discussion. This is a common mistake in the results section, where first-time report writers will 'bury you' in analysis but not use it to answer any research questions. On the other hand, it is equally bad to state conclusions without providing the evidence needed to support those conclusions. This can happen when the report writer believes that the conclusion is true but is unable to find the evidence to support that belief. A lot of first-time report writers do this in their literature review section. In such situations, they may retreat behind vague claims such as "Research has found…" or "It is believed…" without providing any actual evidence, as if claiming that there must be evidence somewhere was enough. Instead, making claims without supporting evidence comes across as wild guesses or personal opinions. The lesson here is that you should never be presenting evidence without a conclusion or vice versa. There are some places in the report where the evidence and conclusion may appear in different sections (See: Argument, p. 119), but doesn't break the rule of always having one if you have the other. The requirement to present both evidence and a conclusion every single time may be frustrating, but the discipline it teaches produces both good writing and good research.

Trying to sound 'academic'

A very common mistake made by first-time report writers is to make radical changes to their vocabulary when they write. They are trying to mimic the style they see in the textbooks and journals, which in their mind involves a lot of large words and complicated sentences. The problem comes from trying to force every sentence into this style by replacing everyday words with technical terms or by using lots of adjectives and adverbs. In this style, bigger and more complicated is always better, as if "The doctor walked into the room" would sound better if you said it as "The dispenser of remedies proceeded henceforth into the designated vestibule". In reality, instead of sounding more 'academic', it sounds bizarre and artificial, like a bad computer translation from another language.

While you may need to use some technical terms, there will typically only be a handful of those that are essential and must be used. These essential terms are usually the names of concepts or theories which are also used by other researchers to refer to important elements of the research area or theoretical model. The rest of your language does not need to be complicated to be suitable for an academic writing style.

As a good rule-of-thumb, if you are using words in almost every sentence which most people would find odd or unfamiliar, and they are not a technical term used by other researchers, then the chances are you may be trying too hard to sound 'academic'. If you can communicate an idea clearly and effectively using simple language then you should do that. This does not prevent you from making some additions to your vocabulary or using a less common word if it has a specific meaning that is important to the idea you are trying to communicate, but additions like that should be gradual and used sparingly.

Too conversational

While you do not need to completely reinvent the vocabulary that you use every day when writing reports (See: Trying to sound 'academic', p. 201), it is also possible to go too far in the other direction, make no changes at all and sound too 'conversational'. The bulk of the vocabulary you use in report writing should be similar to what you might use in everyday conversation, but there are a few important differences. One type of everyday vocabulary that does not belong in an academic writing style are colloquialisms or slang. A 'colloquialism' is an everyday expression which is being used figuratively, not literally. For example, if you were to call something "lousy", you probably mean it is badly done or poor quality, but not "infested with lice", which is the literal meaning of lousy. Another example is describing a choice as a "cop out" or "soft option", meaning a choice that was made to avoid a more difficult or unpleasant option. Our everyday language contains many of these expressions that we have forgotten are colloquialisms because they are understood by everyone around us. The problem with colloquialisms is that they only make sense to people who grew up in the culture that uses them, which can limit your audience. This undermines one of the aims of academic writing which is to be accessible to the widest possible audience. As such, an academic writing style should aim to use its vocabulary in as literal a way as possible and that means no colloquialisms or figures of speech. If you wish to avoid colloquialisms, a helpful thought exercise is to phase everything you are writing as if you are speaking to a tourist who has only just arrived in the country.

Say it again, but with less explanation

A common problem among first-time report writers is that they spend too much time explaining their points. This is a writing style they have seen in teaching materials such as textbooks and lectures, both of which spend a lot of time explaining things, much like the book you are reading right now. While that style is entirely suitable for textbooks or lectures, as explanation is often the main purpose of most teaching materials, explanation is not the main purpose of a piece of academic writing. The main purpose of academic writing, as mentioned before, is to answer a question using academic argument, presenting evidence and then drawing conclusions from that evidence. While some explanation is necessary to achieve this purpose, it should be kept to a minimum.

For this reason, when adopting an academic writing style, the writer should always be seeking to reduce the amount of explanation they provide to the bare minimum needed to understand the evidence presented or the conclusion being drawn. As well as leaving out explanations that are not needed, it is about being efficient with language, never using four words where three would do. While it is possible to take this practice too far and leave out an explanation that was important, this happens much less frequently than including too much.

The never-ending sentence

As you read a sentence it will present you with a number of points which you have to keep in mind until the end of the sentence. If there is only a point or two, such as you find in a simple sentence, this is not hard. The more points a single sentence 'throws at you', however, the harder it is to keep them all active in your mind at the same time. If the sentence goes on too long or 'throws' too many points at you, then you're going to forget some of the points made, which means the overall point that the whole sentence is making will be lost.

For this reason, as a rule-of-thumb, if you are writing in a size-12-pt font, you should try to avoid your sentence extending beyond three lines on the page. With smaller or larger font size that target length should be shorter or longer, respectively. Another way in which you can overcomplicate a sentence is with an excessive use of commas. We tend to use commas to mark the boundary between two parts of sentence in which we are usually making two different points, much like I am doing in this sentence. For this reason, more commas will usually mean more points within the same sentence. As such, two or three commas, which can mean three or four points in a single sentence, should be your upper limit in a single sentence.

If you find that any of your sentences are too long then they should be broken up. A longer sentence making multiple points can be broken up into two or more sentences with each sentence now making only one point. Often this can be easily done by replacing some of the commas with full stops. When breaking one sentence into two in this way, it may help to add a signpost word like 'Therefore' or' However' to the second sentence to show that the points in the two sentences are related (See: Signpost words, p. 207). These rules on sentence length are not carved in stone, but they can be useful guidelines to warn you when a sentence may be running on too long as well as what you can do about it.

Being too short

Almost all forms of academic writing have a recommended word length. Many first-time report writers make the mistake of assuming the recommended word length is like a speed limit; thinking they are following the rules as long as they don't go over it. However, it is worth double-checking with your supervisor or publisher if that is the case with the report you are writing. In some cases the recommended word length should be viewed as a minimum not a maximum, and you are encouraged to aim for somewhere in between 100% and 110% of that recommended length. Whether the rules suggest you aim for just under or just over it, you should always aim to be close to this recommended length. By comparison, handing in a report that is a lot shorter than the recommended length is almost always a bad sign.

This should not be seen as an argument for quantity over quality. Instead, you should think of the shortness of the report is a symptom of a problem, not the problem itself. The reason why you should want your report to be close to the recommended word length is because that suggests you are including all the points that are necessary in the report and discussing those points in the right amount of detail. If your report is too short, on the other hand, that suggests that you are leaving out something important.

A common reason offered by first-time report writers when their report is too short is that they have run out of important things to say. The worst thing to do in such a situation is to try and 'pad out' your report to get it up the recommended length. Adding material that you do not think is important or saying the same points in a more long-winded way can actually make your report worse, not better (See: Say it again, but with less explanation, p. 202). Instead, if your report is to too short you should use this book as a trouble-shooting guide, double-checking you have covered all the basics in each section. If that still leaves you short, it may then be time to consider some of the recommendations in the various 'refinements' sections throughout this book. Alternatively, you can consult your supervisor and either share a draft or discuss what you are doing in each section with them to see if they can help you pinpoint the missing elements. If nothing else works, and you report is still too short, then the only option left is to hand in the report as it is. The feedback you get should help you identify what is missing so that the next time you will know what to include. In the end, as you become a more experienced report writer you should begin to find that the far greater challenge is to keep your report from being too long.

Personal pronouns

There is some debate over the question of whether it is correct to use personal pronouns when discussing your research. Some commentators believe that personal pronouns such as I, we, my or our do not belong in a research report. They would prefer that the passive voice was used throughout. Instead of saying, "I approached two hundred train drivers and invited them to participate in my research", you would write, "Two hundred train drivers were approached and invited to participate in the current research". There is no absolute right or wrong in this issue, it is entirely determined by the preferences of the course or publisher for whom you are writing the report. For this reason, it's always a good idea to get an official response from those individuals on what they consider the proper use of pronouns.

▶ REFINEMENTS

Drafting and re-drafting

When it comes to academic writing, no one gets it perfectly right on the first try. Take this section you are reading right now, the current version of which is very different from the original version I produced in my first attempt at writing it. As part of the process of writing this section, I will have had several attempts at writing each sentence, writing the sentence, reading it back to myself and then often re-writing it to make it clearer or to remove things that sounded wrong when I read them. Each attempt at writing something is referred to as a 'draft', with the first attempt being the first draft, the second attempt being the second draft and so on.

This is not some special effort I made with just this section; it is something I have done throughout the book. In case you were wondering how much of a difference this process makes, I've preserved my first attempt at writing this section so you can read it below.

> *No-one gets it exactly right on the first try. Take this sentence you are reading right now on this page. Chances are the version of the sentence you are reading is very different from the version I wrote down when I first wrote it. I may have had several goes a*

writing the sentence. Writing it, reading it back to myself and then re-writing it to make it clearer or to remove things that sounded wrong when I read them. Each attempt at writing something is referred to as a draft. Often people will number their drafts to help keep track of them; 1st draft, 2nd draft, 3rd draft and so on.

As you can see, this first draft is different from the final draft, although still recognisable as the same section, making approximately the same points. Sometimes the changes are only minor, as they appear to be here, but other times the changes are more dramatic, moving large chunks of text around or adding some and removing others. In reality, the changes to this section are more extensive than they first appear, as you need to consider that everything I am writing here, following the preserved copy of my first draft, is entirely new. The first draft of the entire section ended with "...3rd draft and so on", but in this final draft I realised there were other points I wanted to add.

One of the most effective methods to re-draft your own work is to read it to yourself out loud. For some reason, actually hearing the words spoken out loud can give you an entirely new perspective compared to saying them to yourself inside your head. When reading out loud, you are much more likely to hear mistakes, poor phrasing, overly long sentences, points that don't make sense and a host of other issues that are completely invisible to you up to that point. Reading out loud also helps you to take on the point of view of your audience, and you will find yourself asking questions such as "What is the point being made here and why was it included?" There is one catch to this approach of drafting and re-drafting though, it is time-consuming. Unless you plan this in advance, leaving enough time to write, read, re-write and then possibly repeat before the submission deadline, then this option is off the table. Procrastinators who leave their work to the last minute end up needing to submit their first draft, not because they think it is perfect, but because they have run out of time.

If you can build in the time for re-drafting your work into your timetable, it offers you a number of advantages. One such advantage is that your first draft can be as messy as you like. When faced with any section of the report, you can literally write the first thing that pops into your head and not worry about how it sounds or how much sense it makes because you know you are going to change it later. Don't worry about how much sense it makes or the structure at this stage, just get all your ideas out on the page. Fussing too much over the details at this point can actually get in the way and inhibit your creativity. Once you have all the ideas out there on the page, you can worry about how it all fits together. This can also be a great way to get past that horrible 'blank page' phase that most writers find so intimidating.

You will find that re-writing is so much easier than writing for the first time. Even if you find the first draft is a complete 'write-off' and you don't want to keep any of it, that draft still served a purpose. This is because once you have something written on the page, the whole report seems a lot less scary and a lot more manageable. The other big advantage from drafting is that it helps you to catch a lot of your mistakes before anyone else sees them. Most examiners and reviewers will tell you that the overwhelming majority of mistakes they correct would practically 'jump off the page at you' if you read back through your work carefully enough. So, finish your first draft early, find somewhere you can read out loud to yourself without feeling foolish and let the re-drafting commence.

Signpost words

When writing a paragraph, the most common approach is to present a series of points, with each of these points provided as evidence, all of which get drawn together in the conclusion at the end of the paragraph. In order to make sense of the conclusion, the audience will need to remember each point presented in the paragraph, but if these points are presented as independent from each other it will be hard for your audience to keep them all in mind. The relationship between the points, which may be so clear in the mind of the report writer, may not be clear to the audience.

One way you can help the audience to remember all the points made is to provide signals, called 'signposts', which tell the audience how the points fit together. As the name suggests, these 'signposts' tell the reader where you are going next by revealing at the start of the sentence how this point relates to the point that came before it. In this way, 'signpost' words and phrases help the audience to construct their own picture of the overall point that the paragraph is making as they go along. In doing so, the audience are less likely to forget points and they will be prepared for the overall point that the conclusion is making, which should make it easier for them to understand it.

In the table following you will find some examples of signpost words and expressions which include explanations of what they mean and examples of their use. These are just some of the words that can be used as signposts; there are many others with similar meanings, and so you should feel free to use whichever ones feel like the best 'fit' for your writing style. It is also a good idea to avoid using the same signpost word repeatedly, as this can become very noticeable and distracting; rotating between a few options for each type of word every time you use one is recommended.

Words/Expressions	What they signal	Example
Similarly/In the same way/In addition/In keeping with researcher X's findings...	This next point is going to agree with the point that came before it.	Lamas (2011) found that taller male students were rated as more attractive. Similarly, Mortell (2012) suggested that shorter men would be less likely to be chosen as prospective mates.
Nevertheless/Even so/Despite this...	This next point is going to fail to support the point that came before it.	Lamas (2011) found that taller male students were more attractive. Nevertheless, Shabot (2013) could not reproduce this finding in the workplace.
However/Yet/But/On the contrary/Conversely/On the other hand...	This next point is going to contradict the point that came before it.	Lamas (2011) found that taller male students were more attractive. However, Kranzel (2014) stated that wealth, not height, was the main factor in most women's choice of a life partner.
Next/Then/Following on from this/Furthermore/Subsequently...	This next point is a development of the point that came before it.	Lamas (2011) found that taller male students were rated as being more attractive. Next, Harrison (2015) found that height affected the attractiveness of younger but not older men.
Firstly, Secondly, Thirdly, Finally...	All these points are part of one larger point.	Firstly, Lamas (2011) found that height affected attractiveness. Secondly, Kranzel (2014) highlighted the importance of financial resources. Finally, Harrison (2015) showed age was also a factor.
Therefore/Hence/For this reason/It follows that/As a result/Thus/Consequently...	You are about to state a conclusion that is based on the point(s) that have proceeded this one.	Therefore, it would appear that a combination of height, age and wealth is the best explanation of attractiveness in most men.

As well as helping to link the various points within a paragraph together, signposts can be used at the start of a paragraph to help signal how the overall point of that paragraph relates to the overall point of the previous paragraph. In this way you can link the overall points from various paragraphs within a section together, thereby helping your audience to remember them and make sense of your conclusion for that section.

Table of contents, list of tables and list of figures

For longer pieces of academic writing, it can be helpful to add some lists at the start of the work which indicate the page numbers for various key features. The most common example if this kind of list is the 'Table of contents', which contains a list of all the sections and sub-sections in the piece along with their names and page numbers. You can find a table of contents at the start of this book. Other examples are the 'List of tables' or the 'List of figures', which contain the names and page numbers for each of the tables or figures found in the piece of writing. The purpose of these lists is to make it easier for your audience to navigate their way through larger pieces of writing as well as helping them to locate a section or table they are looking for.

Not all pieces of academic writing have these lists; in fact, most shorter pieces don't include them. There is no rule as to how long a piece needs to be in order to require these lists. You may wish to inquire with your supervisor or editor if they think your piece requires them or not. If that doesn't settle the matter then a rule-of-thumb is that a piece shorter than ten-thousand words almost never needs them, between ten and twenty thousand occasionally needs them, between twenty and forty thousand usually needs them and above forty thousand almost always needs them.

Because these lists contain page numbers, they are typically something you create after all other drafting is complete, so that there won't be any changes to the locations of any of the features you are listing. The contents of each list are presented in the same order that those contents appear in piece of writing. The name of each item appears on the left-hand side of the page, justified left, while the page number appears on the right-hand side of the same line, justified right. Sometimes there is a line of dashes or dots between the name and the page number to make it easier to see which name links with which page.

These lists usually appear in between the title page and the first page of the piece itself. Typically, the page numbering for the pages which contain these lists is not part of the page numbering used in the rest of the piece. To indicate this, the pages containing the lists are often numbered with lower-case Roman numerals (i, ii, iii...). On the first page after the final list, which is usually the first page of the rest of the piece, the page numbering begins again, this time using Arabic numerals (1,2,3...).

Labelling tables and figures

If you are including a table or a figure in a piece of academic writing you will need to include a label for it, explaining to your audience what the table or figure contains. A 'table' is a grid of boxes, known as 'cells', arranged in rows and columns with each cell holding a separate piece of information. A 'figure' is any kind of image, including pictures, diagrams, charts and graphs among other things. The reason that both of these need a label is that it is often less obvious to the audience than it is to the report writer what the table or figure contains. For this reason, any table or figure should always come with a label.

Both the tables and figures should be numbered, with one series of numbers for the tables and a separate series for the figures. As such, the first table to appear anywhere in the piece of writing is Table 1, the second is Table 2 and so on. The series for the figures is separate, and so the first figure would be "Figure 1" and so on. The numbering in each series is continuous throughout the entire piece of writing and never restarts. It is for this reason that, for example, the number for first table in the appendices follows on from the number of the last table in the rest of the report (See: Appendices: Tidy up those statistical appendices, p. 161).

The label should state the type of object, table or figure, followed by the number for that table or figure, then followed by a description of the contents.

"Table 1: Average number of goals scored by each striker in each team."

The descriptive section of the label should explain what the figure or table is presenting in clear and simple terms and should aim to be no longer than two lines on the page. Finally, the location of the label is different for the two types of content, with the label appearing above a table and below a figure.

Effective quotation

The amount of quoting from other sources that you see in academic writing varies from subject to subject, but what they all have in common is the desire to only use quotations when necessary. In some subjects, you don't see many or even any quotations from other sources, and even in those subjects that do use quotations they are used sparingly. The reasons for this are that quotations are often unnecessary and inefficient. Unless the exact words used in the quoted source matter somehow, then a quotation is not necessary. The inefficiency of quoting another source comes from the fact that a quotation will use more space to make a point than it would take for you to make the same point in your own words and simply cite the source as a reference. Part of the reason they use so much space, as we will see later, comes from the need to explain the point the quotation is making. Thus, make the point using your own words and citing the source will always be a more efficient use of space than quoting and having to explain the quotation. The other big advantage of making the point in your own words, over using a quotation, is that a point made in your own words will fit in much better with the surrounding sentences. A quotation will often disrupt the flow of the section, making it harder to connect to the points that precede and follow it and so make it harder to connect all the points in that section together into the overall point that the section is making.

As such, when you are considering the use of a quotation you should always be asking yourself why a quote is necessary? One such situation where quoting can be necessary is in defining key concepts. This is because, when you are defining a concept, the exact words used do matter. In fact, many of the great debates in any given research area hinge on competing definitions of the same concept, with the various definitions differing by only one or two words. As such, using a quotation to both identify the specific definition you subscribe to and the exact words used in that definition is both necessary and efficient. The other situation where quoting another source becomes necessary is when the source is one of the things that the research is analysing, such as in a documentary analysis or research which takes place in a literary subject, such as English Literature. In these cases, quoting the source is much like quoting a participant in your research. Therefore, you should approach quoting that source in the same way and for the same reasons as you would quote the response of a participant (See: Summary data, tables and graphs, p. 104).

In those situations where a quote is necessary there are some rules to follow to ensure you make that quotation as efficient and effective as possible. First, try to only include the essential elements of the section of work you a quoting. Using the same techniques that are used to manage quotations from participants, you can cut down a large quotation into just those elements that are really necessary (See: Summary data, tables and graphs, p. 104). Any context needed to make sense of the quotation can be provided in your own words. Second, after using a quotation, it is always necessary to add an explanation of the point the quotation is making and the way in which that point relates to the overall point being made in the section where the quotation is being included. By following these rules, you can make sure that those few times you do use a quotation, it has all the impact it should.

Personal opinion vs. informed opinion

Some academic writers feel they have no 'voice' in the pieces they write, that they are not allowed to express an opinion and are instead reduced to repeating the views of others. In reality, though, the academic writer does have a voice and their opinion is actually an essential component of the academic writing style as long as that opinion is an 'informed' opinion. An informed opinion is a point of view which the opinion-holder has arrived at based on the evidence they have reviewed. As such, it is the evidence that is informing that opinion. This could be an informed opinion on a topic within the literature review that has been informed by the findings of previous research on that topic. It could also be an informed opinion as to the correct answer to a research question based on the results of the analysis. As we can see from both of these examples, an informed opinion could also be called an interpretation of the evidence. 'Interpreting' means reviewing the evidence and then stating the outcome of that review, usually also offering a reason for making that specific interpretation. For example, if there was a disagreement in the previous research on some issue, after reviewing this evidence, your interpretation might be that you agree more with one side of the debate because they have more convincing evidence. This is something we do every time we offer a conclusion on some evidence, and since evidence and conclusions are essential to academic writing, we can see why informed opinions are also essential to academic writing.

If that doesn't sound like an opinion to you, then it is likely that what you are thinking of is what might be called a personal opinion. 'Personal' opinions can exist before you have gathered any evidence, based on your personal experiences or things you have heard from non-academic sources, such as the internet, social media or casual conversations with friends and family. The problem with this kind of experience/opinion is that it is vulnerable to bias, misunderstandings and limited scope. One of the reasons we engage in research in such a formal manner, reviewing literature, gathering and analysing data, is to get a better more reliable form of evidence on which to base our conclusions. For all of these reasons, personal opinions do not qualify as evidence or a conclusion in academic writing. At best, personal opinions are unreliable; at worst, they are little more than prejudice dressed up as something respectable. The writer E. B. White put it best when he said "Prejudice is a great time saver. You can form opinions without having to get the facts".

The one place where a personal experience or observations can play a role in academic writing can be to illustrate a point; providing an example to help explain a piece of evidence or conclusion and make it clearer. For example, you might say

> Freud claimed that we can end up projecting our unacceptable desires onto others. I have seen this in some young children who are prone to making up stories but tend to call other people liars when those stories are shown to be untrue.

The personal experience here is being used to offer an example of what Freud was saying. It doesn't offer any evidence to say that Freud is correct about his claim.

▶ ADVANCED

Insight

You may have noticed how often throughout this book we have talked about looking "beneath the surface" and about things being discovered or revealed. It is as if the researcher is a magician, constantly pulling rabbits out of hats or finding coins behind your ear. The 'magic' that research reveals to you is universe that surrounds you, but a research report is aiming to offer more than just a list of things you didn't know about that universe. The hope is that sharing this new information will give you a new way of looking at the universe. This new perspective is called 'insight' and if the universe is the magic trick, then insight would be someone pulling back the curtain to show you part of how the trick is done.

Insight is something you would hope to include any time you are offering a conclusion. In a literature review, this means you would aim to offer insight in all those places where you share conclusions as part of an academic argument (See: Argument, p. 119). Examples of this include in the results section, you would hope that key findings from the analyses will provide an insight into the issues that the research questions are asking about (See: Relevance of the findings, p. 97). Another example would be in the wider implications sub-section of the report, where you hope the answers to your research questions will offer a new insight into both the research area and wider context (See: Wider implications, p. 118). The aim here is to go beyond merely pointing out that your findings are relevant to the research questions or wider context, but rather that they offer an entirely new way of looking at those things.

Providing insight is one of the most challenging aspects of academic writing. To begin with, in order to share insight, you need to achieve it yourself. You need to discover a new perspective through the activities mentioned above: reviewing literature, analysing data or reflecting on your research. While there is no simple recipe for achieving insight, there are a few thought exercises which can potentially help to spark some insight. At the most basic level, insight can arise from learning something new. As such, after reviewing some literature or analysing some data you should be asking yourself what you know now that you did not know before? If you have learnt several things you may need to evaluate their relative importance and identify the most important one. How you judge that relative importance is up to you, but among the possible methods would be to value new knowledge for being exciting, original, practical, challenging or provocative. It is important that you are able to explain to your audience what makes your chosen insight important and what new perspective it offers, as these are the details that will help your audience to share in that insight with you. Another potential route to insight would be to consider if your research reveals a deeper knowledge, which is not represented by any one of those things you learnt but rather a realisation that only came to you when you considered several of those things together. It is more challenging to achieve insight via this second route, but the reward can be a deeper more important insight. Still, this route may be one to leave until you have a little more practice at achieving insight.

Criticality

Any academic course or publisher will tell you that criticality is a vital element in the submissions they receive, although if you ask them to explain what criticality is, the answers are not always as informative as they should be. Explanations regarding the nature of criticality often make it sound like you are required to review strengths and weaknesses or present the views of two sides who disagree. While criticism and debate are valid examples of criticality, they are not essential. Criticality can still be demonstrated even if all the perspectives you find are in agreement and without you needing to find fault in any of them. Instead, the most essential element of criticality is scepticism, which can be thought of as maintaining doubt or reserving judgement. Thus, criticality means not accepting things at face value and not settling for the first answer you find, but instead, to double-check the validity of that answer and comparing it to others.

Criticality can be demonstrated in different ways depending on which section of the report is being written. In the literature review section, demonstrating criticality means that any topic being discussed needs to include contributions from more than one perspective (See: Structuring your review, p. 38). This means locating different sources who are all discussing the same topic and exploring what they each have to say about it. If they happen to disagree, then you have a debate and you can try to resolve it (See: Debates in the literature, p. 53). But, even if they all agree, that is still demonstrating criticality as you did not settle for the first source. That being said, it would be unusual for multiple sources to all say exactly the same thing. Each of the sources may agree on the essentials, while still offering different evidence to support their answer or including additional details not considered by the others. Where possible, you should indicate what each additional source has to offer above and beyond what the others had already contributed.

In the other sections of the report, criticality is more often demonstrated through taking a critical perspective on the methodology of your research. For example, in the method section, criticality can be demonstrated in those situations when it is necessary for you to justify certain choices in your research design (See:

Design, p. 64). Another example of criticality in the method section is when you discuss the reliability or validity of your materials (See: Materials, p. 68). This form of criticality can also be demonstrated in the results section, where reliability analyses for your research may be reported (See: Additional testing, p. 106). Finally, in the discussion, these issues and others can be reflected on further when discussing methodological issues (See: Methodological issues, p. 120). All of these are examples of criticality, as they indicate that you are double-checking your method both pre- and post-data collection, and that you are presenting the results of those checks to your audience for further public scrutiny.

▶ CHAPTER 9: EXERCISES

Exercise I: MCT

1) What is the main purpose of the academic writing style?
   A. To clearly explain the theories and concepts behind the piece.
   B. To find the correct answers to the questions at the heart of the piece.
   C. To present all the evidence and allow the audience to draw their own conclusions.
   D. None of the above.

2) Even though the structure of a report is complicated, why should it still be seen as helpful?
   A. It gives the writer a place for each piece of information, helping them to spot if something is missing or in the wrong place.
   B. It gives the reader a way of finding things within the report.
   C. It gives each section of the report a job to do, which helps the writer to decide which information belongs in each section.
   D. All of the above.

3) In order for something to be considered an academic argument there needs to be both _____ and _____.
   A. evidence, an explanation of that evidence
   B. evidence, conclusions based on that evidence
   C. questions, conclusions which answer those questions
   D. questions, evidence which is relevant to those questions

4) When faced with a choice between the type of language you use every day and the type of language which uses more formal terminology, you should...
   A. Stick with the language you use very day because you understand it better.
   B. Aim to include as much terminology as you can so as to avoid sounding too conversational.

C. Use a mixture, employing some simpler everyday language and some terminology when needed.

D. Not worry about it, as long as the spelling and grammar are both correct.

5) While there are things about the way that I have written this sentence, which may be a problem, depending on the rules which govern the piece you are writing, there is one thing about it that is a clear example of poor academic writing, and so should definitely be avoided every time, what is it?

A. The use of a personal pronoun.

B. Too many commas.

C. Stating an opinion.

D. Too much explanation.

6) Including an opinion in a piece of academic writing is....

A. only acceptable if clearly identified as an opinion.

B. only acceptable if it is based on the evidence.

C. a good example of criticality.

D. a bad example of trying too hard to sound 'academic'.

7) When drafting and re-drafting a piece of academic writing, it is very important that you _____ but you also want to make sure that you _____.

A. leave enough time to do it, do not worry about how rough your first draft is.

B. read it aloud to yourself, avoid making too many changes so that you don't lose sight of the first draft.

C. leave enough time to do it, try to get it right in the first draft to save time.

D. get someone else to read the first draft, be prepared that you might need to repeat the drafting process several times.

8) When you want to indicate that a sentence will be contradicting the previous one you would start it with "_____...". On the other hand, if a sentence is supposed to offer a conclusion based on the previous sentences, you would start it with "_____...".

A. Furthermore, Finally

B. Even so, Nevertheless

C. Subsequently, Thus

D. However, Therefore

9) Which of the following can be considered an example of criticality?

A. Presenting two sources that disagree on a point.

B. Double-checking the methodology of your research.

C. Presenting a number of sources which all agree on a point.

D. All of the above.

10) In what way are tables and figures that appear in the appendices different from those that appear in all the other sections of the report?
   A. There are no differences, the rules for both remain the same throughout the report.
   B. They are not included in the list of tables and figures at the start of the report.
   C. They use letters instead of numbers to indicate the order of tables or figures.
   D. The label for the table or figure in an appendix does not need to describe the contents of that table or figure.

Exercise 2: How serious are these mistakes?

A common problem faced by many of those attempting an academic writing style for the first time is judging the relative importance of all the different rules and requirements involved. How important is it to use as much of the recommended word length as possible? How serious a problem is it to offer a conclusion without providing matching evidence? With this in mind you will find, in alphabetical order, 11 common mistakes made by those attempting the academic style for the first time. You need to put each of them into one of three categories of importance: serious errors, moderate errors and minor errors.

- Including information which does not help to answer the main question behind the piece you are writing.
- Including more than three commas in a sentence or writing a sentence that is over three lines long.
- Including lots of quotations.
- Including lots of complicated words or colloquial expressions.
- Not following the recommended structure for the type of piece you are writing.
- Offering a conclusion without providing any evidence.
- Providing evidence without offering a conclusion.
- Spending a lot of time explaining your points.
- Submitting the piece you are writing after only one draft.
- Using personal pronouns.
- Writing a piece that is a lot shorter than the recommended word length.

CHAPTER 9: ANSWERS

Exercise I: MCT

Q1: Ans = B (See: The basics: Purpose, p. 198)
Q2: Ans = D (See: The basics: Structure, p. 198)

Q3: Ans = B (See: The basics: Argument, p. 199 ↔ Failing to form an argument, p. 200)

Q4: Ans = C (See: Trying to sound too 'academic', p. 201 ↔ Too conversational, p. 202)

Q5: Ans = B (See: The never-ending sentence, p. 203 ↔ Say it again, but with less explanation, p. 202 ↔ Personal pronouns, p. 205 ↔ Personal opinion vs informed opinion, p. 211)

Q6: Ans = B (See: Personal opinion vs informed opinion, p. 211 ↔ Trying to sound 'academic', p. 201 ↔ Criticality, p. 214)

Q7: Ans = A (See: Drafting and re-drafting, p. 205)

Q8: Ans = D (See: Signpost words, p. 207)

Q9: Ans = D (See: Criticality, p. 214)

Q10: Ans = A (See: Table of contents, list of tables and list of figures, p. 208 ↔ Labelling tables and figures, p. 209)

Exercise 2: How serious are these mistakes?

Serious errors

(Not following the recommended structure for the type of piece you are writing. ↔ Offering a conclusion without providing any evidence. Providing evidence without offering a conclusion. ↔ Submitting the piece you are writing after only one draft.)

All of these are serious errors, either because they completely undermine the central purpose of the academic writing style, which is to answer the question behind the piece being written using academic argument, or because they will lead to serious flaws in that piece. To begin with, it does not matter whether it is the evidence or the conclusion which is missing; in either case, it is not an academic argument and without academic argument you cannot offer a valid answer to the question behind the piece. Also, it is a mistake to think that evidence without a conclusion is less serious than the other way around, both are equally serious. Second, although ignoring the structure of a piece is not always a serious mistake for some types of academic writing, with the report it is serious because of how much information a report contains. Often the structure of the report is the only thing that makes it all manageable to the audience, and so ignoring that structure can make the piece impossible to follow. Finally, a one-draft submission is almost guaranteed to contain so many serious mistakes and poor choices that is practically sabotaging the report before anyone has had a chance to read it. The first draft should never be the final one.

(See: The basics: Argument, p.199 ↔ Failing to form an argument, p. 200 ↔ The basics: Structure, p. 198 ↔ Drafting and re-drafting, p. 205)

Moderate errors

(Including information which does not help to answer the main question behind the piece you are writing. Including lots of quotations. Spending a lot of time explaining your points. Writing a piece that is a lot shorter than the recommended word length.)

All of these are moderate errors owing to the fact that, while they do make your writing much less effective, they don't fatally undermine it the way serious errors do. The one thing that all of these errors have in common is that they are not making efficient use of the space available in the piece being written, and this is likely to leave the writer short of space to do the things that are necessary to answer the question behind the piece. This is most obvious if you are including information which is not relevant to answering the question, but it also applies to excessive explanation, which is not the purpose of the piece and so also represents a tangent from answering the question. It is less obvious how quotations waste space, until you consider how inefficient they are, requiring both the quote and an explanation of the point behind the quote. Finally, it is just as wasteful to leave space unused, as is the case with a piece that is much shorter than it needs to be.

(See: The basics: Purpose, p. 198 ↔ Effective quotation, p. 210 ↔ Say it again, but with less explanation, p. 202 ↔ Being too short, p. 204)

Minor errors

(Including lots of complicated words or colloquial expressions. ↔ Including more than three commas in a sentence or writing a sentence that is over three lines long. ↔ Using personal pronouns.)

All of these are minor errors in the sense that, although they have a negative impact on the effectiveness of your writing, the extent of their impact is much more limited than the moderate errors. For example, trying too hard to use complicated words and colloquialisms runs the risk of making your writing harder for some in your audience to understand. However, we need to remember that there are legitimate uses for these types of words and expressions in certain places, such as a complicated word which is needed as important terminology. As such, they are not always mistakes when used, but are more likely to be a mistake if used too often. Regarding sentences which run on too long or contain too many commas, these will contain too many points and so will be challenging for your audience to recall. However, while it does mean that some of the meaning in the sentence will be lost, most of the points being made will be remembered. Finally, using personal pronouns is not always an error as it depends on the guidelines for the piece you are writing. Even so, using them where the guidelines prohibit it may prove to be an irritation to some of your audience, but they will not obscure any of the meaning or prevent the piece from answering the question behind it. Overall then, these are mistakes you should generally try to avoid making, but you should not worry too much about it if you do end up making one.

(See: Trying to sound 'academic', p. 201 ↔ Too conversational, p. 202 ↔ The never-ending sentence, p. 203 ↔ Personal pronouns, p. 205)